THE GREAT SCOTT

A Novel

By

Adam Poe

ISBN: 978-0-9849895-1-5

Published By Yellow Bottle Publishing LLC

Cover Designs By Peter J. Gargiulo

THE GREAT SCOTT

To my wife Dana for her never-ending love, support and encouragement.

To my mother for finding the original manuscript for this book in her closet in Florida and sending it to me all those years after I first started it. It's truly amazing what you can find in a closet in Florida!

To my friends, teammates, coaches and opponents over the years—thank you for all the memories. You obviously remain very close to my heart to this day.

"I am the Philosopher King!"
- A Basketball Sage

CHAPTER 1

The clock ticks down the final seconds of the game—Taylor Scott, the greatest basketball player ever to come out of Davidson County stands at the top of the key and stares straight into the eyes of his opponent. Dripping of sweat and breathing heavy with fatigue, he tucks the ball underneath his arm as his heart races. The picture of strength and grace, he stands seemingly alone among the chaos and noise swirling all around him. With the clock inching toward zero and the score tied at 58, the sold-out crowd of 2,500, packed into a gym meant to only seat 2,000, instinctively rises to its feet and waits in nervous anticipation.

Fearless, confident and arrogant, Taylor lets out a sly chuckle as he begins his move to the basket with six seconds left on the clock. He jabs right, then left, as some unknown and less talented high school basketball player tries to keep up. The seventeen-year-old living legend then takes two lighting quick dribbles to his right, before stopping on a dime and rising thirty-eight inches straight up in the air. The ball jumps off of his fingertips as his wrist once again snaps down in picture perfect form.

"Gotcha, boy!" he yells at his helpless defender.

The home crowd collectively gasps as the ball hangs in the air for a full heartbeat.

With the final buzzer echoing throughout the gym, the ball drops softly out of the sky and straight through the net, sending the crowd into a deafening roar. Taylor, on the other hand, stands calmly just above the foul line, admiring his work. Still holding his arm outstretched from his game-winning shot, he preens for the crowd as a small evil smile spreads across his face. *At this moment, the world is his and he knows it!*

Within seconds, the crowd rushes the court in a crazed celebration of teenage adrenaline as a whirlwind of bodies mob and hug Taylor from all directions. At the same time, up in the stands, parents and teachers high five each other in celebration as another long week in the normally quiet Northern New Jersey suburb of Longwood Hills ends on a high note.

The other team can do nothing but walk off of the court in defeat. *"Losers,"* Taylor thinks to himself as he watches them slowly leave the court. *"Total losers."*

The Great Scott has done it again

CHAPTER 2

Managing to pry himself free from the crowd, Taylor escapes through a small opening between two celebrating classmates and sneaks off into the locker room virtually unnoticed. For a brief time, he's the only one in the empty locker room. Putting his head into his hands, he takes a long, deep breath and replays in his mind the game's exhilarating and spine-tingling ending. Pumping his fists and dancing in place with joy, he relishes the perfection of the moment...*Tonight was his night! His game! God, he loves basketball!*

Within seconds, the door to the locker room flies open and the rest of the Longwood Hills Wildcats pour inside in one big swooping flood of emotion and joy.

"There he is! There's the man!" Jimmy Williams yells as he runs at Taylor with his arms spread open and the look of an attacking animal in his eyes. Taylor braces his 6'9" frame for the oncoming attack of love as Jimmy lifts him high into the air and it seems for instant he's going to put him straight through the ceiling. While only 5' 10" and a reserve, Jimmy is hard working, intense and passionate. He also happens to be Taylor's best friend on the team or anywhere else in the world. The two have been inseparable since they were the first kids dropped off at kindergarten on the first day of school. Once Taylor became "The Great Scott," as the media started calling him in the eighth grade, he also became Taylor's biggest protector.

The Great Scott nickname was at first temporarily mocked by friends and teammates; however, by the end of eighth grade, everyone knew Taylor was different. He possessed the type of raw athletic talent they'd only ever seen on TV. He truly was one in a million.

"Yeeeeaaaahhhhh!!! You did it again, Taylor! That's my man!" Jimmy screams as he attempts to squeeze the life out of Taylor's 190 lb. body.

"The Great Scott is in the house, in the house! The Great Scott is in the house, in the house!" the Wildcats chant in unison.

"Yo! I knew you weren't going to let us down! I just knew it!" Eric Goodwin screams with joy at Taylor.

"Never do, my man," Taylor coolly responds. At the same time, he quietly laughs to himself at how calm he is only moments after letting go of the game's gripping intensity. *If they only knew how much pressure he feels each day...If they only knew.*

"The Great Scott is in the house, in the house! The Great Scott is in the house, in the house!" the team chants over and over again as the frenzied locker room celebration continues unabated. As Jimmy finally lets go of his bear hug on Taylor, the rest of the team mobs him in a flurry of hugs and high fives. The greatest player any of them would ever step on a basketball court with simply grins and smiles from all the attention.

Just then, the door to the locker room flies open and in walks the Longwood Hills High School boy's varsity basketball coaching staff. Like they did after every game, they walk into the locker room in order of importance. First in is Head Coach Jack Waters, followed closely by Junior Varsity Coach Walter Preisler, with Freshman Coach John Matthews right on their heels.

Head Coach Jack Waters is a middle-aged man of forty-five who looks more like fifty-five as thick lines run across his forehead and stretch out from the corner of his eyes toward his temples. After twenty-two years of teaching basketball and U.S. history to teenage boys, the constant stress and tension of trying to shape tomorrow's leaders has recently caught up to him and aged him before his time.

In the world of high school basketball, Jack Waters' reputation is one of an educator and a good man, but not necessarily a great coach. He teaches the fundamentals of the game the only way he knows how, which is to say he teaches them from his heart with compassion. If push comes to shove, he will always teach his boys a lesson by talking to them, rather than yelling and screaming at them like they're idiots. His ultimate goal is to see his boys grow up to be good men, whether they turn into car mechanics, lawyers, teachers or in the case of this year's senior class, a potential first round draft pick.

Coach Waters' quiet confidence is wholly supported by the beliefs and attitude of Longwood Hills, a town that's both nurturing and protective of its own, even to a fault. So while he might not be a living legend like his star player, he's a very good high school basketball coach, a great teacher and a pillar of the community, as much a part of the identity of Longwood Hills as the old stone church on the northern part of town that draws local tourists on the weekends. He also fits perfectly into the framework of high school basketball, a place where the games and the end results matter, but the most important thing is the players enjoy their high school years to the fullest. With over 250 wins during his career, he has coached his share of good teams and won some great games, but this year's team, just like everything else that involves Taylor Scott, is different. *It's something special.*

"Settle down, guys!" Coach Waters begins from behind an ever-present warm smile that is both welcoming and stern at the same time.

"Taylor, you broke that poor kid's ankles, yo!" someone yells from the back of the locker room in an effort to get in one last word.

Standing at the front of the Wildcats' locker room, which contains all the familiar smells of dirty socks, old sweat and heat rub, Coach Waters feels a sense of calm and satisfaction from tonight's big win. With his team spread out on the benches in front of him, and Coach Preisler and Coach Matthews standing to his right, wearing small but very distinct smiles, Coach Waters slowly runs his fingers through his black and grey peppered hair and begins to squint from behind his wire frame glasses. A seasoned master of the post-game speech, he's about to pull out a few of his favorite tricks to hammer home some important points to his team.

"That was a really nice win tonight, guys, but there are some bigger issues at stake we need talk about," Coach Waters starts, before taking a big breath and pausing for effect. "Taylor has just bailed us out from what was another, and I mean *another*, very poor defensive game. I'm severely disappointed with our lack of help-side defense and overall lack of communication. You have to help each other out and cover for each other. Especially if you get beat by your man. We are a team. Five guys with one goal, not five guys with five different goals. We're going to have to work hard again in practice on our help-side rotations. Ball-you-man! Ball-you-man! I don't know how many times we need to go through this, but clearly it's not sinking in!"

On this last note, some of the players squirm in their seats in the hope of not being singled out.

"If you guys ever want to win another state championship this year, and I *know* you do, we have to play better defense. On offense, our effort and intensity are there, but on defense, it's another story entirely. You have to have heart to play this game. Except for Taylor, we didn't show much heart out there tonight."

Just like everyone else in town, Coach Waters is a fan of Taylor's.

"Don't get me wrong, tonight was not an easy game. Roxford came ready to play. They deserve a lot of credit. They knew where we wanted to go with the ball and did everything they could to stop us. Truthfully, I think we're lucky to come away with a win." This last comment stings Taylor somewhat, even though he doesn't fully know why. "We have a lot of work to do to get better as a team. But as I said earlier, tonight was not all bad, so let's also take a moment to enjoy this victory."

Upon hearing this last comment, Coach Preisler and Coach Matthews jerk their heads up from staring at the floor and nod encouragement to the team.

"I believe in you guys, we believe in you guys," Coach Waters tells the players as he gestures to Coach Preisler and Coach Matthews. "But *you* guys have to believe in yourselves for this season to turn out the way we know it can. We only get one shot at this, so let's not allow this opportunity to slip through our fingertips!" With this last point, Coach Waters grows silent as he catches his breath.

Picking up his intensity again, he now goes in for the kill: "This is our year! We're the best team in the state! No one is better! We control our own destiny! So let's go! Let's make this school and let's make this town proud! What do you say? Everyone, hands in one last time! Wildcats on three!"

Jumping out of their seats as if they were shot from a cannon, the entire team throws their hands into a circle in the center of the locker room. They explode with emotion, "ONE-TWO-THREE WILDCATS!"

Letting go of the players' hands, the three coaches turn and walk out of the locker room together, leaving behind their undefeated and #1 ranked team to absorb the magnitude of the moment. Rather than spend any time concentrating on Coach Waters' words, the instant the locker room door closes, the Wildcats continue their post-game celebration. Nothing can restrain the joy and excitement they feel right now.

As Taylor's teammates celebrate all around him, he stands in the center of it all taking it in. To the outside observer, it looks as if he's watching a movie or a television show, instead of his own life unfolding right before his eyes.

After a few more minutes of celebrating, the players' yelling and laughing winds down as they start to get dressed and begin to turn their attention to other things. With the locker room now quiet with reflection, each player goes over the game in their head, whether they contributed to the team's success or simply watched the action from the bench. A moment later, the door to the locker room flies wide open again. Not bothering to wait until everyone is looking in his direction, Coach Waters lets his voice take control of the room, "Practice, tomorrow, two o'clock! And don't be late! Also, be smart out there tonight, whatever you do!" With that, Coach Waters turns and leaves the locker room in dramatic fashion, letting the old steel door slam shut behind him with a loud bang.

After hearing this announcement, all twelve players simultaneously let out a loud groan, even though they knew it was coming. They were just secretly hoping they would be awarded the day off for tonight's big win. As for the groan itself, it was an absolute necessity, otherwise they couldn't call themselves players.

Within seconds, it seems everyone has already forgotten about Coach Waters' announcement as the conversation turns to the night's post-game festivities. David Smith, known simply to his friends as Smitty, shouts to the locker room, "Yo! I heard there's *big* fiesta at Susan Jamison's tonight! I mean, *big* fiesta!"

"Who told you that?" Eric Goodwin shouts back.

"Let's just say it's a reliable source," Smitty yells with a grin. "You two going?" he turns to Taylor and Jimmy who are dressing side by side.

"Without a doubt, we'll be there," Jimmy answers for the both of them. "And I'll bring the Big Man, you just get the girls to show," he shoots Smitty a playful smile.

"Alrighty then, that's what I like to hear!" Smitty answers loudly, then leans in and smacks Jimmy a high five. "I guess I'll see you boys later tonight, 'cause I'm *outta* here. I want to jet before Coach makes any more announcements." Grinning to himself, Smitty slaps Taylor a quick five and nods goodbye to Jimmy as he heads for the door.

The rest of the players slowly follow Smitty out of the locker room, but not before each one of them stops by to give Taylor props for his final shot and say goodbye to Jimmy.

As the last two players in the locker room, Taylor and Jimmy make sure everything is securely put away before heading for the door. Without saying a word, the two inseparable friends, who at this moment look more like David and Goliath, turn away from the locker room and head in the opposite direction of the gym and its still hovering fans. The game is over, the speeches are over, *it's their time now*. With practice looming tomorrow, each second counts more than ever and they can't waste any of it on boring and uncomfortable conversations with the people still left standing in the gym.

The long hallway just beyond the locker room reeks of mildew and sweat as Taylor and Jimmy make their way through the semi-darkness in search of their sweet freedom. Yet there's still one problem. Their special way out of the school leads them right by Coach Waters' office and its two large windows; and just like the rest of the people still standing in the gym, they can't get sucked into a conversation right now with Coach Waters, especially one that involves help-side defense, offensive spacing or rebounding position. *They just can't.*

As they walk down the half-lit hallway, their teenage energy practically overflows with giddy anticipation at the challenge ahead. Stopping just around the corner from Coach Waters' office, they stand in the shadows and whisper to each other, without being seen or heard. They've been playing this game on and off for almost two years, yet somehow it never gets old. It's the two of them versus the world, just the way they like it. Smiling in anticipation of the moment ahead, they stand side by side with their backs against the wall, waiting for the right time to make their move.

For his twenty-two years of service to the school and the community, Coach Waters has been granted an old office that is both bare and unflattering. With dull grey walls and a green linoleum floor, the cramped office holds two beaten-up wood desks that have been scraped and chipped from years of use, along with two large grey file cabinets that look as if they've been standing in the same spot since the school was first built. Behind the two desks is a door to a private, yet uninviting bathroom, and above the file cabinets are two large cork boards plastered with all kinds of junk and outdated posters promoting one thing or another.

As the two friends wait in the hallway to make their move, somewhere off in the distance a pipe slowly drips water onto the floor below, making the situation seem even more dramatic than it is. With the anticipation of the moment building to its unscripted conclusion, Taylor and Jimmy quietly laugh to each other at the ridiculousness of the game they've invented.

After only a few seconds of waiting, and filled with over-confidence and impatience, Jimmy decides to make a break for it. Watching him walk boldly in front of Coach Waters' office without any cover, Taylor curses him under his breath, but quickly follows suit.

Shuffling forward, the two players stare at the floor and hold their breath, hoping for the best. They're almost completely past Coach Waters' office, when they luckily notice his familiar voice is nowhere to be heard. Simultaneously letting out a big sigh of relief, they grin at their good fortune, while Taylor sneaks a peek inside the office, only to see all three of the Longwood Hills coaches laughing and goofing around with each other like teenagers.

"Coach Waters sure seems upset about tonight's win," Taylor thinks to himself, while shaking his head at the hypocrisy between Coach Waters' earlier locker room speech and his behavior now.

Once safely past the office, Taylor squares up and punches Jimmy in the shoulder with a loud pop, punishing him for his silent jail break.

"Had to be done, Big Man," Jimmy laughs as he rubs his shoulder.

"If you say so, Little Man," Taylor laughs back with a big smile.

Just then, the phone inside the office makes a loud noise. Grabbing it on the second ring, Coach Waters' voice dramatically changes from uncontrollable laughter to his most serious and professional tone, "Coach Meyers, how are you doing tonight?"

"Almost definitely another call for me," Taylor thinks to himself and knows there is a long list of calls also waiting for him at home. All from college coaches around the country just dying to know...How did tonight's game go?...How's he feeling?...Has he given any more thought to their school? *Desperation* is the only word that pops into

his mind when he thinks of all the time and energy these coaches spend trying to talk to seventeen-year-old and eighteen-year-old kids like him. But as one of the last uncommitted top basketball prospects in the country with passing grades, he knows he's a hot commodity. *It's just the recruiting never stops. It's relentless.*

After reaching the end of the long hallway, Taylor pushes open an old steel door as he and Jimmy step out into the freedom of the parking lot. Immediately, they're hit in the face by the nasty winter air swirling all around them. The wind howls and shakes the barren trees that line the woods directly behind the school and feeling a quick shiver run through his body, Taylor automatically closes himself up for protection. Pulling the collar of his four-year-old varsity jacket in tight, he suddenly forgets everything else he's thinking about and can now only concentrate on one thing, "Where in the world did Jimmy park his car?"

After taking no more than four steps, Jimmy mumbles something undetectable in Taylor's direction and starts running across the parking lot toward his beat-up army green sedan. Within seconds, it seems his keys are out of his pocket and he's sitting comfortably inside his car with the engine on, waiting for Taylor to join him.

Even though he's freezing and wants to also run through the parking lot, Taylor walks—or rather strolls—to the car at his own pace, because deep down he believes the world will always wait for him.

CHAPTER 3

The green sedan coughs and churns along Northfield Avenue before turning right onto Wingate Drive toward Taylor's house. With over 102,000 miles on it, Jimmy's car is already an ancient relic that struggles to get everywhere, yet it never seems to let him down.

Stopping in front of #31 Wingate Drive, Jimmy puts the car into park as the two friends sit in silence and listen to the radio while their minds drift off into space. The small white house Taylor shares with his mom sits on a nice but unassuming block and while the house has its share of curb appeal, it's obvious from the outside there isn't a lot of money to go around. The snow that has blanketed the town covers the front lawn of the house and its trees, but not the walkways, as Taylor cleared those away before yesterday's game. A basketball hoop sits at the far end of the driveway, illuminated by two spotlights attached to the side of the house, and in front of the hoop, the snow is shoveled away in a near perfect 15' x 8' square, leaving just enough space for Taylor to perfect his jump shot in the freezing cold.

"Best present I ever got," Taylor thinks to himself as he fixates on the hoop and remembers the months of prolonged begging he had to endure the summer before

fifth grade just to convince his mom she should buy him this invaluable gift.

Turning down the radio, Jimmy decides to do the unthinkable. He voluntarily breaks the rules. After every game, regardless of the outcome, Taylor and Jimmy ride home from the gym in silence. This rule exists because of a monumental fight they got into last year after a heartbreaking loss. It was so bad they didn't speak to each other for almost three days, the longest they've ever gone without talking as far as their moms can remember.

As Taylor reaches for the car door, Jimmy crosses this invisible line, "Real nice shot, man." That's all he says.

Closing the door, Taylor glares at his best friend through the passenger side window, while shaking his head in mock disappointment. At the same time, Jimmy looks back smiling proudly and nodding in contented victory. A moment later and still smiling, Jimmy puts the car into gear and pulls away from the house, his old sedan grunting and moaning as it heads down the street.

Moving quickly up the main path of the house, Taylor steps inside, shutting the front door in a hurry. Turning to the side, he hangs his varsity jacket on one of the hooks that line the small foyer just beyond the door and kicks off his shoes.

"Is that you, honey?" a voice yells from the kitchen.

"Yeah, it's me, Ma."

"Oh, good, come here and give your mother a big hug and a kiss for that great performance tonight."

"Damn," he mutters to himself as he heads down the hall. "Sometimes it seems everything I do in my life is directly related to basketball and how well I play."

Deborah Jones is a very pretty woman who stands 5' 3" and appears to be in her early forties. She switched back to her maiden name a few years after her divorce was finalized and has kept it that way ever since. She wears her dark blond hair at shoulder length and keeps herself in real nice shape; and while men are constantly making themselves known to her, she hasn't seriously dated anyone in almost ten years, not too long after her marriage to Bill, her high school sweetheart, ended. Originally from South Carolina, she moved with her family to Longwood Hills at the beginning of tenth grade and has never left, even though she dreams of one day going back for good. Her southern accent, which is mostly gone by now, tends to show up only when she's upset or concerned and while she's never given Taylor a reason why she doesn't date all that much, he's also never asked. If Taylor had to take a guess, he would say his mom has never really gotten over the heartache from her failed marriage and it's just easier for her this way. A paralegal for a small family law practice fifteen minutes outside of town, Deborah wants, like all loving parents, for her only child to have the happiest and most successful life possible.

When Deborah sees Taylor, she reaches up and grabs him by the neck, squeezing him with all the love and compassion in the world.

"Hi, Mom," he says in a flat voice.

"What's wrong?" she asks, letting go of her embrace. "You sound really tired."

"Tough game tonight, that's all. Those guys were pushing and grabbing me all night."

"I know, especially that number thirty-four. He was being a real mean son of a you-know-what. I didn't like him *at all*. He was all over you. Bumping and hitting my poor baby. The refs had to warn him *three* times to stop harassing you. But of course, they didn't do anything about it."

"I know, Ma. I was the one he was pushing and grabbing, remember?"

"Ha. Ha. Don't get smart with your mother, young man, or you'll be making your own dinner tonight."

"Yeah, right. You know you would eventually cave in and make it for me. You couldn't stand to see your only child go hungry," he answers, making a sad face to emphasize his point.

"Who, me?"

"Nah, my other mom. The one who waits in the garage 'til you mess up and then comes running in to save the day."

"You have another mom? Why didn't you tell me? If that's the case, can you ask her to help clean up around here more? And also see if she can help with the bills, because I could definitely use a little more help in that department."

Quickly realizing their conversation had taken a turn for the worse, Taylor decides to let his mom win this battle of wits.

"Okay, Ma. That's enough. You win."

"I win? I have beaten The Great Scott? How exciting! This really is a special night for me," she answers with a bright smile.

"Speaking of food, is there anything to eat in the fridge?" he asks, changing the subject.

"Of course, what would you like?"

"Is there any pizza left over from Wednesday?"

"Sure is, I'll throw some in the oven as soon as I hear the shower stop."

"Thanks, Mom. You're the best."

"I know, darling."

Still smiling, Taylor leans down and gives his mom a quick kiss on the cheek before heading up the stairs to the only bathroom in the house for his official post-game shower.

"Before I forget," she shouts after him. "When is Jimmy coming over tonight?"

"The usual!" he yells back. "'Bout an hour or so!"

Just then, the phone rings inside the house for the fourth time in the last hour alone. As the noise echoes throughout the house, neither of them tries to answer it, instead letting the answering machine once again do its job.

Once upstairs and undressed, Taylor steps into a hot shower to try and wash away the rest of the stress and tension from tonight's game.

CHAPTER 4

The bathroom floor is warm and inviting to the touch as Taylor steps out of the shower onto the normally cold black and white floor tiles below. Wiping away the mist from the small mirror above the sink, he looks at his image closely and allows his mind to wander. Replaying every positive thing that happened in the game, from his 29 points to his three dunks, to his four blocks, to his six assists, to his five steals, all the way to his game-winning shot, he can't help but feel invincible, as if he's floating on air.

Moments later, he strains to see the outline of his face in the half-fogged mirror, while trying to keep his adrenaline high. "Not too bad looking either, if I do say so myself," he quietly laughs as he inspects his face in the mirror. Continuing down this same path, he now lets his teenage imagination run wild with inappropriate thoughts about the girls who might be at the party tonight. Somehow, his mom must subconsciously know he's up to no good, since she yells to him from downstairs at that exact moment, ruining his all too real fantasy, "Your food's cooking, honey! Get it while it's hot!"

Grinning in muted frustration at the sound of her voice, he reluctantly gives up his happy fantasy and heads next door to his bedroom to dry off and get ready for the night ahead. Opening his closet, he searches through his clothes, all of which have been meticulously hung up and neatly divided by color and type. Grabbing a pair of lightly faded jeans, a white T-shirt and a black V-neck sweater, he pulls everything on and stares at his image in the full length mirror behind the door. The image that reflects back to him is that of a tall and good-looking young man who's very aware of how he presents himself to the world and how the world sees him in return.

Turning around, he now focuses with longing on the framed photograph on top of his dresser of a five-year-old version of himself smiling and laughing with his dad on vacation down on the Jersey Shore. This is the only photograph in his bedroom. Sitting next to the photograph is a small pile of recruiting letters, whose envelopes have been haphazardly ripped open, and underneath these envelopes is an empty basketball video game box. Instead of having a professional basketball star on the cover, Taylor's own picture has been placed on it for maximum effect. While he's the only one he knows who doesn't play video games, the empty box was sent by a "friend of an agent," along with a handwritten note asking him to *"Imagine his future!"* Breaking his long gaze at the dresser, he turns back to the mirror and studies his image one last time. Still satisfied with everything he sees, he turns off the lights and bounds down the stairs two at a time in search of his hot dinner.

Standing at the kitchen sink, cleaning dishes by hand, Deborah picks up their conversation from before as Taylor inhales four slices of reheated pizza, one can of soda, a banana and some chocolate chip cookies. Enjoying each minute with her son, Deborah instinctively knows that not too long from now these precious moments will become less and less as he evolves from a teenager into a young man. And truth be told, she would much rather just hold him and protect him like she did when he was younger than let him grow up. But sadly, she knows those days are long in the past. Time is relentlessly marching on for the both of them.

"I just checked the answering machine while you were in the shower."

"Yeah, anything interesting on it?" Taylor answers between bites of hot food and gulps of soda.

"Your father called."

"Yeah," he responds with absolutely no trace of emotion in his voice.

"He said he was at the game tonight. Did you see him?"

"Yeah, I saw him."

"Where was he sitting?"

"Opposite corner of the gym from you."

"Really? I didn't see him at all. I only wish it had been the same way twenty-five years ago," Deborah responds with a nervous laugh.

"Come on, Mom! Not again. Okay?"

"I'm just kidding, baby. You know that, right? Plus, if I never met your father, you wouldn't be here with me right now and there's no way I could have that."

Putting down the dishes, Deborah walks over to where Taylor is sitting at the kitchen table and gives him a loving hug. After letting go of her embrace, she picks up the same style yellow office pad she's been using for the last two years to track his phone messages and begins to run down every message left on the answering machine in the last twenty-four hours alone. "There is one message from Tom Horner of Central New York University, one from Wayne Phillips at Arizona Tech University and two messages from that coach whose name I can never pronounce correctly. The rest of the messages are from assistant coaches at what looks like one, two, three, four...sixteen other schools. Wow, that's quite a list. I tell you, you're one popular kid."

"Thanks," he responds unapologetically.

"There is also a message from that man who says he's a 'friend' of an agent in New York City, but he never gives the agent's name," she tells him in a sour tone.

"He's called a runner, Mom."

"Honestly, I don't care what he's called. You're never calling him back. Do you understand me? And if I see him anywhere near you like he was after the North Orange game, I'm going to call the police."

"What are the police going to do? He's not doing anything illegal."

"I don't know. But I do know what he's trying to do is against the rules and I'm not going to let anyone get in the way of my baby's chance at a free college education."

"I hear ya loud and clear. If he calls my cell or texts me again, I will delete it without responding. You have my word."

"Good, that's what I like to hear," she answers with an approving nod.

In addition to the small stack of open recruiting letters sitting next to the picture on top of Taylor's bedroom dresser, a never ending pile arrives in the mail every day as well. But those mostly just get shoved unopened by Taylor into a bunch of sneaker boxes lying underneath his bed.

After taking the yellow pad filled with phone messages from his mom, Taylor studies the long list for about ten seconds, before putting it down next to his plate without saying another word.

CHAPTER 5

By the time Jimmy shows back up at Taylor's house, Taylor is sitting on the couch in the den watching a basketball game on TV. As usual, Jimmy knocks loudly on the front door three times, before letting himself in without waiting for anyone to invite him inside.

Hearing the knocks just above the play-by-play announcer, Taylor yells to him from his spot on the couch, "Yo! In here!"

"There he is! There's the man of the hour!" Jimmy yells as he enters the den and greets Taylor with a loud high five. "What's up, Big Man?"

"Nada, Bro. Just watching your boys from the great state of Texas take a beat down."

"Ha! My boys!" Jimmy responds with a laugh. "I couldn't root for those clowns if they were the only team that played hoops. What's the score?"

"The guys who rode to the arena on horses are down almost twenty," Taylor answers without taking his eyes off the TV screen.

Flopping down next to Taylor on the couch, Jimmy hesitates for a few seconds before starting in with excitement, "Yo! That was a *crazy* game tonight. Absolutely crazy. I can't believe how well Roxford played. They're really not that good."

"I know, but Coach was right, they came ready to play."

"No two ways about it," Jimmy answers. "But no joke, I think that might've been the best game they've ever played."

"If not the best, then close to it," Taylor backs him up. "But just like everyone else, I'm sure they've been gunning for us since we won the state championship last year."

"Without a doubt, it's like we have a giant bull's-eye on our back. If anyone beats us, it's going to make their season."

"For sure. I guess it's lucky for us we were able to take Roxford's best shot and still come away with a win," as Taylor says this, a huge toothy grin spreads across his face.

"Ha! No way, man! Lucky for us we have you!" Jimmy shouts, then leans over and slaps Taylor a high five that echoes off the walls.

"Thanks, man. I appreciate the props."

"Did you ever find out how many points you had tonight?"

"Nah, don't know, really. Probably around twenty-five, I guess."

Taylor knew he'd scored 29 points exactly.

"Cool. But as you know, it's that last bucket that really counts," Jimmy gushes. "That shot was the bomb! I'm telling you, the bomb!"

Standing silently in the doorway with her arms crossed, Deborah gives Jimmy an icy cold stare, before scolding him, "Jimmy Williams! There is absolutely no cursing in my house, young man. But you know that already. So why am I surprised to hear what just came out of your mouth?"

Jimmy has always felt like Deborah's second son so she's never had a problem giving him the same strong guidance as Taylor.

"What? I didn't curse, Ms. Jones. *I swear.* I said bomb. Bomb isn't a curse."

"That's not what I heard and you know the rules of this house."

"I know. But I said bomb. It's not a..." Jimmy gives up his plea and instead throws himself on her mercy, "Yes, Ma'am. I'm sorry. It won't happen again."

"I know it won't," Deborah responds with a soft smile. "And it's okay, I still love you. Now come over here and give me a proper hello."

Jumping up from the couch, Jimmy walks over and gives Deborah a big hug and kiss on the cheek, before settling back down next to Taylor.

Satisfied with having gotten her point across, Deborah is now ready to play 'nice mom' again, "Are you hungry?" she asks Jimmy. "We have plenty of leftovers if you are."

"No, I'm fine. I ate at home."

"Okay, sweetie. But if you want anything to eat, don't hesitate to ask. By the way, I thought you played a great game tonight. You helped the team in so many ways."

"Thanks!" he practically shouts back, happy to receive the compliment.

"Yeah, you did real good, Little Man," Taylor playfully chides his best friend.

After a few seconds, Jimmy's smile begins to fade as the two friends turn their attention to Deborah, who's still standing in the doorway. Since they can't ask her to leave, they simply stare at her, patiently waiting for her to catch on to what they're not telling her. Except the TV announcers calling the game in the background, an overwhelming silence fills the room.

Snapping out of her daze, Deborah finally figures out what's going on and decides to take the hint, "Well, then...I guess I'll just head back to the kitchen. But before you boys run out of the house tonight, make sure you find me to say goodbye. I also want to know where you're going and what you're doing, and don't make up any phony nonsense that you think I don't know is a lie either," she makes an intense face as she delivers this line.

"Yes, Ma'am," they answer at the same time.

"And Taylor, if I send you a text message reminding you it's getting close to curfew, I want a response within fifteen minutes. Do you hear me?"

"Yeah, no problem," he answers, before turning his attention back to the TV.

Instead of heading right back to the kitchen, Deborah takes a moment to linger in the doorway, where she stares at the two young men sitting on her couch. As she thinks about them, an intense smile grabs hold of her face at how lucky and blessed her life truly is.

With their earlier momentum broken, neither Taylor nor Jimmy immediately picks up their conversation from before. Instead, they sit silently in front of the TV, watching the game and gathering their thoughts. When a Texas player gets fouled on a drive to the basket, their concentration is broken by the piercing sound of the phone once again ringing throughout the house.

"I think it's time to get out of here. Let's skedaddle," Taylor tells Jimmy as he gets up from the couch, his internal motor churning again with nervous anxiety.

Still transfixed to the TV, Jimmy ignores him at first as he watches the Texas player miss his free throw.

"Yo, I'm talking to you, Little Man. You hear me?"

"Yeah, let's roll," Jimmy responds as he clicks off the TV.

After a quick detour to the kitchen to tell Deborah their completely made-up plans for the night, the two friends head to the front door and their night ahead.

"Bye, Mom!" Taylor shouts as he opens the front door.

"Yeah, bye Ms. Jones! See you later!" Jimmy yells as he closes the door behind him.

Watching closely from the front window, Deborah stares as Jimmy's car pulls away from the house and begins to make its way down the street. Holding her breath for an instant, she watches as the car's red taillights move out of sight, taking her only child and the best player in the state of New Jersey along with it. Turning away from the window, she returns to the kitchen and her pile of dirty dishes, just as the phone starts ringing again throughout the house.

CHAPTER 6

The engine of the old green sedan coughs and pushes its way through the cold winter night as the two young friends sit in the car bouncing along to the rhythm of the radio. With nowhere to be right now, Jimmy steers the car onto Northfield Avenue and heads toward the diner in the center of town. A regular hangout of the Longwood Hills upperclassmen, the diner is the go-to spot on the weekends for anyone without a plan or the place to be if someone is looking to kill some time.

As they drive down Northfield Avenue, they travel past the town's newly-built library and its small police station, before getting stuck at a red light in front of the community center where five dollars on Saturdays gets you free rein of its two small basketball courts and use of its cramped weight room. Idling at the red light, Jimmy lowers the volume on the radio and wades into a conversation with his best friend that he's wanted to have for a long time, "So, man. Have you given any more thought to where you might want to play ball next year?"

Caught off guard, Taylor hesitates, "What? Nah, haven't thought about it too much, to be honest."

He was playing it close to the vest, even to his best friend. It's actually all he's been thinking about these days.

At which school can he get on the court the fastest?...Where can he get the most recognition?...Does he think he'd really like to play for that coach? These thoughts dominate his every waking moment, while at the same time, the idea that he could possibly make a wrong decision terrifies him to no end.

"It's no big deal, really," he continues casually. "It'll be cool no matter where I go, you know."

"Yeah, I feel ya. I'm not sure what I'm going to do either," Jimmy responds, interjecting his fears into the conversation. "Depending on where my grades come in, I may or may not be able to qualify for some grants. And the thing is, without those grants, I can't really go anywhere besides a local community college."

"I hear ya, man."

"I'm not going to lie. I'm definitely nervous. 'Cause even if I do get a grant, I'm afraid I might not have too many choices. The pickins' might be slim for me. Especially with my folks' situation and all. I mean, you know, money is tough to come by right now with my dad on disability. So wherever I go, I might have to take out some loans or get a part-time job or do something else just to keep my head above water."

"That's definitely legit, but try not to let it get you down," Taylor answers, doing what he can to comfort his best friend. "Things'll work out for the best in the end, you'll see. I'm sure you also killed it last grade period so that's gonna help."

"Thanks, man," Jimmy replies with a small smile, just as the light overhead turns green. "It's good to know you got my back and I can also get this kind of stuff off my chest when I need to."

"Always," Taylor tells him. "Whatever you need, man. I'm here for you."

As the car pulls away from the intersection and continues down Northfield Avenue, Taylor now does his best to quietly end this part of their conversation. This way the questions can't be turned back on him.

"You know what?" he tells Jimmy. "I don't think we should even worry about all that stuff tonight. It's Friday night and we just beat Roxford. It's all good, you know. And these decisions will still be waiting for us tomorrow."

"Yeah, you're right," Jimmy agrees. "We're not going to figure it out tonight, that's for sure. And there's no way I want to spoil our groove right now."

"Definitely not," Taylor responds, and just to make sure Jimmy doesn't ask him any more questions, he turns the volume on the radio back up.

Over the next few minutes, as the two friends continue driving through the empty streets of Longwood Hills in silence, they each wrestle with their own nervous and haunting thoughts about their undefined future. Sitting on the outer edge of innocence, they can feel the inevitable changes coming in their lives and tonight, like most nights, all they want to do is push these scary thoughts as far out of reach as possible. The only things they know for certain are the rest of their basketball season and the final months of their senior year are directly in front of them, inevitabilities that provide warmth and comfort in moments of uncertainty such as this.

With the lights of the town continuing to softly glow all around them, Jimmy makes a right turn onto Southland Avenue and heads toward the diner's pink and green neon sign. Pulling up to the parking lot, his expression immediately changes to disappointment and frustration. The diner's usually packed parking lot is empty. Undeterred by the obvious, he takes a lap around to make sure he's not missing anything or anyone, and after confirming his disappointment, he grumbles out loud, before turning the car back onto Southland Avenue in the direction of the town's twenty-four hour convenience store. Doing is always better than thinking in his opinion, and tonight is no different. They need to get an official plan in motion.

As they pull into the convenience store's parking lot a few minutes later, Jimmy heads toward an empty spot on the side so he can think in peace and quiet.

Once the car is parked, Taylor addresses a visibly frustrated Jimmy, "Hey, man. While you figure out what to do next, I'm going to go inside and get a drink. You want anything?"

"Nah, I'm good," Jimmy responds in a clipped tone. "I'm going to give Eric a call on his cell to see what he's got going on."

"I think that's a good plan, let me know how it goes," Taylor replies, then slips out of the car, striding toward the store.

The convenience store's aisles are bright and shiny as Taylor slowly walks up and down each one of them, looking to kill some time. While he does this, he can feel the other customers staring at him, which simultaneously brings up feelings of dread and excitement at being recognized. Since he's the biggest sports star this relatively small town has ever produced, he rarely goes unnoticed, no matter where he goes, even though there are plenty of times, like now, he wishes no one had any idea who he was.

Before Taylor, there was Noel Davis, the only other local sports hero who came close to capturing the town's imagination in the same way. A hot shot quarterback, Noel had a rifle of an arm and after leading Longwood Hills to its first ever football state championship, all the big name college programs came calling. He eventually landed at a large state university in the Midwest, where he played out a solid, yet unspectacular career in front of rabid fans packed into sold-out stadiums. When his college football career finally ended and with no professional prospects in sight, he decided to give his athletic dreams one more shot by trying to turn himself into a big league relief pitcher.

After signing a free agent contract, he spent a few long and lonely years in the minors, only to flame out unceremoniously for good during a road trip through the Florida panhandle. His family moved out of Longwood Hills not too long after he started playing baseball and no one has heard much about him since.

With Noel now ancient history, the mantle of Longwood Hills' sports hero now sits squarely on Taylor's thin and undefined shoulders. And while at most times he loves the spotlight and the attention, tonight he just wants to buy his drink and get on his way. Especially since he can feel his teenage patience wearing razor thin.

As he walks in the direction of the refrigerators in the back of the store, Taylor spots an old couple slowly approaching him out of the corner of his eye. Urgently looking for an escape route, he soon realizes there is no easy way out. At the same time, he can hear his mom's voice inside his head telling him to be polite and to appreciate all the attention, not everyone is as lucky as he is. Out of options and not wanting to listen to his mom, he tries one last maneuver to see if he can get rid of the old couple. Opening up one of the refrigerator's large glass doors, he crouches down low behind its now frosted glass, hoping they'll walk right by him.

Dressed in a red and black flannel shirt, a dark green down vest and an old grey wool hunting cap, the old man shuffles over to within inches of where Taylor is crouching down behind the refrigerator door and waits patiently for him to stand up. Finally seeing the situation for what it is, Taylor has no choice but to give in. Standing up straight, he towers over the old man.

"Excuse me, son," the old man looks up into Taylor's face, the whiskers from his white beard moving in all different directions as he talks. "But we just wanted to come over and tell you we thought you played a great game tonight."

"You know, we're very big fans of yours," the old woman jumps in. "We go to all of your team's games."

"Thank you," Taylor replies softly. "That's real nice of you."

"We don't mean to pry, but do you think we're going to be state champions again this year?" the old man asks, revealing a mouthful of brown and chipped teeth. "We think you guys are awfully close, but besides you and that Goodwin boy, we're just not sure if this year's team has enough talent to win the whole thing. We really hope you do because we would love nothing more than to see our Wildcats become state champions again. It would mean the world to us."

"Yes, it would be so nice," the old woman chimes back in.

"Great, you two old jerks! I'm so glad you came over to talk to me! Thank you for being so open with your opinions and telling me how talented you think our team is! Don't you annoying people have anything else going on in your lives? Or is worshipping high school basketball all you have? Now go away!"

"I guess we'll have to wait and see," Taylor finally responds with relatively little emotion. "But I think we're going to do okay this year. And keep coming to the games, we appreciate all the support."

Ignoring Taylor's pleasant response, the old man continues his personal assault, "Did you pick a school yet?"

Blinking in amazement at the old man's nerve and since there's no way he's going to answer this question, Taylor just stares down into the old man's wrinkled face as years of silence seem to pass between them.

Sensing the sudden shift in the conversation, the old woman tries her best to end the awkwardness, "Well...We couldn't let this opportunity pass us by to come over and tell you how much we enjoy watching you play. Now come on, Earl, let's leave the boy alone and let him do his shopping. Nice meeting you," she tells Taylor, while slowly moving the old man out of the way by gently tugging on his sleeve.

Frowning in confusion at what just took place, the old man reluctantly starts following the old woman down the aisle, away from Taylor. Right before they turn the corner and move out of sight, the old man looks back over his shoulder and shouts, "Nice shot tonight, son! That one was a doozy!" he belly laughs, while shuffling away for good.

"Thank God! What annoying bastards!" Taylor screams inside his head. *"People are just so free with their thoughts it makes me sick!"*

After thrusting his hand into the refrigerator and grabbing an orange sport drink in frustration, Taylor turns around and heads toward the cash register in the middle of the store, while hoping no one else will want to share their opinions with him or ask him inappropriate questions between now and the car.

The Indian man standing behind the register nods politely when he sees Taylor approaching the counter with his drink in his hand. Looking at Taylor's height, along with the ornate state championship pin attached firmly to his black and gold varsity jacket, just above his heart, the cashier decides now would be a great time to practice his English, "I heard your team played a great game tonight, congratulations," he states proudly in a heavily accented tongue.

"Thank you," Taylor responds curtly, but offers nothing more in response.

Sensing the giant teenager's dark mood, the cashier quickly decides he should practice his English another time, rather than continue to head down the path in front of him. After handing Taylor his change, he watches him leave the store in a hurry, extremely relieved when the glass doors close behind him on his way out.

Once outside the convenience store, Taylor finds Jimmy sitting on the hood of his car, shivering and yelling into his cell phone, "Whatever, man! If you say so! Forget it! You're such a sell-out! You know that?"

Jimmy then angrily ends the call by squeezing the phone tight in his hand.

"What was that all about?" Taylor asks, happy he's not the only one in a bad mood.

"I'll tell ya in a second, it's freezing out here," Jimmy responds, waving Taylor back into the car.

As the two friends slide into the front seat of the car and wait for its old heater to kick in, they stare blankly at each other for a few minutes, neither of them saying a word.

"So what was that all about?" Taylor finally asks again.

"I just talked to Eric."

"And?"

"And they're going to Michelle's first and we can't go there because she still hates my guts. It's so ridiculous, because we broke up three weeks ago. I mean, how long do you have to wait to be in the same room with an ex-girlfriend? It totally sucks, but I think we're on our own until the party starts."

"For real. You're right, that does suck," Taylor answers.

"I know! That's why I was yelling at Eric! He knows Michelle still hates my guts, but he's going there anyway. He's such a sell-out sometimes. I can't wait until I see him later. I'm totally going to rip him a new one."

"Settle down, Little Man," Taylor responds with a light laugh. "You're not going to be ripping nobody nothin'. But seriously, what's our plan?"

"I don't know! That's why I'm so mad!" Jimmy answers loudly.

"Okay! Just chill, will ya? There's got to be something else we can do until the party starts."

"Not really. The diner is completely empty, so our only option, as far as I can tell, is to drive around for awhile and then head over to Susan's early. Other than that, I don't know what to do."

Not caring all that much what they did, since more often than not the action always finds him anyway, Taylor decides to leave it up to Jimmy, "Honestly, doesn't matter to me, Little Man. Just lead the way. It's your call," and gives him a nod of approval.

"Okay, I guess it's settled then," Jimmy responds with a shrug. "Let's take to the streets and see what this weak town has to offer for the next few hours."

With their decision made, Jimmy puts the car into reverse and pulls out of the convenience store parking lot, heading in the direction of the town's empty streets without a clear destination in mind.

CHAPTER 7

Dark houses and mostly open road spread out before them in all directions as Jimmy's car aimlessly sputters around town pumping out hip-hop tunes from the radio. While the two friends sit quietly next to each other staring at the relatively blank canvas all around them, seconds and minutes slowly pass without much really happening. Eventually, they both get bored with the unending silence and decide to turn their attention to their favorite topic of conversation, Wildcat basketball.

This time, it's Taylor and not Jimmy, who starts in first with excitement, "Yo! What did you think of the dunk I had in the second quarter?" he asks. "Did it look as good as it felt? I posterized that annoying dude!"

"Yeah, man. That flush was *nice*."

"I'm telling you, right before that dunk, that dude was talking all kinds of smack to me. Telling me how overrated I was and how good he was. *Pullleeaassee!!* Didn't he know who he was talking to?"

"He better recognize!" Jimmy shouts back.

"I'll tell you what. After that dunk, that dude didn't talk too much more. As a matter of fact, I don't think my man said another word the rest of the game."

"He got, got, yo!" Jimmy tells Taylor.

"He definitely got, got!" Taylor laughs back with a smile.

For the first time since the game ended, Taylor was letting someone else beside his mom know how he was really feeling.

"Settle down, Big Man," Jimmy sarcastically ribs his best friend. "What we need to talk about is your block in the fourth quarter. That was nice! You pinned the rock against the backboard with two hands!"

"Yeah, I almost forgot. Thanks for reminding me."

"You almost forgot? *Whaaaaaaaat?* I thought you cracked the backboard you pinned it so hard. That was impressive, even for you," Jimmy gushes.

"Thanks, man. I appreciate the love."

"Always. By the way, you should've seen the scared look on that poor kid's mug after you blocked his shot. He looked like he'd seen a ghost."

"I guess he'd never been blocked by an All-American before," Taylor responds with a sarcastic laugh, safely letting his ego now run free in front of Jimmy.

At times, it's still a little weird to the two of them that Taylor is as good at basketball as he is, since they both can remember the first time they picked up a ball in third grade gym class.

As the town continues to pass by them outside the car, their post-game discussion rages on inside the car and even though Jimmy played less than half of tonight's game, Taylor makes sure to go out of his way to give him props for every positive thing he did on the court. This way they can talk about all of his contributions in exacting detail.

A little over two hours later, Jimmy slows the car to a crawl along a tree lined street as he strains his eyes to see their exact location. Overhead, the dull lights from the street lamps shine through the car's windshield, but are no match for the pitch black sky above.

"What does that sign say up there?" he asks Taylor.

"I think it says Coddington Road."

"Nah, that's not it," Jimmy grunts back.

"C'mon, man. You told me you knew how to get us to Susan's."

"I do. Well, I thought I did. It's just...I was only there once before and it was daytime."

"You've got to be kidding me!" Taylor's frustration suddenly rises out of nowhere. "You told me you knew where we were going. I've got a good idea, just look for a lot of cars, cars driven by our friends."

"Thanks, Einstein. Thanks a lot," Jimmy tries to deflect Taylor's sarcasm, but knows there's no hiding from it when he gets like this.

"Did you text Smitty? Or Eric?" Taylor asks.

"Did you see me text Smitty or Eric? My cell phone hasn't left my pocket since we left the store."

"Forget it. Pull over. I'll do it."

"Why? I don't need to pull over so you can text someone. You're capable of texting while I drive."

"Don't even go there," Taylor responds with a look of anger. "I'm trying to help us get to the party and you said you knew how to get us there."

"I do. It's just...Just chill for a second, will ya?"

"I asked you to pull over so you can map out the directions on your phone. You at least remember Susan's address, don't you?"

"I don't have internet access on my phone anymore. That was a trial thing that ran out and my mom keeps downgrading our phone plan to save money. I'm barely allowed to text anymore. You do it."

"Right, like my mom's going to pay the overages for me to use my phone's internet. We share an old computer in the den, that's it. She thinks technology is evil."

"So now what?" Jimmy asks with a look of exasperation.

"I'll tell you what. You just keep driving us around and I'll text everyone we know. If anyone gets back to me, I'll be in touch."

"Whatever you say, man. You're the boss," Jimmy responds as he steps on the gas again.

Frustrated by their relatively boring night so far, the two friends sit in silence as they keep driving around trying to figure out how they can to get to the party.

A few minutes later, Jimmy makes a left turn onto Homestead Drive and as they turn the corner, the headlights of his sedan pick up the reflection of a long line of familiar cars. Upon seeing this revelation, Jimmy lets out a giant sigh of relief, before practically shouting in triumph, "Nice, this is it! I knew I would get us here!"

Taylor glares back at him without saying a word.

After Jimmy parallel parks the car between an old station wagon and a new two-door coupe, the two friends, who are barely speaking to each other, get out and head toward the house for what they hope is going to be the best part of their night.

Although it's still early, Susan's party is already crowded and noisy. A sure sign the police will be stopping by later on to break it up.

As they walk around to the back of the house, Taylor and Jimmy finally start to relax and let go of some of the tension from the car. About halfway across the backyard, they run into a group of classmates who are huddled together in a small circle, shivering and smoking cigarettes.

"What a great habit. I just don't get it," Taylor thinks to himself and even though he feels superior, he still gives this small group of smokers a quick nod and casual, "What's up?" as he passes.

Walking up the stairs attached to the wood deck in the back of the house, the two friends enter the party through the kitchen's sliding glass doors. As they glide easily through the crowd, each wearing the distinct look of a triumphant hero, they smile and nod at almost everyone they see. At the same time, Taylor's presence at the party, especially after a Friday night home win, eases everyone's high school fears and anxieties, making them feel as if they too are on their way to a life of bigger and better things.

After grabbing two cold drinks from the refrigerator, the two friends snake a path back through the kitchen in the direction of the den so they can see who's already at the party. As they gulp their drinks, their eyes dart back and forth across the room in an effort to soak in the scene. Only a few seconds later, Jimmy's energy level is already peaking at a high volume, "Yo! A few girls look *reeeaallly* good tonight. I'm telling you, it's gonna be a good one. Oh, my God! Do you see Tammy over there?" he nudges Taylor with his elbow. "She looks *smokin'* in those jeans. I don't think I've ever seen her look that hot. Have you?"

Taylor ignores Jimmy as he seems transfixed on something across the room.

Straining his neck, Jimmy tries to see what Taylor is looking at, but can't see from where he's standing. Hoping to get a better view, he leans to his right and instantly his heart drops into his stomach when he sees Kelly Raymond, Taylor's ex-girlfriend, standing a little too close to another guy. "You've got to be kidding me!" he shouts under his breath. "What's she doing here?"

As if pulled by an uncontrollable force, Taylor suddenly turns his back on Jimmy and starts walking in Kelly's direction.

"Wait!" Jimmy shouts, reaching out and grabbing Taylor by the shoulder. "Where are you going?"

"I'm just going to talk to Kelly. You know, say hi."

"No way, man! Stay away from her. It's over. She'll only drive you crazy again."

"I just want to talk to her. It's been a while since, you know, we talked. Do you think she was at the game tonight?"

"C'mon, man! It's not worth it."

Ignoring Jimmy's warnings, Taylor turns his back on their conversation again and starts walking across the room toward Kelly. Jimmy follows a step behind.

Luckily, Taylor only makes it a few feet before he's surrounded by a small group of sophomore girls, like a school of sharks circling its prey. Staring up at him with equal parts awe and lust, the three lonely and nervous fifteen-year-olds instinctively play with their hair and fidget in place, while trying to look as cool as possible. Thankful for the diversion, Jimmy looks over at Kelly again, silently praying she'll suddenly leave the party.

The girl who appears to be the group's ring leader jumps in first, "You played a great game tonight, Taylor. That was an amazing shot you made at the end. How'd you do that?"

"Uhm...You know, it wasn't that hard," he fumbles for the right words. "I just wanted to win the game, that's all."

"We were very impressed," the ring leader cocks her head sideways and smiles as she says this. "We've never seen so many people cheer at once. Jimmy, you played a good game too."

"Thanks!" he responds with a big smile.

"I mean, I didn't even like basketball until I saw you play this year," the second girl gets over her fears and talks to Taylor. "You're really great. Do you know that?"

Since the second girl is the cutest of the three, Jimmy casually takes a step in her direction, while hoping she will also tell him how great he is.

"Thanks," Taylor meekly responds to the second girl, although he's never really sure how to respond to a compliment like that.

"Seriously, we're your number one fans," the ring leader jumps back in.

"Thanks," Taylor repeats his standard answer.

"How tall are you?" the third girls suddenly blurts out awkwardly.

"Huh?" Taylor answers, doing a double-take.

Blushing bright red, the third girl lowers her eyes and takes a big sip of her drink, while her two friends stare at her with a mix of daggers and embarrassment.

"Ladies, he's a lean, mean, six foot, nine inches," Jimmy responds, taking control of the conversation; and over the next few minutes, as the three girls mainly stare and giggle at Taylor, Jimmy fills in any awkward pauses and keeps the conversation's momentum flowing.

As Jimmy plays emcee, Taylor does his best to seem interested in what the girls are saying, while periodically looking across the room to make sure Kelly hasn't left. She hasn't. He's almost completely relaxed and comfortable again, when out of nowhere, he finally sees him, *"It can't be!"* he shouts inside his head as his heart begins to race. *"Kelly's holding hands with Steven Mason! There's no way! That kid's such a punk!"*

Jimmy catches Taylor once again fixating on Kelly and instantly he knows he has to do something, *but what?*

Without saying another word, Taylor walks away from Jimmy and the three girls and makes his way across the den. Nudging people out of his way as he walks, he strides right up to Kelly and Steven. Towering over both of them, he stares down into their faces with the intensity of a volcano waiting to explode.

Looking up at the exact same time, Kelly and Steven both gasp in horror when they notice the incredible rage on Taylor's face. Having seen this expression before, Kelly tries her best to defuse the situation as fast as possible, "Uhm, Taylor. How are you doing?" she asks. "I heard you guys won your game tonight, congratulations," she awkwardly spits out words that seem to be stuck somewhere deep within her throat.

Standing motionless in response, Taylor does everything he can to try and maintain his composure, *"Calm down! Calm down! Calm down!"* he violently shouts inside his head as his emotions explode underneath the surface like a wild animal backed into a corner. Turning to Steven, he now scowls at him with a bone chilling fixation.

"G-g-g-good game tonight, Taylor. Real g-good game," Steven tries feebly to improve a suddenly frightening situation. "We were there in the first half and thought..."

"Only my friends can call me, Taylor," he grunts back in a cold monotone voice.

"Sorry, I was just..." Steven stumbles.

"Taylor, relax! Steven was only trying to be nice. Besides, you're not scaring us. So just cut it out," Kelly tells him loudly. If nothing else, she could always put him in his place.

"I *need* to talk to you," Taylor responds angrily.

Thinking for a split second which way to answer, Kelly attempts to take the easy way out, "Maybe later, right now I'm hanging out with Steven. We'll catch up another time."

"I *need* to talk to you, *right now,*" he grunts back.

"I'm sorry, but I told you..." Taylor doesn't let her finish. Without warning, he grabs Kelly by the wrist and starts pulling her across the room. Paralyzed with fear, Steven doesn't do anything as he watches Taylor take Kelly away.

"Ow! You're hurting me! Stop it!" Kelly shouts, while trying to plant her heels into the rug to stop Taylor's momentum.

Looking around for help, Kelly starts to panic; with the music blasting loudly, no one seems to be noticing what's happening right in front of them.

Scanning the den in a controlled rage, Taylor swivels his head from side to side as he tries to figure out what to do next. Finding a door on the other side of the room, he moves swiftly toward it. Grabbing the handle with force, he opens the door to find a set of stairs leading down to a basement. Practically carrying Kelly along with him, he descends to the bottom of the stairs in a hurry where he's greeted by a dark room filled with cold air.

Once his eyes adjust to the surroundings, he spots an empty bathroom and heads straight for it. Pulling Kelly inside against her will, he slams the door shut, while still holding tightly onto her wrist. Now in a frenzied state, his adrenaline pumps at full blast, making his temples pound and his mind go white with rage.

"I said, let go of me! Stop it! You're hurting me!" Kelly shouts as loudly as she can.

Positioning himself in front of the door, Taylor finally lets go of Kelly's wrist as she takes two steps backward and braces herself against the wall.

"What the hell are you doing here with that loser?" he shouts, his teenage anger spinning out of control. "That kid is such a wanna-be!"

"We're together now. I'm sorry you had to find out like this, but we've been together for almost a month now."

"A *month*?" he shouts in disgust. "You've got to be kidding me!"

"You're the one who broke up with me, remember? So why do you care anyway?"

"Because I still love you. That's why."

"How can you say that?" she asks with fiery eyes. "You don't love anything except that *stupid* orange ball. You wouldn't know what to do without it. That's what you love, not me."

"That's not true!"

"Then why aren't we together now?"

"We had to break up. Everyone told me I had to concentrate on basketball only this year. No distractions. There's nothing I could do about it."

"Had to break up? Doesn't sound like we had to do anything! Sounds like you chose to be with it, rather than me. Now you can't stand to see me with someone else so you're acting like a lunatic."

"That's not true. I had to do it for my career."

"Your career? That's all you ever talk about. You're seventeen years old, for Christ's sake."

"I had to...You have to believe me," Taylor keeps pleading.

"Maybe, if you thought a little less about your career and a little more about just being a teenager, we'd still be together now. Besides, Steven is nice to me and doesn't disappear for hours to go play ball and work on his 'J'. Especially when I ask him to come over and have dinner with my parents, like somebody else I know."

"But Steven? He's such a wanna-be! How could you?"

"He's not a wanna-be anything. Unless you count wanting to be my boyfriend."

"He's a creep, Kelly. You have to know that."

"No, I don't. He's been nothing but nice to me."

"Yeah, right. All creeps start out nice."

"You mean, like *you*."

"Screw you, Kelly! I still love you!"

"No, you don't! Every time we were together, all you ever wanted to do was talk about basketball. How the game went. What school you might want to play for. How much pressure the coaches put on you. It was always the same. It was never about me or us. It was always about basketball."

"Whatever, Kelly. That's not true."

"You just want to keep the adrenaline from tonight's game going. You don't care about me. All I am to you is your next challenge. It's over, Taylor. I'm sorry. Now please leave me alone."

Gathering up her courage, Kelly swallows hard and takes a step toward the door.

Seeing this step forward as an act of defiance and sensing he's lost all control of the situation, Taylor fights back the only way he knows how, *by using his strength.*

Grabbing Kelly by the shoulders, he pushes her to the ground with a thrust of his hands. Flying backward, she hits the wall with a loud thump and slinks to the ground as a look of terror washes over her face.

Leaning over her in a complete rage, he shakes a finger in her face, "Screw you, Kelly! Don't tell me what I think! Screw you!"

Realizing she's pushed him over the edge, Kelly pulls her knees up to her chest and tries to shield herself from his overflowing anger.

"How can you say those things to me? I just wanted to talk to you! How could you?"

Sitting in a ball on the cold bathroom floor, Kelly now grabs her knees even tighter to her chest and begins to rock herself back and forth as tears start streaming uncontrollably down her cheeks, "Please just go. I'm so sorry. Please just go."

Taylor doesn't hear a word she says.

In a fit of emotion, he leans back and unleashes a primal scream that rattles the walls. Breathing heavily, he stares down into Kelly's face for what feels like an eternity, before lunging forward with lightning quick agility and kicking the wall next to her shoulder. His foot smacks the wall with a loud bang, sending pieces of sheetrock flying into the air.

Overwhelmed by total fear, Kelly buries her face even deeper into her knees as she keeps rocking herself back and forth, but only harder now, "Please just go. Please just go. Please just go," she keeps repeating her plea.

Overcome with emotion and blind rage, he reels back to kick the wall again, but abruptly stops himself cold. Catching his almost unrecognizable image in the mirror, he instantly becomes filled with a deep and undefined sadness, which makes him feel helpless and insecure. Looking down at Kelly huddled in the corner crying, he suddenly realizes she is terrified, *terrified of him*. This sudden flash of reality sends another bolt of raw emotion shooting through his body, forcing him to lean back and unleash another primal scream that rattles the walls. Not knowing what to do or how to feel, he turns around and starts kicking the bathroom door over and over again to try and free himself from these gripping emotions. The bathroom door cracks and splinters in all directions, but somehow doesn't break. Frustrated and angered by this injustice, he turns around one last time and yells at Kelly, "Bitch!"

Bounding up the basement stairs two at a time in search of the nearest exit, he runs right into a group of partiers who've gathered at the top of the stairs to see what all the noise is about. Not being able to tell if what they're looking at is real or not, no one says a word as Taylor aggressively pushes his way past them.

Taylor Scott—town celebrity—then sprints out the same kitchen door he casually walked through with a smile only a few minutes earlier.

Without telling anyone, including Jimmy, he leaves the party and walks home alone in the freezing cold—cursing, kicking and screaming the entire way.

CHAPTER 8

The next morning Taylor wakes up feeling groggy and out of sorts. Still shaken from his emotional roller coaster from the night before, he slowly opens up his tired eyes and stares at his bedroom ceiling in an effort to clear his head. Gazing at the painted ceiling, he tries to focus his thoughts by counting the number of tiny cracks he can find, but it's no use, his head is filled with too much confusion and anger right now to keep a steady count. Emotionally and physically exhausted, he pushes aside the covers of his bed, throws his feet onto the floor and puts on a pair of old grey sweatpants, a long-sleeved black T-shirt and thick white socks, before shuffling listlessly downstairs to get some food.

Once inside the kitchen, he grabs a box of cereal from the cabinet above the sink, a quart of milk from the refrigerator and sits down at the second-hand wood table without bothering to turn on the lights. Pouring himself a large bowl of sugared cereal, he sighs softly and stares off into the distance, desperately trying to force his brain to focus on something other than Kelly and what happened at the party. Yet, it's all he can think about. With each passing thought, the painful knot in his stomach gets tighter and tighter, *"Is Kelly all right? Is word spreading through town already? What if the coaches that are recruiting me find out? If they do find out, will I lose my chance to play big time college ball?"*

One after another these unanswered questions bounce around inside his head as he tenses up from head to toe. Not sure if he should call Kelly to apologize or Jimmy to explain his disappearance or someone else to explain his side of the story, he instead decides to do nothing, except sit in the dark and sulk. His head feels like it's going to explode!

Off in the background, the grandfather clock beyond the kitchen ticks away seconds, then minutes at a time.

Tick-tock. Tick-tock. Tick-tock. Tick-tock.

Staring into space, he thinks himself into a state of paranoia. He's convinced he can see his classmates' scathing social media posts, along with the headline in today's media, "High School All-American Beats Ex-Girlfriend At Party." He tells himself that if this story ever gets out, he will look like just another out-of-control athlete who thinks he can do whatever he wants to whomever he wants. But that's not who he is!

"Calm down! Calm down!" he repeats inside his head, while rationalizing that last night's fight was just a really bad ending to a great night. But it's no use, his mind is spinning out of control, *"Maybe Kelly is at the police station right now, pressing charges? Is that possible? Would she do that?"*

Just then, the lights in the kitchen turn on.

"Hi, honey. You have a good time last night?"

"Huh?" he answers, blinking into the suddenly bright white lights. *"Does my mom know already? Is she playing with my emotions so I'll spill my guts?"*

"Earth to Taylor, are you in there?" Deborah asks, now looking at him with worry. "I said, did you and Jimmy have fun last night?"

Composing himself, Taylor smiles softly, before responding, "Yeah, Ma. It was okay, I guess."

"That's nice, but you should put on some lights in here. Otherwise, you won't be able to see what you're eating."

"Sure...No problem."

"Are you positive you're all right? You look like you're in another world."

"Yeah, Ma. I'm fine. I'm just thinking, that's all."

Not sure if he's just being a teenager or something might really be wrong with him, Deborah continues to look at him with a worrisome frown. Finally deciding it can't be anything catastrophic, she opts to switch the subject, "Did you call your father back from last night yet?"

"Huh?"

"Your father. Did you call him back yet?"

"No. Not yet."

"Well, he called again this morning. You were sound asleep when the phone rang so I told him you'd call him after you got out of bed. Please do me a favor and don't make a liar out of me. Call him back when you can. The last thing I want to be accused of when it comes to your father is being a liar," ten years after the divorce, she still cared what her ex-husband thought of her.

"What time is it, anyway?" Taylor asks, realizing for the first time since he got out of bed that he hadn't looked at a clock.

"Ten-fifteen. Why?"

"We have practice at two o'clock."

"Oh, good. Then you have plenty of time to help me around the house before you leave for the gym. Is Jimmy picking you up? Or do I need to give you a ride?"

"Jimmy is picking me up," Taylor responds without hesitation, even though he has no idea if this is true or not.

"Since that's the case, I'll leave you alone to your thoughts. But as soon as you're done eating, I'm going to need your help cleaning up around here."

"Sure...No problem," he answers again.

Seemingly satisfied with their exchange, Deborah goes to leave the kitchen, but then suddenly stops and spins back in his direction. His heart skips a beat when he sees her do this, *"Is this it? Is she going to tell me she knows about the fight with Kelly?"* He tenses up and prepares for the worst.

"I almost forgot, I brought you the paper. There's a big headline inside about you."

"What? She said it so flatly. Not, I can't believe my son is an out-of-control girlfriend-beater and a disappointment for failing to live up to every lesson I ever taught him, after all of the love and support I provided him, he wastes no time in raising a hand to a woman the first chance he gets?"

Placing the paper down on the kitchen table, Deborah opens it up wide as Taylor gulps down hard and holds his breath.

"There you go, right there!" she points to the article and instantly breaks into a smile that lights up her face. "Big headlines once again, baby! I'm so proud of you!"

The headline running across the top of the high school sports section screams in big bold letters "THE GREAT SCOTT SINKS GAELS AT BUZZER, 60-58." Seeing this positive caption, he lets out a giant sigh of relief.

As soon as Deborah leaves the kitchen for good a few seconds later, Taylor turns his now tightly focused attention back to the paper so he can satisfy what's left of his remaining paranoia. Quickly scanning the paper from the front to the back, and then again, from the back to the front, he frantically searches for anything that might link him to Kelly and the party. Happily, he doesn't find anything that does. At the same time, he makes a plan to jump on the computer in the den to check the local sports websites as soon as his mom is occupied with something else.

Exhaling at his non-discovery, he immediately refocuses his thoughts, knowing that a few days of high school can feel like a few years and anything can still happen.

After rifling through several different scenarios in his head, he settles on the idea that if he can somehow make it through school on Monday without being the center of this weekend's gossip or being called into the principal's office, there's a good chance he can make it through this whole misunderstanding unscathed.

Satisfied with this new plan, he turns his attention to his now soggy bowl of cereal, while off in the background, the grandfather clock beyond the kitchen ticks away seconds, then minutes at a time.

CHAPTER 9

Just after 1:30 p.m., Jimmy stops his car in front of #31 Wingate Drive and honks the horn to pick Taylor up for their 2:00 p.m. practice. Even though they never discussed it, he automatically knows he needs to pick Taylor up today and also watch over him. He also knows they have to talk about what happened at last night's party—it's just, he hasn't figured out how he's going to start this conversation yet.

Hearing the horn from his spot on the couch in the den, Taylor's heart jumps in relief at knowing his best friend can once again read his mind. Within seconds, he throws on his varsity jacket and yells goodbye to his mom on his way out the door. Moving with purpose down the front path of the house, he can't help but look forward to the sanctuary of practice, a place where everything makes perfect sense to him.

When Taylor slides into the front seat of the car, the two friends exchange a quick hello, but don't say anything beyond that. Rather than try and force the conversation right away, Jimmy puts the car into drive and heads toward the gym, while hoping a natural opening to talk will present itself. Sitting next to him, Taylor hopes for the complete opposite.

After a few long minutes of waiting patiently, staring at the snow-covered streets outside the car's windows, Jimmy decides he's had enough of the silent treatment and dives into what he knows is probably going to be an uncomfortable conversation, "Hey, man. What happened to you last night?"

"What do you mean?" Taylor asks, turning away from the passenger side window.

"I mean, what happened to you? Where'd you go?"

Jimmy watched Taylor run out of the party with the rest of the onlookers, but wants to see if he'll tell him on his own.

"Uhm, you know," Taylor responds, trying to deflect the question. "I just didn't feel like staying, that's all. Plus, you were having such a good time with those girls, I decided to hitch a ride with someone else."

"Really?" Jimmy asks with surprise. "Well, you could've at least told me you were leaving."

"Yeah, sorry about that. I just didn't want to spoil your groove. It looked like that girl was really into you."

"Which one?"

"I don't know. The sophomore."

"All three of those girls were sophomores."

"Oh, yeah. Then not the aggressive one, the other one."

"Right, the other one," Jimmy sarcastically responds. "Either way, you should've told me you were leaving. That's not like you."

"Yeah, my bad," Taylor apologizes. "I just didn't feel like staying."

"I hear ya, but who'd you get a ride home with?" Jimmy pushes, wanting to see how far Taylor will take his lies.

"Uhm...Greg Thompson. He was done with the party too, so we left together."

"So you didn't leave with Kelly?"

"What? No way, man! We just talked for like a minute or two and then went our separate ways. I definitely didn't leave with Kelly, that I can *guarantee* you."

"Okay. But the next time you bolt from a party like that, give me a shout and let me know what you're up to. You're my boy. If you're going to bounce, I need to know, even if I'm 'macking on some honey."

"You got it, man," Taylor responds with a reassuring nod. "Next time, you'll be the first to know."

Even though Jimmy wants to ask Taylor a ton more questions, especially about what happened in that basement, he decides to let it go for now, knowing he won't be able to get any more information out of his best friend until he's ready to talk.

Sitting in the passenger seat, looking out at the winter landscape all around him, Taylor smiles deeply at successfully navigating Jimmy's string of uncomfortable questions. At the same time, he knows since Jimmy didn't mention the fight, no one else on the team is going to say anything, either. Which is great, since he still has no idea how he would answer anyone's questions.

CHAPTER 10

By 2:10 p.m., the Wildcats' practice is rolling along at a nice, leisurely pace. It's the perfect Saturday afternoon high school practice, heavy on shooting and goofing around, and light on drills and conditioning. With last night's emotional win still fresh in the players' minds, Coach Waters wanted the team back in the gym handling a basketball one more time before the weekend was over, while also making sure they stay focused on Tuesday night's upcoming game, rather than all the other things teenage boys might be thinking about.

Wearing an old Longwood Hills black and gold sweat suit and a pair of ancient-looking high top sneakers, Coach Waters directs the Wildcats from his spot at center court with a whistle and a clipboard, "Let's go! Everybody, grab a partner and a basket! I mean it! Hustle up or we start running instead of shooting!"

This last threat catches everyone's attention and within seconds, the players are paired up and waiting at the gym's empty baskets for the drill to start. As usual, Taylor and Jimmy find each other, and as they wait at one of the two main baskets, Coach Waters turns to them from only a few feet away and shouts loud enough for everyone to hear, "Taylor and Jimmy! You two separate this time! I don't want to break up your marriage, but let's see if we can make some other friends on this team for you!"

With the team laughing at Coach Waters' joke, the two friends instantly start to plead their case.

"No! No! I've made up my mind!" Coach Waters replies with a shake of his head. "You two need to find other partners! Now stop stalling and let's go!"

Reluctantly giving in to Coach Waters' demand, Taylor stays at the main basket, pairing up with Garrett Chapman, an up-and-coming gangly sophomore who's shown flashes of brilliance, while Jimmy pairs up with Eric Goodwin at one of the side baskets, apparently forgiving him and all his sins from the night before.

The goal of this shooting drill is to recreate game situations and have the players react and not think, with repetition being the key to its success. Guards shoot jump shots from the foul line extended and the corners, while big men work on their post moves down on the low blocks. Due to his unique combination of skill and size, Taylor works on both. This rare combination is what makes all the college coaches drool so much—he can step outside and shoot jump shots over smaller defenders or post up down low and use his quickness to score in the lane. He's a match-up nightmare for high school defenses, the same way he's projected to be next season in college.

As soon as Taylor hears Coach Waters' whistle to begin the drill, he starts working on his outside jump shot. It doesn't matter where on the court he shoots the ball from, shot after shot seemingly hits nothing but net each time it sails through the rim. The repetition of the drill, combined with his need to concentrate on something other than Kelly, eventually starts to calm his still rattled nerves.

When the drill's first two minutes are over, Coach Waters blows his whistle to let the players know shooters and passers need to switch positions. With Garrett now shooting and Taylor passing, Garrett smoothly steps into each one of his shots, making it more than he misses; proving that he can keep up with The Great Scott, if nothing else, at least during a shooting drill.

Two minutes later, when it's Taylor's turn to shoot again, he heads down to the low blocks and begins to work on his post moves. After making a few short bank shots, he decides to take it to another level. Receiving the entry pass from Garrett, he takes one power dribble, spins to the center of the lane and dunks the ball. *Thwump!* Immediately reposting, he takes another pass from Garrett and repeats this move. *Thwump!* He then repeats this same move again and again, each time with more intensity than the last. *Thwump! Thwump!!* The sound of the rim snapping loudly back into place after each dunk catches everyone's attention, including Coach Waters, who tries not to stare at Taylor in awe.

Throughout the entire drill, Coach Waters never leaves his position at center court, and apart from blowing his whistle to alert the players to switch positions, he doesn't do anything else besides yell random instructions when he sees fit.

In addition to Taylor, a few of the other players push themselves hard to improve during this drill, but many of the players, especially the ones that don't play all that much or joined the team for the camaraderie and the exercise, rather than their love of the game, take this time to goof off as much as possible. With Coach Preisler and Coach Matthews having the day off, Coach Waters is the only set of eyes for twelve players spread out over six baskets, a fact that hasn't been lost on the Wildcats, all of whom knew from the minute they stepped into the gym that today's practice was going to be an easy one.

Thirty minutes later, at 3:15 p.m., Coach Waters blows his whistle to end the last serious basketball drill of the day, leaving just enough time for the team to have a little fun, "Let's go!" he yells loudly. "It's time to separate the winners from the losers!"

No sooner do these words roll off his tongue than the Wildcats begin to yell back who they think the real losers on the team are. As the team's laughter fills the gym, there seems to be an even tie for this honor between Jayson Dearing and Alex Geiser, two never used juniors. Coach Waters tries to hide his amusement, but can't quite contain himself, "Okay! Okay! I guess I had that one coming!" he laughs out loud. "Sorry, guys," he tells Jayson and Alex with a smile. "But let's get serious about our fun now! We only have fifteen minutes left before we lose the gym to the wrestling team and I want to find out who the real winner on this team is! Everyone hustle up to center court!"

Running to get behind the center court line, the players fight happily among themselves to stake their positions in line. Coach Waters also joins the fun, sliding in between Taylor and Jimmy, who have somehow managed to find their way back to each other.

"You guys know the drill!" Coach Waters yells. "Four balls total! One shot at a time! First one to sink it in from half court gets out of Monday's suicide sprints!"

Standing at the front of the line, Garrett Chapman continues to box out any would be challengers for the right to shoot first as David Smith playfully talks smack into his ear. When Garrett hears Coach Waters' whistle, he takes one giant step forward and launches the first shot toward the rim with a loud grunt. The ball leaves his hand in a hurry, but just like a wayward missile, it sails clear over the backboard, hitting the back wall with a loud thud. As Garrett chases after his missed shot, he holds his hands over his head for protection as basketballs start ricocheting all over the gym.

Most of the players behind Garrett don't even bother to try and shoot using traditional form, instead they just throw the ball at the rim like a baseball, which only makes their shots fly and bounce around the gym with more velocity. As shot after shot misses the basket, the team's laughter gets louder and more contagious with each passing moment.

With the euphoric absurdity of the drill carrying on in full force, Alex Geiser steps to the front of the line, still smarting from his earlier embarrassment. Grabbing the ball with two hands, he takes three running steps forward and heaves it toward the rim from below his waist. In what can only be described as an act of divine intervention, the ball flies within six inches of hitting the ceiling, before crashing into the backboard and straight through the net.

The instant the ball clears the rim, the entire team turns to Alex and starts playfully making fun of him again, while the players closest to him begin to push him around like a rag doll in mock frustration and envy. Freeing himself from their grip, Alex takes off in a mad sprint around the gym, shooting everyone with his fingers and chanting, "In your face!" As the undefeated and 14-0 Longwood Hills Wildcats cry themselves into hysterics, Alex finishes up his last lap around the gym and then collapses spread-eagle onto the floor in exhaustion.

Once the team's laughter officially dies down, Coach Waters calls the players over to center court so he can get serious one more time. Looking closely into the eyes gathered around him in a semi-circle, he first thanks everyone for a positive and focused practice, before preaching a few words about staying out of trouble the rest of the weekend and making sure to represent the school proudly at all times, no matter where they go between now and Monday. The timing and tone of the speech hits Taylor hard.

The second Coach Waters finishes up his speech, the wrestling team starts wheeling their oversized practice mats onto the gym floor, forcing the Wildcats to retreat to the wood bleachers to change back into their street clothes.

Sitting up high on the last row of bleachers, Taylor watches Coach Waters closely for any kind of sign that he knows about the fight with Kelly.

Without so much as looking back at his team again or asking Taylor to stay after practice to talk, Coach Waters grabs his winter coat and leaves the gym in a hurry through one of its side doors. When Taylor sees this, his wavering sanity immediately gets a huge boost, believing Coach Waters doesn't know anything about the fight. Staring at Taylor from across the bleachers, Jimmy watches him break into a smile for the first time since they walked into the party the night before.

CHAPTER 11

On Monday morning, Taylor's alarm blasts loudly throughout his bedroom, waking him up from another night of restless sleep. Staring at the ceiling through blurry eyes, he lies in the darkness, while once again thinking about the day ahead. Throughout the weekend, he checked the computer in the den repeatedly to see if the fight showed up on anyone's social media posts—*it didn't*—and since no one was talking about it online, he's convinced, now more than ever, if he can just get through the next twenty-four hours without having to discuss what happened with anyone, the whole situation will blow right over. Beyond that, he wishes more than anything he could stay under the covers and wait out this mess beneath the safe and watchful eyes of his basketball posters on the wall. Struggling hard against this instinct, he gets out of bed and stands up straight, while mentally preparing for what the day has in store for him.

Just over an hour later, he enters the high school near the cafeteria and makes his way toward his locker in senior's hall. As he walks through the school's fluorescent lit hallways, his immediate plan remains intact—to test the waters before homeroom. This way he can decide if he needs to run the nurse's office and fake being sick or not. If he has to lie to be sent home today, he's prepared to do so; anything to avoid the embarrassment of hearing his name associated with the fight.

With each passing step, the knot in his stomach grows in intensity as he tries to project his normal persona of cool calm. Using the back of his sleeve to wipe away the small beads of cold sweat that have formed on his forehead, he hopes against hope no one will notice how jittery he seems. As he looks around at all the faces in front of him, he sees nothing unusual—no sideway glances, no hushed comments and no finger pointing. Except for his severe case of nervous anxiety, it appears as if today is no different than any other Monday morning in the middle of a long winter, which is to say, everyone looks to be half-asleep and wishing they were still in bed.

As he sits through his third period English class, he does however start to notice something very weird. Not weird enough for him to go to the nurse's office and fake being sick, but definitely strange enough for him to take notice. While he isn't exactly being ignored by his friends and classmates, he isn't exactly being embraced like usual either. Normally, after a Friday night home win, everyone wants to talk to him about the game and what happened. But today, no one seems to want to talk to him about anything, which is even stranger since he won Friday night's game at the buzzer. Everyone's lack of interest is worrisome, but since he doesn't feel like himself, he pushes any negative thoughts he's having as far out of his head as he can.

What happens next is the best he could've hoped for—the day continues on like any other day except for a few less conversations about basketball. No one mentions the fight or whispers behind his back or says anything unusual. His classmates, the school administration and the coaching staff, all of whom have heard the rumors about the fight by now, say and do absolutely nothing.

Even though everyone knew it was wrong, they separately decided if Kelly wasn't going to press charges, they were going to look the other way. With a 14-0 record and a #1 state ranking on the line, no one wants to be the one to bring down the team's superstar for what was already being labeled a simple teenage misunderstanding.

By the time Tuesday night's game rolls around, the Wildcats' home gym is once again filled to capacity as they run their record to 15-0. Taylor pours in 22 points and grabs eleven rebounds, after what can only be described as a slow and sluggish start. The sportswriter covering the game wrote..."*Taylor spent the entire first quarter and part of the second quarter looking like he was waiting for someone to run onto the court and tackle him. Even as a ninth grader, starting on varsity for the first time, he looked more confident and comfortable than he did in the first half of tonight's game...However, by the middle of the third quarter, he was able to straighten things out and was back to his normal, dominating self, once again scoring at will from all over the court and grabbing what seemed like every rebound and loose ball.*"

The final score was an easy 66-49 victory for the Wildcats, with the article finishing up with this last observation: "*If Longwood Hills can play the rest of the season with the same level of intensity and execution it showed in the second half of tonight's game, there is no reason the school shouldn't bring home its second straight state championship later this year.*"

Kelly never came to school that Monday, telling her parents she was too sick to go, and when she did come back on Tuesday, she avoided Taylor at all costs. As a matter of fact, their paths wouldn't cross again the rest of the school year.

CHAPTER 12

The rest of the winter passes rather peacefully and even though most days are short, cold and grey, every now and then a few streaks of orange sunshine stretch across the sky at dusk, breaking up the monotony and providing a ray of hope that winter will be over earlier than the calendar is letting on. During this same time, the Wildcats continue their dominance inside gyms across Northern New Jersey. Rolling over most opponents with relative ease, the wins begin to pile up as the weeks move on. By mid-February, the Wildcats run their record to 20-0 and remain the number #1 ranked team in the state.

With each win, the media attention increases and soon Taylor is being interviewed by everyone—TV stations, websites, magazines and newspapers. He even gets included in a full page spread in a national sports magazine, along with several other projected high school All-Americans. While he tells everyone the attention isn't getting to his head, he secretly signs up for a free online service to send him an email every time his name appears in the media and also goes as far as to keep the national sports magazine article under his pillow so he can easily glance at it whenever he wants.

As for the college coaches, they never stop calling, their pursuit is unyielding. To try and combat this, when the Wildcats record reaches 20-0, Taylor announces in an interview in the *Davidson County Star-Tribune* that he's narrowed his college choices down to Central New York University, Maryland State University and Burnet State University—New Jersey's largest public university. Although, to be truthful, Burnet State University is just a throw-in to keep the hometown fans happy since he isn't really considering playing for such a mediocre program. *The world of Taylor Scott continues to be a good one and he knows it.*

CHAPTER 13

On the first Sunday of March, Bill Scott honks the horn in front of the house he used to share with his first wife and waits patiently for Taylor to come outside. Rather than ring the doorbell and wade through several minutes of uncomfortable small talk with Deborah, Bill instead sits behind the wheel of his new SUV, thinking yet again how much his relationship with his son has changed over the last ten years. At the time of the divorce, Taylor was only seven years old and idolized everything Bill did, so he naively thought their relationship would always stay the same, no matter what. He was sadly mistaken.

Once Bill moved out of the house, things changed almost overnight. With Taylor no longer blindly seeking his approval and instead unleashing angry outbursts at every opportunity, Bill retreated from their relationship, going weeks and sometimes months without seeing or calling Taylor. This ill-advised reaction by Bill helped push Taylor's feelings from intense betrayal to emotional indifference, so much so, that by the time he was a young teenager, Taylor would often tell people he only had one parent.

During these same important years, Deborah worked extremely hard to piece her life back together until she reached financial independence. This new-found freedom not only allowed her to support Taylor on her own, but also helped push Bill even further out of their lives.

From Taylor's point of view, he thought his dad was selfish and greedy for walking out on his family, but it also didn't help any that he had to watch his mom deal with the fallout from the divorce all on his own. During those first few post-divorce years, he would often hear Deborah cry herself to sleep at night and it was during these late nights of emotional torture that he vowed to make his dad sorry he ever decided to leave. While all of this was a lot to handle as a kid, he simply told himself it was time to grow up, there was no other choice.

His dad, on the other hand, remarried almost immediately and put all of his energy into his new relationship and small but growing real estate development business, while trying to forget his first marriage ever happened.

With the heat gently blowing inside the SUV, Bill is still not sure what he could've done differently besides stay in a marriage with a woman he no longer loved. The whole situation ate at his insides, especially since he was raised to believe a son should always treat his father with love and respect, regardless of the father's actions, while Taylor was taught by his mom to believe a father should have to earn his son's love and respect, that a father-son relationship is a two-way street. Either way, Bill and Taylor's relationship is a far cry from the one Bill had with his own dad. But in Taylor's defense, Bill did leave his family for a secretary in the next office building to start a new life and family twenty minutes down the road from his old one.

At this point in their relationship, Bill has no real idea how to connect with Taylor and has resigned himself to looking at the time they spend together, no matter how difficult or uncomfortable it might be, as better than not seeing him at all. His current approach of watching his words carefully and always listening more than he talks seems to be working better than anything else he's tried in years. It's been so successful he's convinced a level of trust and forgiveness has crept back into their relationship.

At the same time, Bill knows Taylor's world is going to drastically change in the fall when he heads off to college and secretly, he hopes this transition will bring about a greater awareness in him, especially as it relates to what he believes is fair and just. Nothing is as black and white as Taylor likes to make things out to be and soon he's going to see for himself that the world is mostly painted grey between the lines. But aside from everything else, Bill is excited to talk to Taylor today about his plans for the future, as more often than not Deborah keeps him in the dark about what's really going on in his son's life.

As Taylor closes the front door and slowly makes his way over to the SUV, Bill is once again amazed by how much his son is looking more and more like a man each day. With his tall and lean frame beginning to fill out, it doesn't take much of an imagination to picture this same body two or three years from now with twenty more pounds of muscle on it; a sight that will be something to behold. And even though Bill has no idea where Taylor's height and athletic talent came from, since no one else in the family is taller than 6' 2" or good enough at a sport to be called anything other than an average high school athlete, he's extremely happy for all of his son's success.

When Taylor reaches the passenger side door, Bill is suddenly overcome by how much he truly loves his son and how much he misses him in his life. Beaming with joy, he waits until Taylor is settled into his seat, before leaning in for a big hug. Instinctively, Taylor pulls away from this embrace, turning their hug into an awkward half-hug, half-pat on the back greeting that sucks the life right out of the SUV.

CHAPTER 14

Driving along Route 17 North, Bill makes a right turn into the parking lot of Grace's Diner and heads for the first open space he sees. A weathered sign with big red letters and rusted orange corners hangs off the chain link fence running along the back of the parking lot. It reads *For Compact Cars Only*. Ignoring this sign, Bill turns his oversized SUV into the empty space without hesitation, coming within centimeters of scraping his side mirror on a black two-door hatchback as he pulls in.

"Perfect, like a glove," he playfully tells Taylor. "Now what do you say we go inside to get something to eat? I'm starved."

Managing to easily pry himself out of the SUV, Bill is standing on the other side of the parking lot in no time, while Taylor struggles to maneuver his large body out of the passenger side door. Flopping onto the cracked pavement, Taylor smacks his left knee into the ground, sending a jolt of pain running through his leg. Jumping to his feet in defiance, he wipes away the loose asphalt from his jeans as he stares at two large open spaces directly next to where his dad is standing, "Unbelievable!" he shouts under his breath. "This day's going to totally suck."

From the other side of the parking lot, Bill sets the SUV's alarm with a loud chirp as he yells to Taylor, "Come on! Let's get a move on!"

"What a joke," Taylor mumbles as he shuffles in the direction of his dad.

Once inside the crowded diner, Bill and Taylor wait to be seated as the voices around them echo loudly off the walls, creating an atmosphere of white noise and eliminating the need for small talk. At least, Taylor thought so.

Hoping to break down his son's all-too-familiar invisible wall, Bill reaches out and lightly rubs Taylor's shoulders as he talks into his ear, "I'm really glad you agreed to come here with me today. I absolutely love this place. There's nothing better than Grace's."

Taylor tries his best to smile back at his dad, while doing what he can to still move away from his physical touch.

Grace's Diner was built in the 1950's and looks like it hasn't been updated since. With a shiny silver exterior, large glass windows and an oversized "Grace's" sign on the roof, it looks more like a flying saucer from an old science fiction movie than a restaurant. Over the years, it has managed to survive through the loyal patronage of customers like Bill, mixed in with hungry motorists traveling on Route 17 who didn't know where else to go eat.

Scanning the diner's expansive eating area, Taylor notices on the opposite side of the room a long, sit-down counter lined with silver stools, whose red vinyl tops have cracked and torn from years of overuse. Behind this long counter is the restaurant's open kitchen, which lets Grace's customers watch their food get prepared by the perpetually busy cooks and filling the air with a rich aroma of grease and eggs. This enticing aroma only adds to Grace's overall charm.

A few feet from where Taylor and Bill are standing in line next to the register, two glass cylinder cases are filled with an assortment of cakes and pies. In all his years eating at diners, Taylor can't ever recall seeing someone order a piece of cake or pie out of one of these glass cases, yet every diner seems to have them. *He wonders if the cakes and pies are even real.*

As they make their way to the front of the line, a pretty Hispanic girl of no more than sixteen years old smiles at the two of them from behind the register, holding her eyes on Taylor for an extra split second before looking away. A moment later, a deep voice booms out from behind them, "Today is definitely going to be a good day, because I think that's Bill Scott I see!"

Turning around, they watch as a heavy-set man with rounded shoulders and thick black glasses who looks to be in his late sixties, move steadily in their direction. Walking right up to Bill, the man violently thrusts his hand outward as the two men shake hands like long last pals, "Mack, how ya doing?" Bill practically shouts. "I'd like you to meet my son, Taylor. Taylor, this is Maurice Kostopolous or Mack for short. He owns the place."

Immediately looking the man up and down, Taylor notices his dress pants are too big for his body and he's missing a button on his wrinkled white shirt, exposing a swath of hairy stomach below.

"Nice to meet you," Taylor quietly responds with an awkward look on his face.

"Whew! You're tall! You must be the basketball player. It's nice to finally meet you. We've been following your career for years," Mack sweeps his arm across the diner as he says this. "I'm so happy you could finally make it into Grace's. But then again, I blame your dad for that one."

"Thank you," Taylor replies, once again not knowing what to say to an unprompted compliment.

Shifting uncomfortably in place, Taylor suddenly feels weird and somehow violated that his dad has been bragging about him to complete strangers all these years, *"I bet these people think he's dad of the year!"* he starts to get angry. *"I bet they don't even know half the story! Wait! He shouldn't have the right to brag about me! He's got nothing to do with my success!"*

"You have to know your dad's a great guy," Mack tells Taylor in a sincere voice. "Salt of the earth."

"Uh, huh," Taylor grunts back.

"Come on, stop it! You're embarrassing me," Bill jumps in, nudging Mack lightly in the ribs with his elbow.

"Embarrass you? I don't think you have it in you," Mack answers with a gap-toothed smile. "Come on, you two. I have your dad's favorite booth waiting empty in front. Let's get you something to eat."

"It's about time," Bill responds with a laugh as he nudges Mack lightly in the ribs again.

As Mack shows Bill and Taylor to an old decrepit booth at the front of the diner overlooking the flow of traffic on Route 17, Taylor notices the booth's red vinyl is also cracked and torn as pieces of yellow cushion randomly sprout through the vinyl like weeds pushing through a stone path. Before they are even seated, Taylor is struck, yet again, by how nice his dad treats acquaintances and how much they seem to genuinely like him. He reasons, not for the first time, that if his dad only treated his mom half as nicely as he does basically strangers, they all might have a better relationship by now.

A few seconds later, an old waitress, older than even Mack, ambles over to their table with a stack of menus shoved underneath her arm. Wearing Grace's standard issue red and white cotton dress uniform with matching red lipstick, she peers at Bill and Taylor from behind heart shaped glasses and orange frosted hair, "How you boys doing today?" she asks.

"Just great, May!" Bill responds loudly. "How are you doing?"

"Jeez, Bill. I almost didn't see you there," May replies, squinting from across the table. "Nice to see you again."

"You too. Taylor, this is May, the best waitress in all of New Jersey. May, this is my son, Taylor."

"Hi," Taylor politely responds with a wave.

"May, since this is Taylor's first time to Grace's, what do you say we give him the royal treatment?" Bill practically commands.

"It'll be my pleasure. Wait...are you Taylor the basketball player?"

"Yes, he is!" Bill responds loud of enough for most of the other customers to hear.

"Taylor, you have know, your dad brags about you all the time. You're his favorite topic of discussion. Do you know that?"

"No, I didn't," Taylor answers, scrunching his brow in disbelief.

"Well, it's true. Every time he's in here, he tells us all about your accomplishments. We can't quiet him up. Here, take these menus and I'll be right back with your waters. And welcome to Grace's, Taylor."

As May slowly waddles away, Taylor is startled by what she just said. Unsure of how to process this information, his mind starts to wander to weird thoughts about her, *"I wonder if May has been a waitress her whole life? If not, what did she do before this? Does she live in a nice house? In a nice neighborhood? Can someone even afford nice things on a waitress' salary?"*

His dad's voice snaps him back to reality, "How's it going? How's your mom doing?"

"What?" Taylor responds, looking back confused.

"Your mom, how's she doing?"

"She's good, I guess."

"Is she seeing anyone?"

"Seriously, Dad? Come on!"

"Sorry, I know you think it's a weird question for me to ask, but I just want to see her happy, that's all."

"Then you shouldn't have divorced her," Taylor thinks to himself. *"That would've made her happy."*

"Mom's fine," he finally answers in an angry tone. "And I don't think she's seeing anyone."

"Well, I hope she meets someone soon. Your mom's a good woman. She deserves a good man."

"Sure, I'll let her know," Taylor sarcastically answers.

"Uh, oh, wrong turn," Bill thinks to himself and quickly tries to change directions. "So tell me about your plans for next year. Where's your head right now in terms of school and playing ball?"

"Well, uhm...You know," Taylor stumbles through his reply. "I'm just not...I guess, I'm just not sure what I want to do right now."

"What do you mean? Come on, talk to me, I'm your dad."

Somehow hearing the word *dad* come out of Bill's mouth strikes an emotional chord deep within Taylor. Taking a deep breath, he exhales slowly, before deciding to trust his dad with his feelings, "The truth is I've actually been thinking about it *a lot* lately. Too much, really."

"Too much?" Bill answers with surprise. "How can that be? This is a big decision."

"I know. It's just, I'm a little confused right now and these coaches don't stop calling. Every one of them thinks I'm the perfect fit for their school. I...I'm just not sure what I'm supposed to believe anymore. Not to mention, the pressure they're putting on me to make a decision is *insane.*"

"I know it's easier said than done, but don't let them do that to you. They'll hold a spot for you. Trust me."

"You think so?"

"Hi...Sorry...Am I interrupting?" May breaks up the flow of their conversation just as it's starting to get interesting. "I wanted to see if you boys are ready to order?" she asks without taking her eyes off of the small green pad in her hand.

"Sorry, May, we've been talking since you left. We haven't even looked at our menus yet," Bill apologizes. "But don't leave, I'm sure we can decide quickly. As a matter of fact, I don't even need to look at my menu," he boasts.

"Okey, dokey, then shoot," May fires back.

"I'll have the number four. Three scrambled eggs, hash browns and bacon. Coffee, but no juice," Bill rattles off from memory. "Taylor, you're up."

"Wait. What?" he responds, picking up his menu for the first time. *So much for the royal treatment.* "Uhm, I think I'll just have a cheese omelet with some orange juice," he finally answers.

"The number two then?" May asks.

"Sure, as long as the number two is a cheese omelet with some orange juice," he sarcastically responds.

"What kind of cheese?" May doesn't miss a beat.

"American."

"Anything else in the omelet? Tomatoes? Green peppers? Onions?" May's pen is ready to go.

"Uhm...Tomatoes."

"Hash browns or toast?"

"Hash browns."

"Side of bacon?"

"No," Taylor answers, closing his menu, relieved the pressure to order is now over.

"Perfect, be back with your food real soon," May replies with a smile full of red lipstick. Grabbing the two menus, she places them underneath her arm and waddles away toward the kitchen.

As soon as May is out of earshot, Bill dives right back into their conversation from before, "If there's so much pressure on you, why don't you call me more to talk about things? I can help, you know," he seems to be on the verge of almost pleading with Taylor. "Believe it or not, your old man has been around for a while. I've learned a thing or two along the way."

"I dunno. I guess, it's just...I'm trying to figure out what I want to do and since it changes so much, I don't want to bother you. If I called you every time I changed my mind, I'd be calling you every hour."

"So what?" Bill answers. "I don't mind. I'm your father. I'd be happy to talk to you every hour. As a matter of fact, I'd be happy to talk to you several times every hour, if you wanted."

"Come on, Dad! You're a busy guy. I can't call you that much. Plus, when I've called your house too much in the past, Cindy gets mad."

"What? No, she doesn't."

Taylor doesn't respond and stares back at his dad blankly.

"You can call the house anytime," Bill tells Taylor. "Trust me, Cindy doesn't mind. Really, she sees you as her other son."

"A son she can't stand," Taylor thinks to himself.

Not wanting to head down this dead-end path again, Taylor decides to steer the conversation back to his upcoming decision. "I hear what you're saying, it's just, I'm not sure what I want to do," he vaguely looks at his dad as he says this. "It's all so confusing. I mean, I'm leaning toward Maryland State University right now, with Central New York University a close second, but you never know. Mom and I are going to take my last campus visits after the season is over and I'll decide after that."

At hearing this news, Bill's face changes into a disturbing frown.

"The thing is," Taylor keeps going, doing his best to ignore his dad's expression. "I really like Coach McCallom at Maryland State University, at least, so far. He's a Jersey guy, so I feel like he might "get me" a little more than the other coaches, you know."

"Yeah, that makes sense," Bill answers, still disappointed at not being invited along for Taylor's last campus visits. But never one to give up easily, he snaps right back and strikes at his son's soft heart, "I hear what you're saying about visiting the schools with your mom, but don't you want your old man with you too? It's important to have another guy's perspective when dealing with these coaches face-to-face, nothing against your mom and all."

This time Taylor doesn't blink, "Sorry, Dad. I told Mom it would only be the two of us. But we'll call you from the road and let you know how things are going. Really, it's no big deal."

Bill can't understand at all, and wants to stand on the table and yell at his son, *"You're going to need me someday! You just watch! You think you have all the answers? Wait until life kicks you while you're down!"*

Instead, he simply responds in a flat deflated voice, "Yeah, I get it. Don't worry. I'm here if you need me. Call me anytime you want. I mean it."

Once again on the outside looking in, Bill abruptly loses steam for their conversation, but not before he takes the high road, "It's like you said earlier, any of the schools calling you would love to have you. You're great. You're my son. Who wouldn't want you? Next year is going to be the start of something amazing for you."

After listening to this last string of emotionless words, Taylor shakes his head in disbelief at how fragile his dad's ego is and how bad he is at giving advice when he feels like he's been hurt, *"Maybe, May could give me some better advice?"* he sarcastically thinks to himself. *"I think I'll ask her to sit down and talk to me the next time she comes back to our table."*

After a long period of silence, filled with awkward stares at the relentless stream of cars and trucks on Route 17 passing by outside the booth's window, their father-son conversation slowly, but surely improves. At first, they talk about how great things are going for the Wildcats and how much fun Taylor is having playing basketball his senior year and a few minutes later, they shift the conversation to football and the local team's need to replace their aging offensive line if they ever want to have a chance at making the playoffs next season. Somewhere in between talking about the Wildcats and football, May stopped by their table and dropped off their hot plates of food. Neither of them noticed her.

CHAPTER 15

Rat-a-tat-tat. Rat-a-tat-tat. Rat-a-tat-tat. The ball echoes in rhythm off the gym floor.

Rat-a-tat-tat. Rat-a-tat-tat. Rat-a-tat-tat. The world outside the gym begins to melt away.

Rat-a-tat-tat. Rat-a-tat-tat. Rat-a-tat-tat. The rhythm of the bouncing ball transforms Taylor from an everyday teenager into a high school basketball superstar.

It's Saturday night, March 21st and the gym is sold out for the New Jersey state championship game between the Longwood Hills Wildcats and the Morrisville Pirates. Standing just beyond half court, Taylor temporarily warms up alone, while the rest of the Wildcats go through lay-up lines only a few feet away. At 29-0, the Longwood Hills Wildcats are attempting to close out the greatest season in the history of the school without as much as a single loss. Before Taylor entered Longwood Hills High School, the only basketball state championship the school ever won was in 1973, with its second state championship coming last season during Taylor's junior year, when he led the Wildcats to a 27-3 record and a runaway twenty point victory over Badenbrook High School in the title game. In addition to bringing joy to everyone in Longwood Hills, last year's state championship title helped propel Taylor's reputation from the inner circles of New Jersey basketball to the national scene, where it has remained ever since.

The energy pulsating throughout Longwood Hills coming into tonight's game is at a fever pitch. Black and gold banners hang everywhere throughout town and if someone didn't know about the success of the high school basketball team and its star player before they went to the supermarket or some other public area, they knew everything about them by the time they left. The town is in a heightened state of self-congratulations.

As Taylor tries to calm his rapidly beating heart, he breathes in deeply and stares at the gym floor so he can concentrate on something other than the sold-out crowd of 5,000 slowly filling up the bleachers.

Rat-a-tat-tat. Rat-a-tat-tat. Rat-a-tat-tat. The overhead lights from the ceiling create orange and yellow elliptical shadows on the gym floor, reminding him that he'll once again be performing on a stage tonight.

Rat-a-tat-tat. Rat-a-tat-tat. Rat-a-tat-tat. With the bleachers packed and the lights shining their magic, he feels nothing short of a conquering hero. He imagines this is the same feeling every great warrior has felt since the beginning of time right before his biggest battle.

Rat-a-tat-tat. Rat-a-tat-tat. Rat-a-tat-tat. The pit in his stomach squeezes his nerves tightly and attempts to render him lifeless.

More than anyone, Taylor knows tonight's game will help define his legacy at the school. With everything on the line, he wants to go out and do things on the court tonight no one has ever seen or done before. He wants to inspire people and make them revere in his talent, to have them *oooohh* and *aaaahh* at his every move.

Rat-a-tat-tat. Rat-a-tat-tat. Rat-a-tat-tat. The ball bounces between his legs, around his back and in front of his body as the bottoms of his feet tingle with anxiety and beads of sweat slowly drip down the back of his neck.

From across the gym, Taylor stares at Morrisville's own high school celebrity, Xavier Jackson, as he streaks toward the basket during lay-up lines and softly drops the ball through the rim. At 6'2" and 210 lbs., along with lightning quick hands and feet, some media outlets have gone as far as to call Xavier the best point guard to come out of the state of New Jersey in over fifteen years. With a commitment to play next year for one of the best college basketball programs on the East Coast, Xavier's future rise to prominence seems all but assured.

In a few weeks, Taylor and Xavier will also join each other on the New Jersey All-State First Team and while they are familiar with one another from the traveling summer basketball circuit, tonight they are sworn enemies, each standing in the way of the other's dream. *Xavier silently returns Taylor's stare from across the gym.*

On top of going through lay-up lines, most of the Morrisville Pirates use this time to glance over at Taylor standing on the other side of half court. In anticipation of tonight's match-up, the Morrisville coaches have been talking about Taylor's game for so long that most of the Pirates feel as if they're about to go up against a player with superhero abilities. When Taylor broke the Davidson County career scoring record earlier this season, it was the Morrisville coaches who told the news to the Pirates the morning after it happened. At the same time, the Morrisville coaches' strategy to challenge its players to stop Taylor may have also inadvertently psyched a few of them out along the way. Coaching is a tricky business, especially on the high school level where the players' moods can swing back and forth like the wind. Either way, tonight is Morrisville's chance to take down The Great Scott, ruin Longwood Hills' perfect season and bring home its own state championship, a goal most of the Pirates have been dreaming about for as long as they can remember.

Just beyond the baseline, reporters from all over the state are spread out like sitting ducks, with one corner of the gym occupied by TV crews alone. Taylor's mom walked into the gym earlier and like all games, he gave her a quick smile and wave from his position on the court. He also caught a glimpse of his dad as he took his seat in the stands, but as usual, he didn't make any effort to acknowledge his presence. The one person he hoped to see, but didn't, was Kelly. While he's a little disappointed by her absence, he also understands on a very gut level why she's not in the gym. Come to think of it, he realizes he hasn't seen her at all in the last few months and wonders for the first time, in a long time, if she still hates him for everything that happened at the party.

Shaking this thought out of his head, he rejoins his teammates for lay-up lines as just over five minutes remain on the clock before tip-off.

CHAPTER 16

"Let's go! Everybody in! We don't have much time!" Coach Waters yells above the noise of the crowd.

Hearing his voice from across the court, the Wildcats stop their lay-up lines and head over to their bench. Wearing a grey patterned blazer, a black tie and a perfectly pressed white shirt, Coach Waters tries to project a sense of reserved calm as Coach Preisler and Coach Matthews stand next to him, each wearing their best sport coat and dress pants, while also carrying Wildcat clipboards and pens in an effort to look as official as possible. As Taylor approaches Coach Waters, he can't help but notice the lines on his face seem more pronounced than usual.

"Okay, everyone gather in real close so you can hear me!" Coach Waters yells again, signaling for the Wildcats to close ranks and form a tight semi-circle around him. *"Tonight is definitely something special. There's no doubt about it.* We all know what's at stake here, so I'm not going to make things any bigger than they already are. Just remember, if we go out and play our game tonight, the same way we've played all season, it doesn't matter what Morrisville does out on the floor, because we're going to win. We're the better team. We've proven it all season and tonight is just one more opportunity for us to go out and prove it again. Let's run our offense and not get pulled into a run and gun game with these guys. We can't get into a street fight. On defense, let's not forget the ball-you-man principles we've worked hard on all year. Everyone, stay in front of your assignment and don't give up any easy baskets. *I repeat, no easy baskets.* If we do all of these things tonight and we do them with *energy, passion* and *execution*, we'll walk out of this gym as state champions," upon hearing these last words, the Wildcats erupt in nervous claps as chills run down their spines. "Guys, you will remember this night the rest of your lives, so let's make every second count. There are no do-overs. *This is it!* Let's play hard for thirty-two minutes! What do you say? Are we going out tonight as winners?"

"YES!" the Wildcats scream.

"I can't hear you!" Coach Waters yells back.

"YEEEEESSSS!!!!!!!!" the Wildcats scream again.

"Okay, hands in one last time! Wildcats on three! ONE-TWO-THREE WILDCATS!"

The intensity inside the now hot gym grabs hold of the sold-out crowd as the starters from each team are announced. No matter how hard they try, most of the players from tonight's game will never match the adrenaline high they feel right now the rest of their lives, even though many of them will spend years chasing after it. When Taylor and Xavier are introduced to the crowd over the P.A. system, thunderous applause rains down onto the court, creating a level of indescribable expectation for the game ahead.

At the end of player introductions, the coaches corral their teams one last time in an effort to provide last-second instructions as the players bounce around high-fiving each other to try and shake off what's left of their nervous energy. When the game horn sounds over the shouting of the cheerleaders, everyone knows tip-off is only seconds away.

Standing at center court, the referee blows his whistle loudly as he throws the ball high into the air to start the game. Skying for the opening tip, Taylor easily wins possession over Morrisville's smaller center, sending the ball backwards into David Smith's waiting hands. Momentarily placing the ball on his hip, David holds it tightly as Xavier races forward to meet him on defense with an icy intensity in his eyes. Looking right back into Xavier's eyes, David takes one dribble between his legs, before taking a hard dribble to his right to start the Wildcats' offense. He only gets about two feet up the floor before he's stopped cold. No match for Xavier's size and speed, David bounces off Xavier's chest as a look of surprise washes over him. With his pulse now racing with anxiety, David looks into Xavier's eyes again as Xavier playfully stares back at him with a smirk.

Not one to be easily deterred, David puts his head down and figures out a way to slowly dribble the ball up the court as Xavier bumps and pressures him the whole way. Dribbling two steps over half court, David does the unthinkable. Breaking one of the cardinal sins of a point guard, he picks up his dribble with no one to pass it to. Trapped by the half court line behind him and Xavier in front of him, jumping up and down and yelling, *"Ball! Ball! Ball!"* he's stuck! Ten seconds into the game, the Wildcats look to be overmatched.

Eric Goodwin sees David struggle from the other side of the court and makes an alert decision. Sprinting forward, he calls for David to pass him the ball. Recognizing a safety net when he sees one, David throws Eric a one-handed pass over Xavier's outstretched arms and takes Eric's position on the baseline. The Wildcats' first crisis of the game is swiftly averted.

Dribbling hard to his left, Eric starts the Wildcats' offense as David runs across the lane and sets a screen for Taylor on the low block. Feeling the play develop, Taylor takes one step away from David's screen, before quickly spinning back to where he started. Hesitating in the middle of the lane, he plants his back foot and runs hard toward Garrett Chapman, who's waiting with another screen above the foul line. In one fluid motion, Taylor slides behind Garrett's screen, receives the pass from Eric and steps into his jump shot—*swish!* The ball hits nothing but net. The Wildcats strike first, 2-0.

"Nice try," Taylor whispers in his defender's ear as he jogs back on defense.

Wasting no time, Xavier takes the inbounds pass from his teammate and races up the court. Putting his head down, he dribbles hard for the basket in an attempt to score before the Wildcats can set their defense. Watching the play unfold in a panic, David desperately tries to cut Xavier off at the three-point line, but he's too late. He bounces off Xavier's shoulder and falls to the floor. Xavier doesn't even bother to look down at David as he takes two more hard dribbles and lays the ball uncontested into the basket. In the blink of an eye, the score is tied 2-2.

Over the next few minutes, the game takes on a similar ebb and flow as the Wildcats need a lot of time and energy to score each time down the floor, while the Pirates push the tempo and seem to score almost at will. Standing in front of the Wildcats' bench with his arms crossed in frustration, Coach Waters appears very uneasy as a week of sleepless nights looks to be coming true right before his eyes.

The next time the Wildcats are on offense, Eric misses a long jump shot, which is easily corralled by the Pirates center. After taking the outlet pass, Xavier pushes the ball up the court again, before slowing down just above the three-point line. Dribbling two steps above the three-point line, he stares down Jimmy, who checked into the game for David, and waits for a high screen from one of his teammates. Reading the screen as it arrives, Xavier takes one dribble to his right as Jimmy gets tangled up in the Pirate player's arms and legs. Seeing his opening, Xavier pushes the ball forward, just as Garrett Chapman tries to step in front of him. It's no use. Xavier blows by Garrett at full speed.

Watching the play develop from the baseline, Taylor switches off his man and runs over to help out. Reaching the lane at full speed, Xavier rises toward the rim at the exact same time Taylor takes a giant step forward and leaps into the air with his right arm outstretched to try and block his shot. Meeting in mid-air, the two players collide with a loud smack as the referee's whistle pierces the noisy gym.

As the crowd collectively gasps, Taylor flies backward onto the floor as Xavier's shot hits the front of the rim and gently rolls into the basket. *And one! Basket counts and the foul!*

Taking a step in Taylor's direction, Xavier stands above him and whispers under his breath, *"You're real soft, Bro. Real soft."*

Lying on the floor in pain, Taylor does his best to let the embarrassment from the play slowly pass as he watches Xavier walk to the foul line.

"You okay, man?" Eric shouts as he runs over to Taylor.

"Yeah, I'm good. Just give me a second."

"No worries, take as much time you need," Eric answers, ignoring the pained look splashed across Taylor's face.

A few moments later, when Taylor signals he's finally ready to get up, Eric helps him to his feet, while doing what he can to give his confidence a boost, "Don't worry about it, man! That call could've gone either way. Shake it off."

"Thanks, Bro. But it's all good," Taylor responds as he makes his way over to the low block to wait for Xavier's free throw. Gasping for air, he casually rests his hand on his lower back, hoping no one can see how much pain he's in.

After getting the ball from the referee, Xavier easily knocks down his free throw to complete the three-point play and put the Pirates up by a score of 12-6.

With the first quarter winding down, Eric tips in a missed shot by Jimmy to cut into the Pirates' lead, but when the horn sounds to end the first eight minutes, the scoreboard reads Morrisville Pirates 18, Longwood Hills Wildcats 12.

The start of the second quarter brings out the Pirates' full court press as they try to push the tempo of the game and take the Wildcats out of their comfort zone. But after a week of focused practice, the Wildcats appear unfazed and easily handle this increase in defensive intensity without any problems. With a few minutes remaining before halftime, Taylor makes a steal at center court and glides in for an uncontested one-handed tomahawk jam that sends the Wildcats' half of the gym into a frenzy that seems to shake the roof. At the same time, Xavier continues to drive to the basket almost at will to keep the Wildcats at a distance.

When the horn sounds to end the second quarter, the Pirates lead by a score of 34-23. Xavier finishes the first half with 15 of his team's 34 points, while Taylor finishes with 11 of his team's 23 points. The game that was hyped as a colossal battle of stars was playing out exactly the way everyone in the stands hoped it would.

Heading into the locker room for halftime, the Wildcats' emotions are extremely low. They haven't been down many times all season at the break and they've never been down as many points as they are tonight. The thought of trying to erase the Pirates' 11-point halftime lead feels almost insurmountable, since they didn't play badly over the first two quarters as much as they were just outplayed. As they sit in the locker room waiting anxiously for words of wisdom from their leader, what they get in return at first is unfortunately something closer to a nervous ramble.

"I'm going to keep this short, guys," Coach Waters begins, his voice scratchy and hoarse from trying to yell over the noise of the crowd. "It's pretty simple what we have to do to get back into this game. *We have to get in front of Xavier and stop him from driving to the basket.* Even if it means leaving some of their other players open. He's the main reason we're down so much right now. I know it's easier said than done, but we have to figure out a way to stop Xavier from scoring!" the Wildcats involuntarily cringe and sink into their seats when they hear Coach Waters make this demand.

Stopping for a moment to look at the nervous faces in front of him, Coach Waters suddenly catches on that he has to take his halftime speech in a different direction; demanding more effort isn't going to solve the problem: "On a positive note, I think we did a nice job of handling their defensive pressure, so I don't want to make any real big changes on the offensive side of the ball. But I do want to make one change. When we start the third quarter, I want Jimmy at the point guard spot for David. Jimmy, see if you can get Xavier to work a little harder on defense. Hopefully, wear him out some, this way he's too tired to shoot the ball." Upon hearing this news, Jimmy and Taylor share a silent look from across the locker room that says it all.

Turning now to David, Coach Waters directs his attention solely on him, "David, we still need you. You're going to be a big part of what we want to do as a team in the second half, so make sure you're ready to go when I call your name." Even though he has no choice, David reluctantly nods his acceptance to Coach Waters.

Once again looking at the rest of the Wildcats, Coach Waters now finishes up his halftime speech with enthusiasm, "We need everyone right now if we're going to get back into this game and win it! So be ready, all of you! There are still sixteen minutes of basketball left to be played! So let's not hang our heads just yet! Sixteen minutes to see who leaves tonight as state champions! I say it's going to be us! Are you with me?"

"Yes."

"I can't hear you!"

"YES!"

"I still can't hear you!"

"YEEESSSSSS!!!"

"That's more like it!" Coach Waters yells. "Hands in one more time! Let's go! We can do this! Wildcats on three! ONE-TWO-THREE WILDCATS!"

As the third quarter opens up, the Wildcats come out firing on all cylinders, hitting several straight shots to cut into the Pirates' halftime lead. Not to be outdone, the Pirates fight right back and re-establish their commanding lead by stopping the Wildcats on defense and scoring the ball when they have it on offense. With the clock ticking away precious minutes at a time, the Pirates start believing deep in their hearts, perhaps for the first time all night, they really are on their way to knocking off the undefeated Wildcats.

Basketball, however, is a game of runs and tonight is no different. Just when the Pirates seem to have taken back control of the game for good, Coach Waters' halftime gamble begins to pay off. With unending energy, Jimmy forces Xavier to chase him all over the court on offense and on defense; making Xavier give up the ball on offense to his teammates earlier than he wants to. Caught off guard, the rest of the Pirates look almost afraid to shoot when Xavier passes the ball to them, grinding their offense to a halt and propelling the game's momentum back to the Wildcats.

Coming out of an intense timeout, Xavier's frustration boils over as he dresses down his teammates in full view of the crowd. Yelling and swinging his hands wildly to emphasize his points, the crowd watches from the edge of their seats as he seems determined to alienate his own team. But instead of backfiring, his outburst does the exact opposite, *it works like magic.* Wanting nothing more than to make their leader happy, the Pirates immediately snap out of their funk and start hitting their open shots. This sudden change sends the game's momentum swinging back in the Pirates' direction as they extend their lead to 43-31 with just under five minutes left to go in the third quarter.

On the Wildcats' next offensive possession, Jimmy sends a bounce pass into the low post to Garrett, who fakes going baseline, before using a strong power dribble to turn into the center of the lane. Pump-faking his man into the air, Garrett attempts to shoot the ball, but is soundly hit on the arm by his defender.

Awarded two free throws for the foul call, Garrett steps to the foul line to try and cut into the Pirates' lead. Focusing all of his energy on the front of the rim, he calmly takes two dribbles and releases the ball. His first shot hits nothing but net. While he waits patiently for his second shot, the Wildcats clap and yell with excitement all around him. Suddenly aware of his surroundings, his heart begins to race rapidly like runaway freight train and his legs become wobbly. With the ball back in his hands again, he takes two more dribbles and releases his second shot. Unfortunately, the ball is off its mark right from the start. Skipping hard off the front of the rim, it ricochets off a Pirate player's hand, before bounding toward the sideline in a hurry.

Both Xavier and Jimmy see the ball at the exact same time and sprint forward to try and save it from going out of bounds. The details of what happens next has since become folklore in Longwood Hills, growing in size, stature and some would say believability over the years.

Getting to the ball first, Xavier bends down to pick it up in stride as Jimmy comes barreling in from behind him at full speed. Unable to stop his momentum, Jimmy catches Xavier off balance. The collision sends Xavier flying headfirst into the scorer's table, where he lands against the table's legs with a loud crunch. Violently screaming out in pain, Xavier grabs his right shoulder as Jimmy stares down at him in stunned silence.

The Pirates fans sitting behind the scorer's table immediately jump to their feet and start pointing and screaming at Jimmy with venom and hatred in their eyes. Staring in disbelief at their anger, Jimmy turns away from the bleachers, toward the safety of the court, but it's no longer there. The Pirates' starting forward bumps right into his chest, "What'd you do, man?" he screams at Jimmy.

"What're you talking about?"

"I said, what'd you do? What're you deaf?"

"Get out of my face! I didn't do anything wrong!" Jimmy snarls back.

"What'd you say to him?" a second Pirates player leans into Jimmy's shoulder.

"Back off me!"

"What'd you say to me, punk?"

"I said, back off me! What're *you* deaf?"

"Step off, Little Man! I'm telling you, back up!"

"Why? What're you going to do about it? I'm not afraid of you!"

"I'm not asking you to be afraid! I'm telling you to be afraid!" and with that, the second player pops his elbow into Jimmy's chest.

Stunned, Jimmy looks around for help, but the referees are nowhere to be found.

"Try again!" Jimmy shouts as he leans forward and grits his teeth. "You don't scare me!" and retaliates by burying his shoulder deep into the second player's ribs.

"You couldn't guard Xavier so you had to hurt him! I'm going to kill you!" the starting forward shouts into Jimmy's ear.

"What're you talking about? It was a clean play!"

"Clean play? If it was so clean, how come you're standing over here and he's lying over there?" the starting forward points at Xavier on the floor.

"It's called basketball!"

"What'd you say, punk?"

"I said, it's called basketball!"

"You think you're so smart? Smart people don't last too long from where I come from!"

"Then I'm glad I'm not where you're from, because this smart punk isn't going anywhere!"

Finally snapping out of their daze, the Wildcats sprint across the court to help protect Jimmy as the rest of the Pirates and the game's three referees, who are now in a state of panic that things are about to spin out of control, follow closely behind.

"Yo! Get off him!" Eric yells at Jimmy's two tormentors in the middle of a dead run. "I'm talking to you! Don't put your hands on him!"

"Go to hell!" the starting forward returns Eric's threat. "Your man's dirty, punk!"

"Screw you! It was a clean play!" Taylor shouts.

"Screw you, All-American!" the second Pirates player shouts back. "Your boy took out Xavier, now we're coming after you!"

"Step off!" Taylor sneers as he points his finger in the second Pirates player's face.

Seeing the situation unfold, one of the referees grabs Taylor from behind and pulls him away from the argument. It's not a moment too soon.

Moving now without hesitation, the head referee jumps in between the rest of the players and begins to take back control of the game. *"Enough!"* he shouts in all directions, *"I said, enough!"*

Alarmed at the players' still simmering tempers, both head coaches run onto the court to help the referees keep the peace as their assistants stay on the sidelines, yelling to their teams to remain calm and not to leave the bench.

"You better watch your back!" the starting forward taunts Jimmy one last time over one of the referee's shoulders. "I know where you live!"

"You don't scare me!" Jimmy yells back defiantly. "Read my lips, U-DON'T-SCARE-ME!"

Swiveling his head from side to side, the head referee's voice now booms with authority, "*I said, that's enough!* I mean it! No more trash talking! The next guy that says anything is getting thrown out of here! You understand me? Don't ruin a well-played game by being stupid! Now go back to your benches!"

Still fuming with anger, the players reluctantly listen to the head referee and start heading in silence in the direction of their benches. As they do this, both head coaches stand guard to make sure no one gets any funny ideas.

With order temporarily restored, the three referees huddle close together at center court, deciding what they should do next. As a wave of anxiety fills the gym, the three referees whisper quietly to one another, weighing the fate of the players and ultimately, the game in their hands.

Over on the sidelines, some of the players remain quiet, but most slap five with each other to show how proud they are of one another for not backing down.

Not a sound can be heard in the gym when the head referee steps away from the huddle and walks over the scorer's table to make what will be his biggest call of the night. With the crowd watching breathlessly, he signals his momentous call with both hands, a technical foul for each team's bench—*that's it!* The referees collectively decided they didn't want to overact to all the pushing and shoving by handing out technical fouls or ejecting players in the middle of a state championship game, especially since they didn't see any punches or elbows thrown. If Jimmy had the chance to speak up, he would show them the tennis ball-sized bruise now forming on his chest. But instead of complaining, he decides to focus all his anger on making the Pirates pay for their actions.

With Xavier's high school basketball career coming to a shocking end, he's helped off the court by the Pirates' trainers to a standing ovation from both sides of the gym. A sign of sportsmanship that only minutes earlier would have seemed impossible. Watching Xavier slowly walk off the court in agony, everyone in the gym is once again reminded that we aren't always in control of the big moments in our lives, no matter how badly we wish we were.

"Don't worry about it, man!" Taylor shouts, getting up close in Jimmy's face. "You didn't do anything wrong!"

"Yeah, man. I know!" Jimmy shouts back, his face still burning with adrenaline.

"Guys! Over here! Now!" Coach Waters yells.

With the gym eerily quiet with the reality that Xavier isn't coming back, Coach Waters decides to grab this moment by the throat. While he never wants to lead his team to victory because of an injury, he's been around long enough to know the Wildcats' best chance to take home a second consecutive state title has suddenly appeared. Calling the Wildcats in real close so no one else can hear what he's about to say, the volume of his voice is just above a whisper, "Listen up, guys. And I mean, *really listen*. You're about to experience a great lesson in life about taking advantage of the opportunities presented to you. We didn't ask for Xavier to get injured, but he did. Without sounding cruel, odds are the Pirates are going to be disoriented for the next few minutes as they try to figure out how to play without him. This leaves a *very* big opening for us to get back into this game."

Scanning the faces in front of him, Coach Waters senses a level of disappointment at what he just said. But instead of softening his message, he purses his lips and focuses his energy on getting his team to understand, *"Guys, we can't worry about how the other team is feeling.* All we can do is worry about how we're feeling. It might not be fair, but injuries are part of the game. This could've just as easily happened to one of us. It's not our job to make sure the other team doesn't get hurt. As long as we didn't go out and intentionally hurt anyone on purpose, *which we didn't*, there's nothing to feel sorry about. Jimmy didn't do anything wrong. *I repeat, Jimmy didn't do anything wrong."*

"Yes, Coach," the Wildcats collectively respond in a flat tone.

"Are you sure you understand?" Coach Waters asks. "Because it sounds like you might want to hand this game over to Morrisville. I hope I'm wrong. Am I?"

"We want to win," the Wildcats now respond a little louder.

Squinting with his left eye almost closed, as if he's trying to read the players' minds, Coach Waters keeps talking in a low raspy voice, *"Are you really sure? Because this is it.* There are only four minutes remaining in the third quarter and after that, we have eight minutes left to see if we can win this game. There's no room for indecision. We need to go back out there right now and take this game. Are you with me?"

"YES!" the Wildcats now shout with enthusiasm.

"That's what I like to hear. Stay focused over the next few minutes and this game is ours. *Believe me, it's ours.* Let's take it to the Pirates the moment this game starts back up! Hands in one more time! Wildcats on three! ONE-TWO-THREE WILDCATS!"

As the Wildcats step back onto the court, Coach Waters turns to Coach Preisler and Coach Matthews and grins widely, knowing he just got through to his team loud and clear.

When Jimmy reaches half court, he leans back and screams out loud for everyone to hear, "Come on! Let's go! Let's do this!"

"Yeah, man! Let's do this!" Eric screams back.

"This is our game! We got this!" Taylor joins in.

Still burning with anger, Jimmy tells the five Wildcats on the court to throw their hands in one last time, "Let's go! This is our game! Wildcats on three! ONE-TWO-THREE WILDCATS!"

At the same time, on the other sideline, the Pirates struggle to find their emotional balance as their head coach practically begs them to stay focused and not to lose faith.

After each team makes the two technical free throws it was awarded for the fight, the Pirates in-bound the ball to restart the action. As they do this, it looks like they're in a state of shock.

Over the next few minutes of play, the Wildcats do exactly as they were told and take full advantage of Xavier's absence. Basically lifeless, the Pirates try to stop the Wildcats' furious and emotional comeback, but are unable to do so. When the horn sounds to end the third quarter, the Pirates' lead has shrunk to 47-44.

On the first play of the fourth quarter, Taylor follows a missed jump shot by Eric with an easy put back lay-up. As he lets go of the ball, he slaps the backboard with two hands to let everyone in the gym know he doesn't think anyone can guard him. *No one can.*

The next time the Wildcats are on defense, Taylor moves from one side of the lane to the other, to block not just one, but two successive shots. The second blocked shot is picked up by Jimmy who throws the ball ahead to Garrett for an easy breakaway lay-up.

A few minutes of uninspiring play later, the Pirates head coach is forced to call back-to-back timeouts to try and get his team to snap out of its funk. *But it's no use.* The Pirates' sunken shoulders and lethargic energy says it all.

With 3:03 left to play in the fourth quarter, Eric passes out of a double team to find Jimmy standing wide open in the corner, behind the three-point line. Catching the ball in stride, Jimmy steps into his shot and easily knocks down the three-point basket to put the Wildcats up by a score of 57-50. It's their largest lead of the game. The Pirates come right back with a three pointer of their own from the top of the key, only to watch Taylor dribble right down the center of their defense and hit a short jump shot from the middle of the lane. Over the next minute, the teams trade baskets, but for the Pirates, it's too little too late.

With twenty seconds to go in the game, the Pirates take their last shot of the night, a wide open jump shot from the right side that hits hard off the back of the rim. Leaping high into the air, Taylor grabs the ball out of the sky with one hand and officially ends any hope the Pirates may have had for a miraculous comeback.

Smiling from ear to ear, Taylor dribbles the ball over the half court line, before turning to look at the game clock on the back wall. With the last precious seconds of the game ticking away, he begins to explode with an intense joy as a surge of energy shoots down his spine into the bottoms of his feet. Rising out of their seats, the Wildcats fans begin chanting "We're #1!...We're #1!"

When the game clock flashes two seconds left, Taylor throws the ball high into the air and begins celebrating the perfect ending to the perfect season. With a final score of 63-57, the Longwood Hills Wildcats are crowned state champions for the second year in a row and for only the third time in the school's history.

On the other side of the court, Morrisville's state championship dreams come crashing down to earth without Xavier as they are held to only 12 points over the last quarter and a half in defeat.

With the final buzzer echoing throughout the gym, the entire Longwood Hills student body once again rushes the court in a crazed celebration of adrenaline and emotion as Coach Waters hugs his assistants and looks for his wife and daughters in the bleachers. Standing in the middle of it all, Taylor high fives everyone he sees as the incredible weight from this past season slowly rolls off his back.

Watching the Pirates leave the court in defeat, Taylor can only think of one thing, *"We got lucky tonight."*

CHAPTER 17

The Wildcats' championship game celebration flows from the court to the team's locker room, before exploding with unrestrained happiness on the bus ride back to Longwood Hills. Singing, dancing and laughing the entire way home, the players soak up every magical moment as if it's their last on earth, while the coaches sit quietly in the front of the bus sharing stories from this past season. Filled with an incredible sense of pride and satisfaction, the coaches wish every year could be as spellbinding as this one.

As the team bus pulls back into the Longwood Hills High School parking lot, the Wildcats are greeted by what seems like the entire town. Everyone from the mayor, to the school principal, to large groups of parents and students, have joined together with the fire department and police department in welcoming home its conquering heroes. In a captivating display, the town's fire engines and police cars are lined up in a row, sending majestic streaks of red, white and blue lights dancing into the night sky above.

Overcome with emotion, the players leave all their gear on the team bus and run onto the waiting fire engines as Coach Waters, Coach Preisler and Coach Matthews are welcomed into the waiting police cars. As the leader of the Wildcats' championship run, Coach Waters is invited to sit in the passenger seat of Police Chief John Marshalls' cruiser at the head of the victory celebration, along with instructions to start the unrehearsed parade through town, only when he's good and ready. Delighting in the enchantment of the moment, Coach Waters grabs control of the cruiser's loudspeaker, before leading everyone out of the high school parking lot with a deafening roar of "Let's Go Wildcats!"

As the adrenaline from the game and the perfect season keeps flowing, the players shout with delight into the night, while their classmates follow behind the fire engines honking their horns and blasting their music in celebration. Unending rounds of applause and makeshift signs of congratulations greet the Wildcats on almost every street of this normally quiet town as Taylor's high school basketball career closes out in a dream-like sequence. Standing on the back of one of the fire engines, he watches the lights of his idyllic hometown flash by him in waves as he celebrates this once in a lifetime achievement with his closest friend in the world, the rest of his childhood pals and a loving and protective coaching staff. *Meanwhile, an overwhelming feeling of fear and dread starts building up inside him.*

In a few short months, he knows his entire life will be completely different from the only one he's ever known and while he's successfully tricked himself into believing the enormous expectations placed on his shoulders from basketball will be easier to handle next year, as he stands in the dark on the back of the fire engine, he finally admits he's been lying to himself this whole time. *The truth is, things aren't going to be any easier next year, they're only going to be harder.*

With the flashing lights of the parade keeping alive the greatest season in the history of the school, Taylor's excitement about finally being free from the mounting expectations of basketball has already disappeared. At the same time, he can't stop thinking about Xavier. Ever since Xavier knocked him over on the way to the basket in the first quarter, he can't get his size, strength and quickness out of his head, while also wondering how many other players in college will be as good as or better than Xavier.

Without warning, a gust of cold air shoots underneath the collar of his varsity jacket, forcing him to wrap his free arm around his body to fight off the angry chill now running down his spine. Looking over at Jimmy, pumping his fists and yelling with joy into the night, he tries to imagine, not for the first time, what his life is going to be like without his best friend by his side encouraging him and protecting him each day. *This last thought makes him even more anxious and nervous than anything else.*

As this last paralyzing thought continues to linger, new and even more intense feelings begin to bubble up inside him, sending his mind spinning almost out of control, *"Am I as good as everyone thinks I am? Will my mom be okay without me? Has my comfortable life growing up been too comfortable? Am I ready for all of this?"*

All of these unanswerable questions scare him beyond words, yet they won't go away.

112 / Adam Poe

CHAPTER 18

A few days after the state championship game celebration, the post-season awards are announced. As expected, the Wildcats receive more than their fair share for going undefeated and winning their second consecutive state championship. For the second year in a row, Taylor is named to the New Jersey All-State First Team, while Eric Goodwin is named to the New Jersey All-State Third Team and David Smith is named a New Jersey All-State Honorable Mention; an acknowledgement which helps him temporarily feel better about playing so poorly in the state championship game. While Garrett Chapman doesn't receive any official honors, he's designated a "Future Player to Watch," a recognition which puts the burden of trying to become Longwood Hills' next great sports star squarely on his young shoulders, where it will remain with great expectations for the next two years.

For being named to the All-State First Team, Taylor and the other four All-State First Team members have their hand-drawn faces placed on the front page of the sports section of New Jersey's largest newspaper, an honor which dates back almost fifty years and includes some now very famous and not so famous alumni. Joining Taylor on the All-State First Team is Xavier, whose face sits just above

Taylor's on the page. In more ways than one, Taylor is once again angered and frustrated by Xavier's presence, but knows there's nothing he can do about it.

The biggest surprise from the post-season award announcements comes in the form of a lengthy article entitled, "*Good Things Come To Those Who Wait.*" After twenty-two years of coaching the Longwood Hills High School boy's varsity basketball team, Coach Waters is named "New Jersey High School Basketball Coach of the Year." The writer of the article highlights not only the team's achievements from this past season, but also Coach Waters' extensive history of dedication to Longwood Hills High School, his family and the community. The article masterfully captures Coach Waters' positive spirit and good-natured demeanor, along with his big heart. It's an extremely gratifying honor for Coach Waters and not just for being recognized for living an exemplary life based on his core principle of giving more than you receive in return, but the award also allows him to temporarily step out of Taylor's long shadow, which secretly is a thrill even for him.

A week after the post-season awards are announced, Taylor plays in the All-American game in New York City. Playing well in what can only be described as a glorified pick-up game, he scores 8 points and grabs five rebounds, a performance which temporarily helps him feel better about the bright future he's been promised by everyone.

At 9:00 a.m. on the following Monday morning, Taylor sits next to his mom in the front seat of her light blue sedan as Deborah pulls out of their driveway to begin what will be a five-day road trip to visit the last three colleges he's interested in seeing before making a final decision as to where he'll play next year.

As Deborah steers the sedan toward Rt. 78 South, the air flowing through the car's open windows is warm and welcoming. According to the directions sent in an email by the Burnet State University men's basketball coaching staff, the drive to Burnet State University's main campus in Raritack, New Jersey, should take just under an hour and a half door-to-door, leaving plenty of time to safely make it to their 11:00 a.m. appointment without a hitch.

The goal for today's recruiting visit is to get in and out as soon as possible. With over four hours separating Raritack, New Jersey, from Westpark, New York, Deborah wants to get as close to Central New York University tonight as possible before they both get too tired. Intuitively, she knows this isn't the best attitude to have heading into the day, but since Taylor's feelings about Burnet State University haven't changed, she wants to make sure he's fresh and ready for tomorrow's visit to Central New York University, a school he may actually attend in the fall.

Throughout this past season, whenever Taylor was asked by the press if he's still considering playing for Burnet State University, he always said yes, even though there was never a moment in which he ever really considered going to the school. What he decided early on was that if he could somehow convince the other team's crowd, even for a second, that he was going to try to turn around the state university's struggling basketball program, they might go easier on him. During some away games, he was convinced his plan had worked perfectly and at other times, he was convinced the opposing team's crowd didn't know how to read anything, let alone a sports section.

With very little traffic along Route 78, Deborah turns onto the Burnet State University campus as the digital clock in the car's dashboard reads 10:38 a.m. Following the instructions sent in the same email by the coaches, she steers the car through the campus' main gates and heads over to the visitor's registration booth to sign in for the day.

After waiting in line for a few minutes, Deborah and Taylor are greeted with a lazy smile by a heavy set security guard wearing a grey uniform with green trim that appears too small for his oversized body. Approaching the driver's side window, the security guard asks Deborah for her photo I.D. and then instructs her to sign and date the form attached to the clipboard he hands her. As he does this, he looks into the car and gives Taylor a once-over, holding his eyes on him for a full pause, before determining he's not a threat.

Satisfied with Deborah's signature, the guard places a temporary parking pass underneath the sedan's windshield and gives them directions to the basketball arena for their meeting. As he points down the road directly in front of their idling car, the seams of his uniform stretch and pull in all directions.

The Burnet State University basketball arena has served as the on-campus home gym for the men's and women's teams since 1970. Designed and built as a rectangular-shaped block with only a few exterior windows on each side, the arena seems to have landed on the New Jersey soil almost by mistake. Over the years, the 10,000 seat arena has proved to be a decisive home court advantage for the Burnet State University Warriors, but only *if* the building is crowded, *if* the fans are energized and *if* the team is talented enough. For the Burnet State University men's basketball team, there have been way too many *if's* over the years and not enough wins. Taylor Scott or no Taylor Scott, the next season for the Warriors was more than likely going to be a difficult one.

As Taylor and Deborah sit quietly in the car waiting for the clock to move closer to 11:00 a.m., Taylor suddenly becomes overwhelmed by feelings of indifference. While he desperately wants to follow through on his promise to visit this school, now that he's finally here, a big part of him doesn't even want to bother to get out of the car.

"Let's make this quick. Okay, Ma?"

"Sure," she answers, looking over at him quizzically. "Whatever you say, sweetie. It's your college career we're here to explore."

"Yeah, I know. I just don't want to be here too long, that's all."

"Sounds good to me," she tries to read the sudden shift in his mood. "These visits are all about you, but you know that. As a matter of fact, if you want me to pull out of this parking lot right now and head straight to Central New York University, I'm happy to do it. Honestly, I'm not sure what we're doing here anyway. You have no intention of going to this school. I feel like you're wasting these poor coaches' time."

"You're probably right. It's just, I feel like this is something I need to do. This way I'm not leaving any stone unmoved or stone overturned or whatever that phrase is? Who knows, maybe I'll love the place."

"You think so?"

"No, I don't. But I guess I should be completely sure before I cross it off my list. This way I can't second-guess myself in the future, since we both know how much I love to do that."

Frowning softly to himself, Taylor reaches for the car door and slides out as Deborah grabs her pocketbook from the backseat and locks the doors behind her, once again shaking her head in confusion at the inner workings of her son's teenage mind.

At exactly 11:00 a.m., Taylor and Deborah enter the arena and find their way over to the men's basketball team office. Once inside the office, they are greeted with a warm smile by a baby-faced student manager wearing a white Burnet State University polo shirt and neatly pressed khaki pants. The manager wastes no time in welcoming them, before handing each of them a bottle of water and escorting them down a long hallway filled with wall-to-wall beige carpeting, stopping only when he reaches a conference room in the back of the office. On the other side of the conference room door, the Burnet State University coaches are doing everything they can to wait patiently for Taylor's arrival. When Taylor and Deborah enter the conference room, the coaches immediately jump to their feet and begin introducing themselves one by one in a flurry of smiles and nervous energy.

A few minutes later and still smiling from ear to ear, the coaches retake their seats as Taylor and Deborah find empty chairs on the opposite side of the table. Once everyone is comfortably settled in, the student manager picks up a pile of green folders filled with important information about the Burnet State University men's basketball program and begins handing one to everyone seated at the table. After successfully completing this task, the manager quietly closes the conference room door on his way out, but not before he gives Taylor a nod and small smile.

As the Burnet State University coaches whisper final instructions to one another, Taylor lets his eyes drift from the big white 'B' imprinted on the cover of his folder to what looks to be a ridiculous number of framed motivational slogans hanging on the conference room walls. It appears as if every generic slogan ever written about winning and having a positive attitude was found by the Burnet State University coaches and hung up inside this room.

"Does anyone ever get motivated by those things?" Taylor wonders silently to himself. *"I mean, either you have it or you don't. Isn't that simple?"*

As this last question lingers inside his head, he suddenly realizes no one else in the room is talking and everyone is staring at him. Carefully taking his eyes down from the wall, he bites his bottom lip and smiles awkwardly at the coaches on the other side of the table, while praying no one will ask him what he was just doing. *Much to his great relief, no one does.*

Over the next thirty minutes, the Burnet State University coaches make an empowered presentation to Taylor and Deborah about the bright future of its men's basketball program. It's an aspirational pitch, filled with inevitable wins and championships all won in front of national TV cameras and sold-out home crowds just outside these same conference room walls. The coaches tell Taylor there is no better time in the history of the school to become a Burnet State University Warrior than right now. That most of the pieces for winning multiple conference championships and making a run in college basketball's post-season tournament are already in place. *The only thing that's missing is him.*

If it wasn't for the tray of fruit and cookies in the middle of the table to help distract his attention, Taylor still isn't sure how he would have made it through the entire presentation without completely zoning out again.

After this initial recruiting pitch finishes up, the coaches take Taylor and Deborah on a tour of the basketball arena and its strength and conditioning rooms. Over and over again throughout the tour, the coaches enthusiastically describe everything they see in excruciating detail as if they were the ones who designed or built it. This constant "hard-sell" by the Burnet State University coaches grates on Deborah's nerves, but since she doesn't want to say or do anything to cloud Taylor's judgment, she simply nods politely. Taylor, on the other hand, seems to once again be lost in his thoughts, gliding absentmindedly from one room to the next, without saying more than a few words or making much in the way of eye contact.

When the tour of the basketball arena is over, everyone gets on a shuttle bus and heads to the center of campus to join a group of thirty or so other sets of parents and kids for a one-hour walking tour through the campus' well-maintained grounds. The tour guide they are assigned is an enthusiastic and pretty psychology graduate student with shoulder-length dark blond hair and inquisitive green eyes. A two-year veteran of these guided walking tours, she effortlessly keeps their group engaged throughout the one hour they are together by pointing out little known facts about the university, along with some very funny stories about the social habits of its not-so-discreet student body.

During this guided walking tour, the coaches mostly hang in the back to allow Taylor and Deborah the time to enjoy this experience on their own and only make themselves known when they feel the guide has failed to point out something crucial about the university's academic reputation or forgot to highlight an important feature of one of its many historic buildings.

When the walking tour comes to a close, the coaches ask Deborah if they can steal Taylor away so he can survey an introductory macroeconomics class taking place on the other side of campus. Seeing this break for what it is, Deborah happily agrees and as she watches Taylor and the coaches jump on another shuttle bus in search of higher learning fifteen minutes away, she heads for a quiet place to eat lunch alone in the warm spring air.

Once seated inside the large lecture hall, Taylor does his best to appear interested in what is being taught by the macroeconomics professor, while the Burnet State University coaches sit directly behind him staring at the back of his head. With their matching white polo shirts and small giddy smiles, it seems the coaches still can't contain their excitement that Taylor is actually visiting their school. To counter their uncomfortable stares, Taylor spends most of the class ignoring the professor and making up weird and inappropriate stories about the personal lives of the coaches inside his head.

After the macroeconomics class mercifully lets out, Taylor and the coaches get on another shuttle bus and head back over to the basketball arena so Taylor can have lunch with a few of the current Burnet State University players. Over a late lunch of burgers and fries, Taylor starts to relax and let go of some of the tension he's been holding inside all day as the players trade basketball stories and share a few laughs. In between giant gulps of food, Taylor makes sure to ask a lot of questions about what it's like being a student-athlete at Burnet State University, but mostly he focuses his questions on the basketball team and its upcoming schedule for next season.

Once lunch is over, Taylor rejoins his mom inside the same conference room in which their day began less than five hours ago. As they both stare blankly ahead, they listen to the Burnet State University coaches make one last impassioned plea about why their school is *absolutely* the right place for Taylor to bring his immeasurable basketball talents to in the fall. This final pitch is basically the same pitch the coaches have been giving Taylor all day in one form or another. That he could be *the* player to put his state university's struggling basketball program on the map and turn it into a "name" school, the whole time playing close to his childhood home, in a big-time conference and in front of sold-out crowds. The coaches finish up by telling Taylor if he commits to their school, he will become an even bigger hero in the state of New Jersey than he already is.

The strategy for the Burnet State University coaches is simple: They believe if they can get Taylor to come to their school, other big name New Jersey high school basketball players will follow him in the future, creating a pipeline that will literally build their program from the ground up. Unlike other sports, basketball is only played by five players at one time, so one player *can* make all the difference in the world, both on and off the court.

Going into the day, the Burnet State University coaches knew getting Taylor to commit to their school was going to be a long shot at best and frankly, they were still a little surprised he decided to visit in the first place. But now that he was sitting right in front of them, they wanted to do everything in their power to make sure his decision was a difficult one. They only hoped they succeeded.

After this last meeting of the day ends, Deborah and Taylor thank the coaches and leave the Burnet State University campus behind, with a promise to have a final decision within the next two weeks. No less than ten minutes later, as Deborah searches for signs for Route 278 North to begin their four-plus hour drive to Central New York University, Taylor turns to his mom and makes his final decision about the school.

"Hey, Ma."

"Yes, dear."

"While I liked the Burnet State University coaches and its campus was decent and all, I don't think I want to go there next year."

"Really?" she responds with a hint of sarcasm. "I'm very surprised to hear you say that."

"Yeah, I know," he answers with a small laugh. "It's just...I don't think it's the right place for me, you know. I think Central New York University or Maryland State University might be a better fit in the long run."

"Sure, honey, and I think you might be right," Deborah confirms out loud something she knew before they left the house this morning.

"Then it's official! Burnet State University is out!" he announces with great relief.

"If that's the case, dear, you should call the basketball office tomorrow and let the coaches know you're not going to be accepting their scholarship offer. This way they can spend their time and energy elsewhere. There's no need to keep them guessing."

"Yeah, I think you're right. I'll call them next week and let them know."

"Next week?....AAGGGHHHH!!!" she really doesn't understand how his teenage mind works.

CHAPTER 19

The next morning Deborah keeps the car steady in the right hand lane at fifty-five miles per hour as they make their way along Route 81 North toward Central New York University. With the radio softly broadcasting the news, Taylor sits silently in the passenger seat staring out the window with his sneakers off and his right foot propped up near the windshield. While Deborah would never intentionally ruin a day that holds so much promise for her son's future, she nevertheless decided late last night in the hotel the two of them were going to have an extremely important conversation this morning, one she's painfully avoided for months. Taking a deep breath, she smiles softly before beginning, "Taylor, can I talk to you a second?"

"Huh?" he replies, turning from the window.

"I said, I need to talk to you for a second."

Based on the tone of her voice, he instinctively knows this isn't a conversation he wants to have, "Sure, Ma. What's up?"

"I want to talk to you about Kelly."

"What about her?" he asks, the words almost getting stuck inside his mouth.

"I want to talk about what happened between the two of you back in February."

"Back in February?" he shouts inside his head. *"You've got to be kidding me!"*

As a wave of panic rips through his body, he looks at the tall trees running along the highway again and imagines jumping out of the car and sprinting into the woods, never to be seen again. Swallowing down hard on the lump that's appeared in his throat out of nowhere, he steadies his emotions before turning back to his mom, "What do you mean?" he asks coolly. "I'm not following you."

"Rrgghhhh!!" he was getting too good at lying and if Deborah had the time, the two of them would spend the rest of the car ride talking only about that.

"Well, if you don't know, let me tell you," she begins. "Back in February, I was in the supermarket parking lot putting the groceries into the car when Police Chief Marshalls came up to me and asked if I had a minute to talk. At first, I thought I must've accidentally run a stop sign or maybe one of the brake lights was out since I couldn't imagine what he wanted to talk to me about. But it turns out, that's not what he wanted to discuss at all."

"That's good," Taylor responds in a sing-song voice, desperately hoping the rest of the story is also about her.

"What Police Chief Marshalls told me that day shocked and embarrassed me. On top of that, *everyone* could see I was talking to him. I felt like a wanted criminal."

"Okay?" his voice cracks in response. "But why are you telling me all of this?"

"I'm telling you all of this because Police Chief Marshalls told me he had just completed an investigation into a fight at a party, *a fight that involved you.*"

Taylor's eyes almost pop-out of his head when he hears this.

"An investigation into a fight at a party that involved me?" he asks disbelievingly. "Mom, I didn't get into a fight back in February with any guy at a party. *I promise you.* They must have me confused with someone else."

"I didn't say a fight between you and another guy. It seems you like to fight with girls and not guys. Or did the police get that wrong too?"

"Mom, I...I..." he searches for the right words.

"And be careful what you promise me, young man! Don't forget, I'm still your mother. Now should I continue or do you want to tell me the rest of the story?"

Taylor silently shakes his head no.

"Well, it seems after you left Susan Jamison's party the night of the Roxford game, the police came by later on to break it up. Some of your so-called 'friends' got caught with alcohol and tried to deflect attention away from their underage drinking by telling the police they overheard a fight between the town's basketball star and Kelly Raymond."

"They did?" he asks in a severely wounded voice.

"Yes, they did. And don't get me started how you ended up at that party in the first place, since you and Jimmy lied to me about where you were going that night. I asked you to tell me the truth about your plans and you couldn't even do that!"

"Oh, come on, Mom! That's not fair!"

"Don't you give me that it's not fair nonsense," she tells him angrily. "Police Chief Marshalls also told me Steven Mason found Kelly hysterically crying in the Jamison's basement. She was so scared she was unable to leave on her own. Steven had to help her out of the house and take her home that night."

"He did?" Taylor asks in astonishment.

"Yes, he did," she shoots him a menacing look from across the front seat. "Police Chief Marshalls also said a bathroom door and wall had been smashed in. You wouldn't happen to know anything about that, would you?"

"Uhm...I..." he stammers.

"I figured as much. But since the police can't prosecute on stories alone, especially the stories of teenagers who'd been drinking, they didn't have enough evidence to charge you with anything. So it seems you got *very* lucky this time."

Taylor gulps down hard on the lump in his throat again.

"The police tried to talk to Kelly the next day, but as I'm sure you know by now, she wouldn't say what happened to anyone. Not to the police, not to her parents and not even to Steven. So between no one actually seeing the fight and Kelly not willing to share her side of the story, you got away free and clear."

Taylor's heart momentarily leaps with joy at hearing this news, before sinking back into his stomach at the thought of how much he hurt Kelly.

"Again, it's not that the police didn't want to charge you with anything. *They did.* So my question to you is, are you controlling this whole situation and that's why it turned out this way?"

"Huh? What do you mean?"

"I mean, did you threaten Kelly in a way that she was afraid to talk to the police? Are you that malicious?"

"What?" he asks in disbelief. "Come on, Mom! You know I'm not like that, right?"

"I thought I knew who you were. But after hearing Police Chief Marshalls' story, I'm not sure anymore. You fought with a girl and kicked in a bathroom door and wall. Who does that?"

The words dig deep into Taylor's heart.

"Mom, I'm still the same person I've always been. *I swear.* The whole thing with Kelly was just a terrible misunderstanding."

"Honestly Taylor, I'm not sure what to think right now. And you know you're going to pay for the damages you did to that bathroom when we get back home."

"Okay, fine. As long as you tell me you believe me I didn't threaten Kelly in that way."

"What?" she raises her voice. "This is *not* a negotiation! You hear me?"

"Okay, calm down. I'll pay for the bathroom when we get back home."

"Yes, you will. And the only thing I can tell you for sure is deep down Kelly must still love you, because if you're not controlling her, I can't figure out why she wouldn't tell the police or her parents what happened between the two of you. She had nothing to gain by keeping quiet."

Caught off guard, Taylor tries to register this complex thought, but can't quite grasp it.

"You do realize you were *this* close to getting arrested," Deborah holds up her thumb and forefinger for effect.

"I do now," he mumbles back.

"What did you just say? Are you taking a tone with me?"

"Sorry, I didn't mean to. I...I..." he stammers.

"I can't believe what I just heard! I tell you that you were one eye witness away from getting arrested and you respond with an attitude. Who are you? And what happened to my son? I didn't raise you to be so selfish and callous. You're a basketball player. *That's it.* You're not above the law and you're definitely not above being a decent person. As a matter of fact, I expect a lot more out of you. Your actions are a direct reflection of me. Don't ever forget that!"

"Sorry, I...I..." he tries to find the right words again.

"Do you realize what would've happened if you'd been arrested? Forgetting the embarrassment and shame for a second, you probably would've been suspended from the team and there's no way the Wildcats would've won another state championship without you. How do you think your teammates would've felt if you let them down like that? And what about Coach Waters? After all he's done for you."

Taylor stares at his mom in frightened silence. He's never seen her so mad.

"If you were arrested, maybe we wouldn't even be in this car right now! Maybe all those schools that wanted you so badly might not want a girlfriend-beater on their team! Everything could have been so different if just one person had seen that fight. Just one! Do you ever think about that?"

"That's all I've ever thought about!" he wanted to scream back at her, but all that came out was, "Kelly's not my girlfriend."

"Oh, please! Don't tell me you got hung up on the word 'girlfriend' and didn't hear anything else I just said. There is something you need to understand and you need to understand it *right now*. There is a razor thin line between success and failure in this life. Where we finish up at the end can usually be traced back to a few decisions we make during the important moments we face. Without a basketball scholarship, I'm not sure I could find the money to send you to college and your dad sure isn't going to pay for you to go. Then what? What would you do without a college education?"

"Okay, Mom. Please, just relax. I'm sorry," as he says these words he can feel the car swerving in and out of their lane.

"You should be sorry! Don't you dare! You hear me? Now is definitely not the time for you to put up an attitude. Now is the time for you to start learning a little humility."

Looking over at her fuming with anger, Taylor instantly hates himself for making her feel this way. Putting his head into his hands, he turns his anger inward, "I'm so sorry, Mom. Can you please forgive me? Please..."

As Deborah tries to find the inner strength to calm down, she searches urgently for a place to pull over and rest. Luckily, just up the freeway, she sees a giant sign for a fast food restaurant rise into the sky. Heading straight for its parking lot, she pulls the car into an empty space in the back away from the other customers and gradually begins to let go of her death grip on the steering wheel. As the blood slowly returns to her hands, she exhales loudly and forces her rapidly beating heart to slow down.

CHAPTER 20

After shutting off the car's engine in the back of the fast food restaurant's parking lot, Deborah stares straight ahead into an open field of mostly brown dirt and dead yellow grass as she silently explores the right words to continue their conversation. To help combat her pointed silence, Taylor decides to play a game in which he guesses what kind of job each person entering the restaurant has based on the type of car they drive, what kind of clothes they are wearing and how overweight they might be. After counting what he believes is his third car salesman in a row, carrying twenty extra pounds and wearing rumpled dress pants and a mismatched shirt and tie, he desperately wants to say something to make the situation better, but he's afraid that whatever comes out of his mouth next will be wrong. So he instead waits patiently in the passenger seat in silence, counting car salesmen and wishing things could go back to the way they were when he got out of bed this morning.

Finally pulling herself together, Deborah turns and looks Taylor straight in the eyes, "So do you want to tell me about what happened in that basement? Why you were so mad?"

"Uhm…I…I'm not sure," he hesitates, but wants to scream back at her, "*It was Steven, that wanna-be! And Kelly, that cheating liar! She's supposed to love me forever! Even if we aren't together!*"

"What do you mean you're not sure?" she gently pushes. "Try to remember for me, *please.*"

"Uhm…I guess, I was just upset, you know."

"Upset at what? You just won the Roxford game with your shot at the buzzer. What did you have to be upset about?"

"I don't know," he answers with a shrug.

A look of frustration grabs hold of her, "*Please*, try to remember for me. I need to understand. Where did all that rage come from?"

"I dunno…I guess, I just saw Kelly there with Steven and it made me so mad. I don't know why it did, but it did."

"So you hit her?"

"No! I didn't hit her. I swear, Mom."

"As you can see I'm *very* glad to hear you say you never put a hand on Kelly, but who taught you it's okay to treat a woman like that? Men are bigger and stronger than women. Always have been and always will be. That's why you can't ever get physical around a woman like that again. Do you hear me?"

"Yes," he answers with a soft nod.

"Violence is never the solution. It's the same thing I told you when you were in third grade and you punched Scott Pollard on the playground. You don't use your hands to solve problems."

"I know, Mom. Really, I do. I'm sorry."

"I hope you aren't just telling me you're sorry," she focuses her angry stare even harder on him. "I hope you've told Kelly you're sorry too."

"I did. I *promi*…" his voice trails off. "I did, Mom. *Trust me*," he lies through his teeth.

"That's good to hear, but I still don't know where all that anger came from. You weren't raised like that and truthfully, you don't want for anything in this world except for maybe a car, which you're still not getting, by the way."

"I know, Mom. That's why I broke the bathroom door and wall instead of hurting Kelly," he answers with a sarcastic grin.

"That's not even close to funny!" she furiously yells back. "What's wrong with you?"

"It was a joke...I...I'm sorry," he recoils in his seat.

"Stop making bad jokes and stop apologizing," she demands. "And tell me why you were so upset that night."

"It's just...I still love Kelly. At least, I thought I did. And when I saw her at Susan's party with Steven, I just got so mad that we weren't together anymore and she was there with him. I kept picturing them, you know...being together."

"I'm sure that must've hurt your feelings. Seeing your ex with someone else can be extremely painful. There's no denying how much love has hurt me in the past. But that doesn't in any way excuse your behavior. You won't solve anything or win someone's heart back with violence."

"I know, Mom. I do. The funny part is I don't even want Kelly back. She was just there with someone else that wasn't me. It made me so mad, that's all."

"So that's it? Kelly shows up at a party with someone else that's not you and you turn into a raging madman?"

"What? No...I mean, that's not all," he swallows hard and tries to comprehend what might happen next if he finally shares his true feelings.

"So?" she asks again.

"It's just...It's just...Everyone puts so much pressure on me *all the time*. Sometimes, I feel like I'm going to *explode!*"

A look of shock spreads across Deborah's face.

"There are days I just want to rip my own skin off so I won't have to live my life as me anymore," he keeps talking in a hurried voice. "And the night I saw Kelly and Steven together, even though we won the game, I was angry at the world."

Suddenly terrified, Deborah scrambles for the right words, "I...I'm not sure I completely understand. Who puts so much pressure on you?"

"Well, *you* for one."

"Me?" she responds in surprise.

"Yes, *you*...And Coach Waters...And my teachers...And Dad...And the people from town who corner me in stores...And the college coaches who never stop calling...And a lot of other people...You know, *everyone*."

"What do you mean we put pressure on you?" she asks as calmly as possible. "All we want is what's best for you. You have a gift. We just want to see you reach your potential."

"Well, it's tough being me some days. I know I asked for all of this, *but I'm only seventeen, for Christ's sake*. You try walking around with everyone's hopes and dreams tied around your neck. I'm sure you wouldn't like it much either. To be honest, I don't think you could even handle it," before the words are even out of his mouth, he wishes he can take them back. "It's a lot of pressure, even for me. Some days, I guess, I just don't do a good job handling it. I'm not perfect, you know," with his breathing now heavy, his words are coming out chopped and somewhat hard to understand. "I just got so mad at Kelly. She's supposed to always be true to me, no matter what. Even if we aren't together. I know that doesn't make much sense, but I just never expected her to date anyone else. I don't know why I thought that, but I did. And everyone, including you and Coach Waters, told me I had to concentrate on basketball *only* this year. It was too important for my future. I'm not stupid, you know. I know everyone wanted me to break up with Kelly, *so I did*. But I didn't really want to. She was my girlfriend. No one asked me what I wanted. How come what I wanted didn't matter?"

"You could've said no," Deborah responds, almost in a whisper. "You know that, right?"

"No, I couldn't have!" he yells back. "That's not true at all!"

"Yes, it is. You could..." her voice trails off as this crushing revelation hangs in the air.

While Taylor has always been under a lot of pressure, Deborah has always assumed he could handle it. Even as a kid, he seemed stronger than most adults, including her.

"I am very sorry, Taylor. I had no idea you felt this way. We were all very wrong to pressure you to break up with Kelly. It's your life and you should be able to date anyone you want. Basketball or no basketball."

"Thanks, Mom. But it's too late. It doesn't change anything."

"I know, I know," she softly admits.

Taking a deep breath, she now places her own truth out in the open, "If we're being completely honest with each other, part of the reason I pressured you into breaking up with Kelly is that I didn't want to see you make a mistake. You were in such a serious relationship at such a young age that I became fearful for you."

"Fearful?" he asks with a scrunched brow.

"Yes, I just didn't want to see you and Kelly get pregnant by accident and put any unnecessary stress on your future."

"Mom!" he shouts in disbelief.

"I know. It's a terrible thing for me to think and do, but I couldn't help it. I'm your mother. I just want what's best for you."

"How could you? From now on, why don't you let me tell you what I want, rather than you telling me what you think I should want. That's a good place for us to start. Mom, I need you in my corner and not against me."

"I know, baby. I'm so very sorry. Do you think you can ever forgive me?"

Even though his anger and disappointment are almost too much to bear, he wants nothing more than to make her happy, *now and always*, "It's okay, Mom. I know you want what's best for me. But from now on, you have to ask me what I want and not assume you know what I want. I'm almost an adult, you know."

"You're absolutely right. I promise from now on to always ask and also see how I can help alleviate some of the pressure you feel every day. After all, that's what moms do," she smiles compassionately as she says this.

"Thanks...And I'm going to hold you to it."

"I hope you do. And while all of this talking is good for the both of us, it still doesn't excuse your behavior toward Kelly at that party. I never want to hear about you losing your temper with a girl like that again. Are we clear?"

"Yes, it won't ever happen again. I promise."

"Especially with you going away to college in the fall. You're going to have a lot more unsupervised chances with women once you get on campus and I'm counting on you to always do the right thing."

"You have my word..."

As soon as their conversation ends, Taylor turns the phrase *unsupervised chances* over and over again inside his head and while he desperately wants to ask his mom what she meant by it, he decides it's probably best to leave it alone for another day. His instincts toward women are showing signs of improvement already.

CHAPTER 21

It's not even nine o'clock in the morning yet, but the emotions from the day have already been draining. While it's true some part of Deborah will always remain conflicted about the timing of this morning's conversation, she knows deep in her heart she did the right thing. She couldn't be responsible for introducing to the world an uncaring young man that believes a woman can be treated like an object. It's also her job as Taylor's parent to both understand and protect him, even if it means sometimes protecting him from himself.

After straightening up inside the fast food restaurant's bathrooms, Deborah and Taylor walk back to the car feeling emotionally tired, yet happy. About halfway across the parking lot, Taylor leans over and throws his arm over his mom's shoulder in a warm and affectionate embrace. Eagerly grabbing hold of this affection, Deborah squeezes him back with all the love in her body as a soft tender smile spreads across her face.

With a much lighter air filling the car, Deborah once again steers it back onto Route 81 North to complete what's left of their drive to Westpark, New York. Just over thirty minutes later, they exit the highway and start heading up the hill to the Central New York University campus. When they reach the first intersection, Deborah makes a right turn at the light and starts winding the car toward the field house and the offices of the men's basketball team.

Sitting deep within the field house, inside his personal office, along with his top two assistants, is Central New York University's long time Head Basketball Coach Tom Horner. A former player at 6' 7", Coach Horner is a tall and lanky man who looks more like an accountant or a lawyer than a big-time basketball coach. With a quiet confidence and fiery determination that contradicts his outer appearance, Coach Horner has built the Central New York University Cougars into a conference power and a Top 25 program, year in and year out. In addition, once or twice a decade, he guides the Cougars on a deep run through college basketball's post-season tournament to challenge the other elite schools for the championship. To put it another way, Coach Horner has built the Central New York University men's basketball program into the type of program Burnet State University wishes it could someday become.

While the evolution of Central New York University into a household name has mostly been a smooth one, there have nevertheless been a few bumps along the way. With some of Coach Horner's teams not collectively performing up to the talent level of its individual players, a very vocal group of frustrated fans has built up right alongside the team's twenty win seasons. A victim of the absurdly vicious cycle of success breeding the need for more and more success, the pressure the fans now place each year on Coach Horner and the Cougars has no limits. This never-ending pressure, coming from the same die-hard fans he helped create, has led Coach Horner to grumble to his staff, on more than occasion, that he may have been better off becoming an accountant or a lawyer after all.

Recruiting is the lifeblood of any successful college basketball program—*it's serious business*—and Taylor's visit today is no different. With the future of its men's basketball program at stake, the Central New York University coaches are ready to convince Taylor that his future playing days belong right here in Westpark, New York, tied to a program and campus that are as big as his ambitions.

Much like the Burnet State University coaches the day before, the Central New York University coaches arrived an hour early this morning to collectively discuss any last-minute preparations for Taylor's visit. As they anxiously await his arrival, they decide to focus their thoughts by playing the *"What if?"* game. *"What if he decides to come to Central New York University next year?"*...*"What if he's really as good as advertised?"*...*"What if he can contribute as a freshman at both guard and forward?"*...*"What if?"*...*"What if?"* Each *"What if?"* scenario ends with Central New York University having more wins next season, which of course makes all the coaches tremendously happy.

Just before 10:00 a.m., Taylor and Deborah enter the field house and make their way over to Coach Horner's office. Knocking loudly on the outside of the door, when they step inside, they are once again greeted by a room full of smiles and nervous energy. While the energy today is more manageable than it was yesterday at Burnet State University, Deborah can still sense the *unbelievable wanting* of her son and she hates it.

After a few minutes of relatively painless small talk, the coaches ask Taylor and Deborah to join them outside in the field house parking lot. A long time ago, the coaches decided the best way for them to show off their school to recruits is to let Central New York University's impressive campus speak for itself and the best way they know how to do this is to give each recruit a personalized driving tour led by the one man who knows more about the school than almost anyone else alive: Coach Horner himself. Separately, this approach also allows the coaches to address head-on the one big myth about their school, a myth perpetuated by its rivals, that its campus is too big and intimidating for anyone to ever feel comfortable so why bother enrolling?

When their small group reaches the field house parking lot, they stop when they see a bright red sign that reads, *"If Your Name Isn't Coach Horner, Don't Bother Parking Here!"* Smirking playfully at Taylor and Deborah, Coach Horner opens the doors to his shiny new silver luxury sedan with a chirp of the keyless remote, before asking Taylor to sit up front in the passenger seat so they can get to know each other a little better. Once Deborah and the two assistant coaches are comfortably situated in the backseat, Coach Horner turns his luxury sedan out of the field house parking lot and begins driving around Central New York University's campus at a relaxed pace. In no time, Taylor notices how down-to-earth Coach Horner seems as he flawlessly alternates between his duties as resident tour guide and sharing funny stories about former players who are now playing professional basketball.

When asked, Taylor does his best to give Coach Horner answers about what he wants from his future, while also making sure to ask return questions of his own when he can think of them. Sitting in the backseat, Deborah politely makes small talk with the two assistant coaches, while doing her best to eavesdrop on what's being said between Coach Horner and her son. She knows Taylor desperately needs a strong and consistent male role model in his life and that wherever he chooses to go next year, the relationship he's going to have with his head coach is going to have a profound effect on him. She did the best she could to raise him without much help from her ex-husband, but now that he's becoming a young man, there are too many things as a woman she can't teach him or possibly understand. So whoever coaches Taylor next year is going to have to be equal parts coach, father and friend. But more than anything, he's also going to need a lot of patience. There are still plenty of demons screaming at Taylor and while he believes he's already grown up and ready to take on the world, his transition into college freshman is going to be a difficult one at best. He doesn't do anything easy and Deborah can't imagine that just because he leaves for college, he's suddenly going to turn into a different person. Chances are things will probably get worse before they get better.

After a peaceful hour spent driving through Central New York University's picturesque campus, Coach Horner temporarily parks his luxury sedan near the English Department, so the coaches can pretend they're deciding what they should do next. At the end of this brief conversation, the two assistant coaches ask Taylor if he would like to go with them to survey an introductory English class before lunch, which opens the door for Coach Horner to invite Deborah to go downtown so they can talk to each other on a more personal level, parent-to-parent. Later, over coffee and pastries, Coach Horner lets Deborah know how much he understands and appreciates the responsibility of looking after someone else's child and how well he believes Taylor will be taken care of should he come to Central New York University in the fall.

When Taylor and the two assistant coaches reach the doors of the English class, the coaches encourage Taylor to go inside and find a seat on his own. Hesitating when he hears this, Taylor turns and asks why no one will be joining him. Laughing playfully at his question, the coaches tell him there's no need for them to go inside, since they already have a great grasp of the English language, perfected through a lifetime of talking to recruits just like him. Smiling confidently as they deliver this line, the coaches let Taylor know they'll be waiting for him right outside these same doors when the class lets out. As Taylor turns and heads into the classroom alone, he's both relieved and angered by the coaches' seemingly flippant attitude.

After a painful hour and a half spent listening to a lecture on a novel he's never heard of, Taylor emerges from the class feeling even more distracted than usual. When the two assistant coaches see him from across the hall, they greet him with a few lighthearted jokes about the lecture and also tell him there's going to be a short quiz later on, so he should start getting prepared now. Grinning uncomfortably in response, Taylor somehow manages to shake off the overwhelming social anxiety that plagues most of his new interactions with adults and successfully lobs back a few sarcastic jokes of his own. As he strikes the right balance between arrogance and humility, he beams with confidence at being able to temporarily overcome his inner fears.

When the back and forth jokes die down a short while later, Taylor gives way to the coaches' now more serious tone as they head across the street to the student center so Taylor can have lunch with a group of hand-picked Central New York University basketball players. As Taylor greets the players in the middle of the food court, he slaps each one of them five with a calculated coolness reserved only for those who are on the inside of an elite club and inherently know its unwritten rules without having to talk about them first. While the players casually talk to each other in a small circle, everyone in the food court turns and stares at the tall and athletic young men in grey sweat suits, talking to the equally tall kid in jeans. It's immediately obvious to Taylor from everyone's stares that the Central New York University men's basketball players are *stars* on this campus and he couldn't imagine why he wouldn't want to become one of them.

Once lunch is over, the assistant coaches walk with Taylor back outside into what is now a bright and beautiful warm spring day. As they head across campus toward the university's crown jewel—the Cougars home gym—they pass another special building, the university's chapel. A masterfully built non-denominational house of worship, whose brick and limestone architecture dates all the way back to Renaissance Italy, the university's chapel is just one more impressive building on an already impressive campus. When Taylor first arrived today, he was unsure of whether he could fit in at Central New York University, but now that he's spent the last few hours meeting the coaches, meeting some of the players and exploring its iconic campus, he fully understands the intense appeal of the place.

On top of being the home field for the varsity football team, the Cougars home gym is also one of the most intimidating places to play in all of college basketball. Holding over 24,000 screaming fans on any given night, it's a basketball player's dream, a gym that energizes and immortalizes its own team, while annihilating the spirit of its opponents.

At just past 2:30 p.m., Taylor and the assistant coaches reach the doors of the gym, where they find Coach Horner and Deborah waiting for them just like it was planned when they separated earlier in the day. As they walk together inside for what the coaches hope will be the highlight of the day and something they believe has convinced more recruits to commit to Central New York University than all of their nationally televised basketball games combined, the coaches silently cross their fingers they can pull off one more notable showing for today's guest of honor.

After a short fifteen-minute meeting with the team's athletic trainers and its strength and conditioning coach, Coach Horner escorts Taylor onto the floor of the Cougars gym. When the two of them reach the oversized Cougars logo that covers most of center court, the lights of the cavernous gym begin to dim. Taking his cue, Coach Horner takes a few steps backward and slips quietly into the darkness behind Taylor.

What comes next is something Taylor will remember for the rest of his life, something he may never even be able to put into words. Starting with a slow steady beat...*fa-whump...fa-whump...fa-whump*...and then increasing with intensity and volume...*fa-whump...fa-whump...fa-whump*...like a runner desperately trying to reach the top of a long flight of stairs...*fa-whump...fa-whump...fa-whump*...the noise rattles the floor...*fa-whump...fa-whump...fa-whump*...making his heart pound inside his ears and his mouth turn dry with anticipation. Then, almost as quickly as it began, the noise suddenly stops.

Surrounded by complete blackness, Taylor looks around for clues as to what's going on, but can't see beyond his face. Without warning, the oversized LED screen hanging above his head unexpectedly bursts to life, illuminating the massive gym with its brilliant intensity. Looking up at the LED screen, he sees his name and number emblazoned on the back of a Central New York University basketball jersey in larger-than-life reality. A booming voice—*a voice it seems louder than God himself*—next rains down from the sky and echoes off the walls. Welcoming everyone to another night of heart-stopping Central New York University men's basketball action, the voice introduces the other four Cougars starters, before asking everyone to put their hands together and say hello to the team's new starting small forward...#23, a 6' 9" freshman from Longwood Hills High School in Longwood Hills, New Jersey...The one, the only...TAYLOR SCOTT!

The recruiting visit finishes up an hour later back inside Coach Horner's office, where Taylor and Deborah are given the Central New York University version of the "hard-sell." During this intense close to the day, Coach Horner lets Taylor know three scholarship players will be added to the team next season to offset the loss of two senior starters and one key reserve to graduation. With these gaping holes to fill, he guarantees Taylor he'll have the chance to compete for quality minutes right away, should he accept Central New York University's scholarship offer. Nodding along with a big smile, Taylor's heart skips a beat when he hears the magic words come out of Coach Horner's mouth every recruit dreams of...*quality minutes right away.*

CHAPTER 22

The Cougars gym and the rest of the Central New York University campus slowly drifts into memory as Deborah and Taylor travel south on Route 81 toward Harrisburg, Pennsylvania. With today's recruiting visit over and Thursday's visit at Maryland State University still a day away, Deborah can only hope the almost seven-hour drive down to Washington Springs, Maryland, will be a lot more leisurely and enjoyable than their rushed trip up to Westpark, New York, on Monday night. She also hopes this drive will provide even more quality mother-son bonding time, since she loves this more than anything else.

When Taylor first stepped off the Central New York University campus, a huge grin was plastered across his face and he was buzzing with energy and excitement. But now that each mile pulls him further and further away from the school, there once again seems to be a shift in his temperamental mood. Staring out the passenger side window, he replays in his head everything he saw and felt during today's recruiting visit, yet he can't truly get a grasp on how he feels.

A little over two hours later, somewhere just south of Scranton, Pennsylvania, and with the silence in the car still deafening, Deborah decides she's has to get him to share his feelings, "So Coach Horner and his staff seemed nice," she opens up the conversation casually. "And it looks like they really want you to come play there next year. I don't know about you, but overall I thought it was a very inspiring school. How are you feeling about it?"

"Okay, I guess."

"Just okay?"

"Yeah, I mean, their gym is no joke. That place is definitely legit. And they sure pulled out all the stops for me. I'm just...I'm just not sure I want to go to such a big and cold place, you know. It snows there *all* the time."

"It definitely snows there a lot, baby. And you need to consider their cold winters when making your decision. But I promise if you go, I'll buy you a much warmer winter coat," she tells him with a smile, it seems almost begging him to choose Central New York University. "The school also has it set up so you don't have to walk outside too much during the winter, unless you decide you want to."

"Yeah, I guess you're right."

"I think it's also important to keep in mind that besides basketball, Central New York University has a great academic reputation. I really liked it, if you can't tell."

"So you want me to go there?"

"*No*, that's not what I said. It's your decision, you know that. You're the one who has to go to the school you choose, not me. I just want to see you happy. That's all I've ever wanted for you."

All day long, Deborah's been thinking that if she'd only been given the same opportunity to attend a school like Central New York University when she was younger, she would've jumped at the opportunity with both feet and never looked back.

"So the cold winter up there is the only thing that's not sitting right with you? You sure there isn't anything else?"

"I liked the place. Really, Mom, I did. I'm just not sure I *loved* it, you know. I want to *love* the school I decide to go to. Is that crazy?"

"No, that's not crazy. But what would make you love it?"

"I don't know...I guess, maybe, I mean, I had lunch with some of the guys on the team and I'm just not sure about them, that's all. They were kind of nice, but I could tell they didn't like me. They kept looking me up and down funny. If we're going to be teammates, shouldn't we be friends like in high school?"

"I'm not sure. But you have to remember, you also just met them."

"*I know*, Mom," he responds in a frustrated voice. "Give me some credit, will ya? And I know when someone is looking at me funny. I've been around long enough to recognize when it's happening."

"Sorry, you're absolutely right. If I had to take a guess, I would say the other players see you right now as a threat and not as a potential friend. If you go there, I'm sure that will change with time."

"Still. They didn't hide it very well."

"Try not to take it so personally."

"Whatever, we'll see."

"What does that mean?"

"It means, I'm not sure about the place right now, that's all."

"All right. Fine. I didn't mean to push. I just thought it looked like a beautiful place to go to school and the coaches seemed genuinely interested in seeing you do well, both on and off the court. However, I didn't meet the other players, so I can't speak to their attitudes. But you have to remember, friendship can't always come as easily as it did for you and Jimmy. Your friendship is something special."

"Yeah, I know," he answers just as he turns away from their conversation and refocuses his eyes back on the world outside the car.

Recognizing this far-off stare all too well, Deborah decides to leave him alone to his thoughts, rather than keep pushing their conversation to a place he doesn't want to take it to.

With the tires of the car humming along at a nice even pace, Taylor watches as the white lines of the road slide underneath the front wheels and out of sight, sending his mind drifting further and further into the future. It only stops drifting when he once again reaches a place of paralyzing thoughts and intense fears about this next stage in his life.

CHAPTER 23

A red brick archway stretches across Armstrong Avenue, high above the street, displaying the words MARYLAND STATE UNIVERSITY FOUNDED 1840 in big block letters. While there are seemingly hundreds of other entrances to the Maryland State University campus, the "Arch on Arm" as it's called by students and faculty is the school's unofficial main entrance, as well as the official separation point between the university's leafy campus and the outside world. On most nights, the "Arch on Arm" also serves as the central meeting spot for students heading down to Armstrong Avenue to grab a cold drink and blow off some steam by listening to one of the many independent bands that dominate the area's small but thriving music scene.

Pulling off Route 13, Deborah follows the printed directions on her lap and steers the car north onto Armstrong Avenue. Passing directly underneath the "Arch on Arm," she turns right at the corner of Washington Avenue and drives onto the Maryland State University campus in the direction of the basketball arena. With the saga of finding Taylor a school to call home next year almost over, she can't help but smile to herself at the thought of the phone *not ringing* inside her house, something she's desperately been looking forward to for almost two years.

As the car makes its way down Washington Avenue, an overpowering sense of awe suddenly grabs hold of Taylor when he sees the overall beauty of the campus stretching out in front of him in all directions. From the school's lush green grass, to its blooming white flowers, to its cobbled walkways, to its manicured trees, it seems as if the images lying dormant inside his head about what a college campus should look like are suddenly matching up with the reality before his eyes.

Opening up his window to get an even better look, Taylor sees that every building is identical to the one next to it, giving the entire campus a uniform feeling of togetherness. Designed and built in the same timeless Georgian-style and using the same red Williamsburg-style bricks, each building has finishing touches of eggshell white painted doorways and window trim set against architectural details that reflect the school's colonial heritage. With his excitement about what the day ahead might bring continuing to grow with each building they pass, he squints hard against the bright blue sky above and stares off into the distance at a large quad lined with giant oak trees. The quad is filled with students laughing, playing casual games and lounging around, letting time peacefully pass by. The whole scene appears to be lifted straight out of the school's promotional catalogue and staged just for him.

"This is nice," Deborah states out loud for no other reason except she too really likes what she sees. At the same time, a sense of calm washes over her knowing that her son would be perfectly safe and happy in a place like this, even if it's further away from home than she would like it to be.

As they turn into the parking lot of the Liberty Arena, Maryland State University's new home gym, Deborah and

Taylor are both blown away by the sheer size and magnitude of the building. The arena has been placed in the exact center of campus and while it looks almost identical to every other building in terms of architecture-style, it practically screams, *"Look at Me!"*

After finding a parking spot marked 'visitor,' Deborah shuts off the car's engine and stares through the windshield at the arena. With the weight of the moment resting heavy on her mind, she sighs softly to herself, realizing a lot of basketball wins are needed for a university to justify building a striking monument like this. She also hopes, especially after their heart-to-heart talk earlier in the week, she's not once again voluntarily throwing her son to the wolves.

Sitting next to her, Taylor is captivated by the arena as visions of greatness dance in his head, "Now this is a home gym!" he suddenly shouts out loud, provoked by nothing more than the feelings of giddy excitement running through his veins.

"It's definitely impressive, baby. There's no doubt about that." Falling deep into thought, the two sides of Deborah's brain immediately pull her emotions in opposite directions, *protect him versus let him go.*

CHAPTER 24

Standing under the shade of an oversized elm tree, just outside of the Liberty Arena, waiting for Deborah and Taylor's arrival is Maryland State University's top assistant coach, Sean Banks. Wearing a red, white and blue Maryland State University men's basketball warm-up suit and a matching pair of brand new high tops, it looks as if Coach Banks is waiting for a pick-up game to break out at any moment and doesn't want to be unprepared for it when it does. At 6' 1" and 185 lbs., he has an athletic frame, dark brown skin and wears his hair shaved remarkably close to his head. A member of the Maryland State University coaching staff for less than two years, he has already proven himself to be an invaluable asset and tireless recruiter; and while he and Head Coach Rory McCallom come from very different walks of life, he has risen in his short time on staff, much to the dismay of the other assistant coaches, to become his boss' most trusted advisor. A very intense man, Coach Banks knows what he wants out of life and isn't shy about going after it. He backs up these burning desires with an unending work ethic that makes it seem inevitable that no matter what he wants, he will eventually get.

Since most of Taylor's contact leading up to this point has been directly with Coach McCallom, he has no idea what to expect from Coach Banks when he sees him lightly jogging in the direction of their car wearing a super wide grin and waving enthusiastically, "Ms. Jones! Welcome to Maryland State University!" Coach Banks starts in with passion and enthusiasm before he even reaches the driver's side door. "I'm Coach Sean Banks! It's a pleasure to meet you!"

"Thank you," Deborah responds through the open window, fixating her eyes on Coach Banks' perfect smile as he holds the car door open for her. "It's nice to meet you too. But please, call me Deborah."

"It'll be my pleasure. And Taylor, it goes without saying, we're very excited you've decided to come visit us today. We're very proud of the program we've built here and we can't wait to convince you to become a part of it."

Coach Banks' blatant salesmanship oozes out of every pore, yet somehow it comes across as genuine.

"Sounds good to me," Taylor replies as he leans forward in his seat to get a better look at Coach Banks' face.

"We have a full day of activities set up for you both, followed by dinner with Coach McCallom and his wife. We know this is a lot for one day, but since we only get you this one time, we want to make sure we provide you the best Maryland State University experience we possibly can. We don't want you leaving here thinking any other school is the right place for you."

"Uh, huh," Taylor grunts back from across the front seat.

"Do either of you need any help with your bags? Or would you like to keep them in the car?"

Surprised by Coach Banks' generous offer, Deborah instinctively smiles, before responding, "That's nice of you to ask, but our bags can stay in the car. To be honest, what I could really use is a short trip to the ladies' room."

"I don't think that should be a problem," Coach Banks winks casually in her direction as he responds. "Why don't we head inside the Liberty Arena? This way I can also steal a few minutes alone with Taylor before we make our way up to Coach McCallom's office."

As Taylor and Deborah follow Coach Banks around to the front of the Liberty Arena, they are once again blown away by the size and magnitude of the building. With no detail left to chance, a beautiful cobblestone pathway leads to the arena's main entrance, where giant glass windows stretch skyward for two stories. At its highest point, the windows blend seamlessly with the surrounding red bricks in a perfect match of old and new. Designed as a symbolic portal from the past to the future, the arena was meant to both impress visitors and intimidate opponents. A goal it easily achieves.

Hanging above the main doors of the arena, a permanent sign reads, *"Maryland State University Welcomes You To The Liberty Arena...Go Revolutionaries!"* and hanging high above this sign, to the right of the windows, is an oversized banner displaying the Revolutionaries' menacing-looking mascot.

To fulfill his duty to protect the Liberty Arena and its home teams from its sworn enemies, the Revolutionaries' mascot wears a tri-corner hat on top of his long flowing black hair, a full length battle coat open at the waist, white pants, black boots that sit just below the knee; he's armed with a musket slung tightly over his left shoulder and a long curved sword with a gold handle, hanging from his belt. The mascot practically growls at passersby from his elevated perch high above the ground.

As Taylor continues to take everything in, he can once again feel his heart race with excitement, while Deborah stands next to him, trying to swallow her emotions one breath at a time.

"Where did you drive in from?" Coach Banks breaks up the silence as they walk to the front door of the arena.

"Last night we stayed in York, Pennsylvania," Deborah answers. "We were on our way down from visiting Central New York University."

"Central New York University? Now why would you want to visit such a place?" Coach Banks playfully asks.

"I don't know, maybe it's because they have a small basketball program up there that has expressed a lot of interest in my son," Deborah responds as they step inside the arena.

"Yeah, go get him, Ma!" Taylor laughs inside his head, suddenly impressed with his mom's biting sarcasm.

"I'm just kidding," Coach Banks replies nervously, a step behind Deborah. "It was a small joke. I hope I didn't offend you. We both know Coach Horner runs a top-notch program at Central New York University and any player, including Taylor, would be lucky to be a part of it. Although, we really do hope he likes it here better."

Coach Banks quietly thanks God under his breath Coach McCallom wasn't here to watch him stumble through this awkward exchange.

"No offense taken," Deborah responds through closed lips. "As for the other, let's just see how the rest of the day goes, before we compare notes."

"Yeah, Ma!" Taylor laughs inside his head again. *"Keep after him!"*

As the three of them walk in the direction of the ladies' room, they stop and pause for a minute when they reach an expansive glass display case built directly into the wall of the arena. A glass display case that can only be described as a shrine to the Maryland State University men's basketball program and its long history of success.

Starting on the shelves closest to the ground, the Revolutionaries' numerous regular season and conference tournament title trophies are lined up next to each other, almost piling up one on top of another, while its most prestigious trophy, the one handed to Coach McCallom immediately after leading Maryland State University to its only post-season college basketball championship six years ago, sits alone high up in the dead center of the case. This way visitors need to crane their necks to look at it or some more cynical students and fans have come to suggest, look up to it as if you're praying to it.

Right next to the championship trophy is a framed photograph of the Revolutionaries' winning team standing at center court, celebrating the school's monumental victory in full glory. The day after the Revolutionaries took home college basketball's post-season championship, the photograph appeared on the front page and home page of every major media outlet from Washington Springs, Maryland, to Seattle, Washington, and back again. Magically capturing the team's raw emotion from accomplishing something it once thought was improbable, if not impossible, the photograph suspends time and place in the way only sports imagery can. It has since become an integral part of Maryland State University's athletic legacy and an indelible memory for its fans, so much so, the grown men these championship players will one day become will be forever compared, whether they like it or not, to the younger versions of themselves celebrating in the photograph.

"Please take your time looking at everything," Coach Banks once again breaks up the silence. "But Deborah, when you're done, I want you to know the ladies' room is just down the hallway to your right."

"Thank you," she responds and after few more seconds of staring into the glass case, heads down a glistening hallway filled with advertisements that seem to cover every available inch of wall space.

"Now that your mom has left us for a moment," Coach Banks addresses Taylor. "Tell me, how was your drive down from Central New York University?"

Even though these situations always make Taylor extremely uncomfortable and he knows full well what Coach Banks is doing, he has no other choice but to wade cautiously into their conversation. "It was fine, I guess. Not much to look at, you know."

"Well, at least you had your mom to keep you company. Long rides can be dull without some good conversation. Especially if you've just left somewhere you were excited about."

"If you say so..."

Based on this unemotional response, Coach Banks knows he's probably going to have a tough time pulling any worthwhile information out of Taylor about his visit to Central New York University. At least, anything he can report back to Coach McCallom. So he decides to try a different approach, determined, if nothing else, for the two of them to be on solid ground before they reach Coach McCallom's office, "You know my grandmother lived in New Jersey. Elizabeth, New Jersey, to be exact. I always had a lot of fun visiting her as a kid. As far as I'm concerned, New Jersey has always done right by me."

"Yeah, it's a cool state, I guess," Taylor answers with a shrug. "Where'd you grow up?"

"Philadelphia. Born and bred. I got Philly cheesesteaks running through my veins. Wait, are you a football fan?"

"Yeah, I live and die by New Jersey's team. Why?"

"Uh, oh," Coach Banks playfully responds. "I think we might have a problem."

Even though Taylor hasn't shown his sense of humor yet, Coach Banks takes a calculated risk that underneath his stiff exterior, it's there. "I'm from Philly, Taylor. You have to know I love my Huskies something fierce!" he grins from ear to ear as he says this.

"Oh, come on now!" Taylor responds loudly as he loosens up a little bit. "What have you guys ever won? Tell me, do you even have a quarterback who can throw twenty yards downfield?"

"Ha. Good one, young man. But you'll see. This is our year to bring home the title. We've waited too long already."

"Spoken like a true Philadelphia fan. You're all the same, *crazy delirious*. Do they teach you guys that somewhere? Or is it just passed down from generation to generation?"

"Ouch!" Coach Banks responds as he pretends a fake arrow is piercing his heart. "I'll tell you what. I'll bet you five suicide sprints on each game our teams play this year. Winner can yell insults at the loser as he runs his sprints. Deal?"

"I don't know. How will you know where to find me to collect?"

"I'll bet you another five suicide sprints I know *exactly* where to find you next year," Coach Banks answers with a smile.

Watching from a safe distance down the hall, Deborah feels a sense of satisfaction and comfort at seeing her son and Coach Banks interact so naturally with each other. Besides her reaction to first seeing the Liberty Arena, today's recruiting visit was off to a very good start. "Are you two arguing over football already?" she cheerfully scolds from behind.

"Yes, Ma'am," Coach Banks turns around in the direction of her voice. "It seems I have an enemy football fan in my midst."

"Amazing. You leave two men alone for five minutes and inevitably they start arguing over sports. But mostly, they seem to like to argue over football. What is it about that sport that turns men into little boys?"

"I don't know," Coach Banks replies. "But I believe it's as close to a national religion as we have in this country."

Too busy turning to look back at Taylor's face, Coach Banks doesn't notice Deborah softly frown at the mention of football and religion in the same sentence, "Either way, Taylor," he finishes up. "I love me my Huskies something fierce! Don't ever forget it."

"So sorry to hear that..."

Moments later, Coach Banks smiles broadly as he changes the direction of the conversation, "Now that we've gotten the football argument of today's recruiting visit out of the way, what do you say we head up to Coach McCallom's office to see if he's in?"

"I think that's a wonderful idea," Deborah responds, excited to meet the Revolutionaries' head coach for the first time.

Sitting in his office two floors up, Coach McCallom stares impatiently at his watch, trying to remain calm as he waits for his star recruit to be hand-delivered to his door. Ever since he watched Taylor play in an invitation-only basketball camp last summer, he's believed Taylor could be the missing piece to take Maryland State University back to the top of the college basketball world. Not to mention, line his pockets with a big contract extension if he can deliver another post-season college basketball championship to the Revolutionaries faithful.

To make sure Taylor doesn't slip through his fingers, Coach McCallom has put Coach Banks and the rest of his coaching staff through an intense regimen of meetings, role-playing and more meetings, leading up to today's recruiting visit. And while preparation is always the key to success, when Coach McCallom woke up this morning and saw the sun rise over the bay from his back porch, he felt a big sense of relief, knowing it was going to be another beautiful day in Washington Springs, Maryland; nothing is worse than trying to show off Maryland State University's scenic campus to a new recruit in the middle of bad weather.

With bright blue skies now stretching as far as the eye can see, Coach McCallom is once again convinced God is personally looking out for the success of the Revolutionaries' basketball program. All that remains is for Coach Banks to hurry up and deliver Taylor to his door already, this way he can start his part of today's show.

CHAPTER 25

The bell for the third floor chimes lightly in the background as Coach Banks holds open the elevator doors for Deborah and Taylor to step into the impressive lobby of the Revolutionaries men's basketball team. On the other side of the doors, the words *Maryland State University Men's Basketball* are etched into the blue carpet which runs from one side of the room to the other. A few feet beyond these words, the school's bright and colorful crest sits at the base of an oversized dark wood reception desk, giving the entire space a feeling of dramatic importance.

As the three of them walk through the lobby, Coach Banks introduces Deborah and Taylor to everyone he sees, from the secretaries to the students helping out in the office, to the women's head basketball coach who happens to be dropping by. The whole scene has been staged by Coach McCallom to show his prized recruit and his mom, the men's basketball team office is always hard at work, even in the off-season.

At the end of a hallway lined with the same blue carpet, Coach Banks stops when he reaches Sherri's desk, Coach McCallom's loyal secretary for the past fifteen years. A plump middle-aged woman with bleached blond hair and a gentle smile, she's wearing large gold hoop earrings, a blue sweater and white linen pants for today's special visit. After a brief exchange in which Sherri makes sure to go out of her way to compliment Deborah's hair and outfit, Coach Banks leads them over to the office of the man in charge.

Knocking lightly on the outside of Coach McCallom's door, Coach Banks opens it up three-quarters of the way and pokes his head inside without entering, just like they practiced it the day before, "Got a minute, Coach? I think I have some people here you might want to meet."

Breathing a small sigh of relief, Coach McCallom delivers his well-rehearsed line loud enough for everyone to hear, "Sure, Steve. Come on in."

Sitting behind a large mahogany desk with a pair of reading glasses hanging off the end of his nose is Maryland State University's long-time head basketball coach Rory McCallom. A heavy-set man with round broad shoulders and a thick neck, he has thinning dark brown hair which he's pushed across the top of his head to try and hide the fact he's in the middle of going bald, yet he isn't fooling anyone. While he looks every bit of his fifty-eight years, you can still see the handsome and dynamic young man that took over the Revolutionaries men's basketball program all those years ago right underneath his now-aging skin.

While outwardly warm and friendly to almost everyone he meets, percolating directly below the surface is a simmering intensity that never really leaves. Luckily for the outside world, Coach McCallom doesn't show this side of his personality too often, reserving this special part of himself mostly for his players and assistant coaches. His temper is legendary, but you have to ask the right person about it or it will just be shrugged off as another rumor running through the never-ending mill of speculation surrounding the Revolutionaries men's basketball program, a favorite pastime on Maryland State University's campus and throughout the state.

Before they even say hello to Coach McCallom, Taylor can't help but notice the gold watch on his wrist and the diamond-encrusted post-season college basketball championship ring on his hand. The embodiment of success, Coach McCallom wants you to know this about him from the instant you meet him. However, he offsets this desire for recognition with a homespun charm he's developed over the years into movie-worthy perfection. This charm says, *"I'm one of you,"* even if you aren't wearing a $15,000 watch and a special ring given out to only a few people every year. This is all part of his great success as a coach, because in the rare air of college basketball that Maryland State University and the other top programs occupy, being a head coach is as much about winning basketball games as it is about shaking hands, making speeches and connecting with fans. In Coach McCallom's own estimation, he's spoken at every community hall, special event and booster club gathering within two hundred miles of the Maryland State University campus. All in an effort to let everyone know he's just one more guy in the state of Maryland working hard to do a good job and get home to his family at night.

"Coach, I would like you to meet Taylor Scott and his mother Deborah Jones," Coach Banks officially introduces their special guests.

Standing up from behind his desk, Coach McCallom graciously welcomes them into his office, "It's a pleasure to meet you both. I'm so glad you chose to come down and see our little school for yourselves today. We think you're going to really like it. The administration has built a beautiful campus in our small corner of the world and a nice little gym behind me that I hope Taylor will one day call home."

After hearing this last part, Taylor peers over Coach McCallom's shoulder and notices for the first time the entire back wall of his office is one large glass window that looks out into the now empty Liberty Arena and its alternating red, white and blue seats.

"While I wish I could take all the credit for the beauty of this building," Coach McCallom sees Taylor is staring over his shoulder, "I have to hand it to our talented group of architects and engineers. They are the ones that deserve all the credit for turning it into a special place to be envied."

"They sure have," Taylor and Deborah respond at the same time as if they'd rehearsed it.

"Taylor, I think I may have mentioned this to you during one of our initial phone conversations, but I also grew up in New Jersey," like any good salesman, Coach McCallom was trying to create an even deeper connection with his audience. "My parents moved me, my three brothers and one sister from Brooklyn to Vinewood, New Jersey, when I was only five years old. My parents stayed in that same house in Vinewood until my father passed away twelve years ago."

"Yeah, I think you told me that a long time ago," Taylor answers, preferring to skip over the father comment and concentrate on the thing he can relate to. "And I guess, if you were able to make the transition down to this school, it can't be that difficult, right?"

"Difficult? Not at all. This is one of the easiest places to transition to. In no time, you'll appreciate the slower pace of life. Not to mention, the natural ebb and flow of the seasons."

"That's cool," Taylor replies and then asks a question he considers almost as important as what life is like on Maryland State University's campus. "Where did you play high school ball? Vinewood High?"

"Oh, no," Coach McCallom responds with a shake of his head. "Vinewood High's teams weren't very good back then."

"Still aren't," Taylor snickers.

Ignoring Taylor's snide remark, Coach McCallom continues talking, "Coming out of middle school, I was lucky enough to get a scholarship to a private high school a few towns over from Vinewood. During my senior year, we won the state championship in basketball, which helped me get another scholarship to play basketball right here at Maryland State University. But that's all ancient history at this point and I'm sure you don't want to hear any more about me. So please, sit down," Coach McCallom extends his right arm, inviting Taylor and Deborah to sit in the two stately-looking leather arm chairs on the opposite side of his desk.

Taking his cue, Coach Banks moves out of the way and gets comfortable on the small box-patterned couch near the door normally reserved for informal conversations.

By the time Coach McCallom begins talking again, Taylor is already envisioning himself being introduced to a sold-out Liberty Arena home crowd. Not to mention imagining his jersey hanging from the rafters next to the rest of the Revolutionaries' basketball legends who also once called Maryland State University's campus home.

"Before we begin," Coach McCallom momentarily turns his eyes to Deborah. "I want to let you know that even though we are sitting inside a basketball arena, I and the rest of the coaching staff care deeply about your son's education. Getting an education is the number one priority for all of our players. We have mandatory study halls, as well as tutors assigned to the team to make sure none of our players ever fall behind, even when classes are missed due to our travel schedule. If nothing else, I promise you Maryland State University will provide Taylor the opportunity at a world-class education."

"While that's nice to hear," Deborah tells Coach McCallom from across the desk. "I can assure you, Taylor won't need any tutors to help him keep up with his studies. He's well prepared for college classes."

"Sounds very nice to me," Coach McCallom answers with a smile. "We have some good students on our team, but not everyone has the educational foundation Longwood Hills has provided Taylor. Having an excellent high school background really does provide a student-athlete a huge advantage when entering college. In this case, our academic team will be here to help Taylor if he wants it, but we won't count on him needing any assistance."

"I think that sounds like a very practical approach," Deborah responds with an approving nod.

"Taylor, do you have an idea what you want to major in?" Coach McCallom turns his attention back to his prized recruit.

"Business, I think."

"Great, you can't go wrong there. Even if you never wind up going into business, the foundation it provides will benefit you in anything you choose to do with your life."

"Yeah, I figured you can't really know too much about money," Taylor answers with a small smirk.

"Spoken like a man well beyond his years. Any idea at this point which area of business you would like to concentrate on?"

"Uhm, no...Just general business, I think?" *He didn't know there was more than one area!*

"Well, you actually don't have to decide anything for a while. Not until at least your sophomore year. Isn't that right, Coach Banks?"

Hearing his name from his spot on the couch near the door, Coach Banks leans forward in his seat, happy to be invited back into the conversation, "Absolutely. You don't have to choose your major until your sophomore year. Then, you still don't have to select a narrower path of study until the start of your junior year. There's plenty of time to decide a lot of things between now and then."

"Okay, cool," Taylor responds, while making a plan to look up what areas of business exist as soon as he gets home.

"You'll be happy to know our Business Department is well respected both nationally and regionally," Coach McCallom picks up the thread in the conversation. "In addition to its outstanding academic reputation, it also has strong connections to the Baltimore and Washington, D.C. business communities. Most students find these connections invaluable for networking and internship opportunities. Remind me later when we're taking our tour of campus to knock on Dr. Stark's office. He's the head of the Business Department. We both sit on the board of the Student-Athlete Advisory Council, so we know each other quite well. If he's around, I'd love for you to meet him in person."

"I think that sounds delightful," Deborah answers, excited at the idea of meeting someone else besides a coach or trainer on one of these recruiting visits.

"I'm glad to hear it," Coach McCallom replies. "Now I think we should leave this office behind, especially since today's sunny blue skies really are a gift from above."

Deborah and Taylor both nod in agreement.

"We'll start downstairs with a brief tour of our nice little home gym here and then head outside shortly after that. I will also introduce you to the other assistant coaches later in the day. I gave them the morning off as I didn't want to make this visit feel any bigger than it is," Coach McCallom grins ever so slightly as he says this.

Deborah and Taylor both nod in agreement again as if this is smartest thing they've ever heard.

"Shall we?" Coach McCallom stands and politely points to his office door.

Before turning to leave, Taylor takes a moment to stare again out into the empty Liberty Arena. As he does this, he's unable to imagine anything going wrong in such a perfect building.

CHAPTER 26

After a relaxing night having dinner with Coach McCallom and his wife, Deborah and Taylor wake up early the next morning and get back into the car to start their four and half hour drive home to Longwood Hills, New Jersey. With all the recruiting visits now over, a sense of finality hangs in the air as Taylor sits in the passenger seat trying to sort through his feelings about which school might be best for him. At the same time, his never-ending fears about taking the next step in his life keep circling back on him, playing tricks on his mind. An hour later, with his silent mood still dominating the car, Deborah tries to snap him out of his funk the only way she knows how, by being his mom, "I spy, with my little eye, something that is red!" she practically giggles.

"What?"

"I spy, with my little eye, something that is red!" she repeats.

"Come on, Mom! I'm not eight anymore."

"Just up there on the left is a red pickup truck!" she exclaims.

"Sounds great. You know playing a silly game isn't going to stop me from being in a bad mood. It's not that simple."

"Look, the red pickup truck is three cars ahead of us on the left! Don't you see it?"

"Mom, enough. I have a lot on my mind, okay?"

"I know you have a lot on your mind, baby. You went to bed last night smiling and woke up this morning with a black cloud hanging over your head. You haven't said two words to me all day. I know I don't have to tell you this, but when you were eight, you used to love this game."

"Just in case you forgot, I'm definitely not eight anymore. So knock it off."

"No, you need to talk to me."

"No, I don't."

"A nice game of I Spy will get the conversation going," she ignores him.

"It's not going to help, Mom. Okay? This is a big decision. I just need some time to think, that's all."

"Thinking is definitely good, but don't go looking for something that might not be there. What does your gut tell you?"

"My gut tells me I like Central New York University and Maryland State University the same."

"I'm sorry, sweetie, but that's impossible. You have to like one school more than the other. Do me a favor and close your eyes."

"Huh?"

"I want you to close your eyes for a second."

"Only if you do the same."

"Very funny. I'm driving."

"I know."

"Please, close your eyes...For me."

"Why?"

"Humor your mother, will you?"

"Fine."

"Are your eyes closed?"

"Yup."

"Now take a deep breath and concentrate. Picture yourself playing in a game next year. Do you see yourself?"

"Yeah. Why?"

"What name is on the front of the jersey?...And don't hesitate!"

A feeling of intense satisfaction spreads through Taylor's body as he clearly sees the name of the school on the front of the jersey.

"I'm not sure what I see," he lies. "It's just, one school is the right choice and one school is the wrong choice. But there's no way to know if I'm right until I'm already there. *Then it's too late.* I think I should just stay home next year and go to a local community college," he grins uncomfortably as he says this, revealing much more than he intended.

"While you know I would love for you to never grow up and live with me forever, the one thing you will not be doing next year is staying home with me."

"Why? You just said I loved playing games when I was eight. This means I was fun then. I can be fun again."

"Sometimes I wish you were still eight, *believe me*. At least when you were eight, I could solve most of your problems by giving you a hug or taking you out for ice cream. Now there isn't much I can do except encourage you to follow your heart."

"Sorry...I guess."

"You just grew up so fast."

"So those days are behind us, huh?"

"Yes they are, baby. But that doesn't mean I can't wish to go back to them every now and then. It's a mother's right to dream, so please don't deny me that."

"I would never."

"I also want you to know, even in spite of all this Kelly nonsense, I'm very proud you're my son and how you've turned out."

"Thanks, Mom."

172 / Adam Poe

Seizing the moment, Deborah decides to get weighty one last time, knowing it could be a while before they have the chance to talk like this again, "I want to tell you something else and please don't interrupt me until I'm done."

"Okay," he replies with unease, the tone of her voice once again revealing this is probably a conversation he doesn't want to have.

"I want to say thank you."

"Huh? You want to thank me? For what?"

"I just asked you to not interrupt me. Please Taylor, let me finish."

"Okay…Sorry."

"I want to say thank you for helping me through the time when your father and I split up."

"No! Please, stop!" Taylor suddenly wants to scream back at her.

"I've never said thank you for being there for me. I know you were only a kid back then, but you were also my friend. It meant everything to me."

Taylor squirms in his seat and looks away as a rush of emotions he forgot were even there begin to bubble inside him.

"It was a tough time in my life and you were so strong. Your strength was an inspiration to me. Do you know that?"

The muscles of Taylor's chest tighten as if a cold sheet of ice is hardening inside his lungs and his entire chest might crack wide open at any moment. Keeping his eyes fixated on the world outside the car, he silently shakes his head no, afraid that if he looks into his mom's face, he won't be able to hold back his tears.

"I figured if you could be that brave for me," she tells him with sympathetic eyes. "The least I could do is get myself better and start being a parent to you again."

The tears that have pooled in the corner of Taylor's eyes want to escape, but he refuses to let them.

"Thanks, Mom," he finally turns back in her direction and responds through clenched teeth. "I was just so *mad* at Dad, you know. And I also wanted to see you get better. That's all I cared about."

"I know, baby. None of it went unnoticed. I promise you."

"Thanks," he answers, continuing to force his raw emotions back down into the abyss.

"I wanted to tell you all of this before it's too late and you were off to college. It's extremely important to remember the past when heading into the future. Because no matter how difficult and painful the past might have been, without it, we wouldn't be who we are. I hope that makes sense?" she glances over to see his face, wanting to remember him exactly as he is right now.

"Yeah, that makes sense. I'm just glad we still have each other, you know. Because I can't count on Dad for anything real. The only thing I can count on him for is to brag to other people about what a great father he is and how much credit he should get for my success. Success he has nothing to do with. He only shows up when the spotlights are on. When the lights are down, he's nowhere to be found. You know what I mean?"

"Yes, sweetie. Unfortunately, all too well...I know your father can be a real inconsiderate jerk sometimes, but to be honest, I have to take some of the blame for your poor relationship. Looking back at it, I made too many decisions about your future without involving him."

Taylor sits up straight in his seat and stiffens his spine when he hears this.

"I'm also sorry that I discouraged him from coming by and seeing you more when you were younger. Especially when the two of you were having problems. That was my doing, not his."

Using the back of his sleeve, Taylor wipes away a few tears that have suddenly fallen out of his eyes against his will.

"Baby, I was just so angry and upset at your dad. I couldn't even look at him without wanting to throw something at him. He took my heart and walked all over it. I wasn't about to let him do the same thing to you. Then when he remarried so quickly and started having a second family with *that* woman. The pain was too much for me to take, so I pushed him as far away from us as I possibly could."

"Okay? But why are you telling me all of this *now*?"

"Because I want you to forgive him."

"You what?" he asks in disbelief.

"I want you to make more of an effort to get to know your dad. Even though you'll be going away to school in a few months, I think it's important for you two to build a better relationship."

"How can you say that? You just agreed with me he can't be counted on and is nowhere to be found when things get difficult. Why should I?"

"Because I think you might need him in the next few years more than you think."

"No, I won't. I don't need that guy to do anything *except* stay away from me."

"Baby, I know this might be difficult for you to hear and understand right now, but your father isn't all bad. There was a time in my life when I loved him unconditionally. I would've done anything for him. I can't be that poor of a judge of character. So please try, if not for yourself, then for me."

After listening to this last plea, Taylor stares straight ahead out the window with a look of confused anguish, trying to digest what his mom just said. Taking some time to gather his thoughts, he finally turns to her, "I'll think about it, okay?"

"That's all I can ask..."

With the small green signs that mark off each tenth of a mile along Route 95 North rolling past the car at a steady clip, Taylor's mood slowly turns for the better, "I spy, with my little eye, a yellow hatchback," he whispers under his breath.

"Did you say something, sweetie?"

"Me? No, it must be the tires of the car or something."

CHAPTER 27

On the last Wednesday of April, Taylor stands behind an old wood podium inside the Longwood Hills High School gym and looks out at a small audience filled with reporters, school faculty and a few students who were given permission to attend his press conference. Holding the best microphone the A/V squad could find tightly in his enormous right hand, his mom, dad and Coach Waters sit behind him on a makeshift stage, each wearing a proud smile. After flattening out the script his dad wrote for him the night before across the cracked wood of the podium, he pauses dramatically and scans the eager faces looking back at him before beginning...

"After spending the last year evaluating the many generous offers from the schools who thought enough of my basketball skills to recruit me and after discussing everything in length with my family, I have come to a decision about my future." Looking up again, he fixates his eyes on the front row, where he sees the head writer from the nation's leading prep recruiting newsletter, sitting next to the high school sports reporter from a major online media company, both sitting two seats down from Jimmy. "While it's been a long and difficult road to reach this decision, I feel in my heart I've landed on the right school for me. So without any further delay, I want to let everyone know, starting next season I will be taking my basketball talents to..." pausing one more time for effect, he reaches down into the base of the podium and pulls out a red, white and blue baseball hat and firmly places it on top of his head. As the crowd applauds, he slowly mouths the words into the microphone, "Maryland State University."

After waiting patiently for the applause to die down, Taylor turns and looks directly into the TV cameras to finish what's left of his speech, "And I can't wait to get down to Washington Springs, Maryland, to begin the next chapter of my life. But more than anything, I look forward to working with my new coaches and teammates so I can improve and contribute to the ongoing success of the Maryland State University program. Thank you."

Within minutes, the town of Longwood Hills is abuzz with word of Taylor's announcement and thirty minutes later, after receiving his signed scholarship acceptance via fax, Coach McCallom, Coach Banks and the rest of the Maryland State University men's basketball coaching staff celebrate their good fortune with a round of twenty-five-year-old whiskey Coach McCallom keeps in his office for special occasions just like this. *The living breathing trophy of next year's recruiting class is all theirs and they couldn't be happier.*

After hearing the news on their own, the current Maryland State University players scramble around to find out as much information about Taylor Scott as they can, trying to calculate, what, if anything, his presence on campus may mean to their playing time next season.

CHAPTER 28

The final days of Taylor's senior year fly by in a hurry as the spring air changes from cold and rainy to warm and sunny. During this time, Longwood Hills' graduating class walks through the halls, just like every graduating class before it, in a constant conversation about its limitless future. Having outgrown the school, the teachers and the town, the world is waiting for them and they can't dive in head-first soon enough. Some were off to college, others to trade schools and some to the armed forces, with mostly everyone going somewhere else besides Longwood Hills. As the happiest days of their lives come to a close, Longwood Hills' graduating class can't say goodbye to them fast enough.

The day after senior prom, Taylor, Jimmy and the rest of the basketball team head down to the Jersey Shore for a few days of mandatory relaxing, goofing-off and lying on the beach. In what seems like a blink of an eye, Taylor is sitting across from Jimmy in the back seat of Eric's convertible, shortly after graduation ceremonies, wearing big white sunglasses and a silly grin of accomplishment splashed across his face. While the always present pit of intense self-doubt remains squarely lodged in his stomach, he's once again found a way to push it below the surface and pretend it doesn't exist; proving yet again that denial may be the most powerful human emotion of all.

As Eric's convertible races through town with its radio blasting and black and gold streamers flowing off the back, Taylor doesn't say very much to either Jimmy or Eric, rather choosing to once again take everything in during this big moment of transition. Life is still very much a mystery to him and he's only now beginning to see all of its nuances.

With the finality of the moment sinking in, Taylor can't help but stare with nervous discomfort at Jimmy only a few feet away, much like he did the night they won the state championship. Even though they'll only be two hours away from each other in the fall, it might as well be two days, as apart is apart and the space between them is already starting to feel much greater than it actually is.

CHAPTER 29

The phone echoes throughout #31 Wingate Drive, but as usual Taylor doesn't bother to try and answer it. After years of ignoring the phone's constant ringing, he's only recently gotten used to picking it up again without a coach being on the other end, talking through a rapid fire sales pitch. Splayed out on the couch, with his feet propped up on the coffee table, he stares at the ringing phone and hopes against hope his mom will answer it. After the fourth ring, he gives up this wish and slides across the couch to grab the receiver, "Hello," he grunts.

"Is this Taylor?" the voice on the other end asks.

"Yeah, it's Taylor...Who's this?"

"It's Emmet," the nasally high-pitched voice introduces himself in heavily accented English.

"Emmet? I don't know anyone by that name. Sorry, Bro," and immediately goes to hang up the phone.

"No! No!" the voice on the other end says with a laugh. "It's Em-mit, not Em-mut. It's like your famous American frog."

"Okay, my bad, Em-*Mit*," Taylor over exaggerates this last syllable. "As I said before, I don't know anyone by that name. I'm hanging up now."

"Wait! My name is Emmet McShay. I'm going to be your roommate next year."

"What?"

"Yeah, didn't you get an email from Coach McCallom telling you this?"

"No, man. I'd remember something like that."

"No wonder you sound gobsmacked. My email arrived last week."

Taylor sits up straight on the couch and tries to recall what he found online about the foreign recruit Maryland State University signed. He remembers he's from somewhere in Europe, but beyond that, his mind is a big blank. Reaching for the remote, he puts the TV on mute as a huge wave of discomfort begins to set in, *"There's no way this is happening!"* he shouts inside his head. *"A Euro! They have me rooming with a Euro! How can they do this to me? Euros are soft and smelly and wear their jeans way, way, too tight. At least, that's how the ones who play in the pros look."*

"Hello?" Emmet asks over the silence. "Taylor, are you still there?"

"Yeah, I'm still here," he softens his voice for the first time. "So we're going to be roommates, huh?"

"Yes, we are," Emmet enthusiastically responds. "And teammates too. It's all very exciting."

"Yeah, I guess it's cool for me too," Taylor replies, although he doesn't come close to matching Emmet's excitement. "Sorry I sounded so surprised before, it's just...I don't remember getting any email from Coach McCallom."

"No problem, mate. And I'm sure this won't be the only thing that vexes us about college."

"Hey, what kind of accent is that? Where you from?"

"Dublin."

"Like Dublin, Ireland?"

"Exactly like Dublin, Ireland. Do I sound like I'm from Dublin, Ohio?"

"Nah, you definitely don't sound like you're from Ohio. That's for sure."

"The email from Coach McCallom says you live in Longwood Hills, New Jersey. I went online, it looks like it's in the upper half of the state."

"Yeah, we call it Northern New Jersey. You ever been to Jersey before?"

"I've been to Jersey Island, off the coast of Great Britain, but not New Jersey. Do you think those two are the same thing?" Emmet laughs out loud as he asks his question.

"I think it's safe to assume they're a lot different," Taylor finds himself laughing along with Emmet. "Do you live in Dublin now?"

"No, I've spent the last two years playing high school basketball at a private school in Nashville, Tennessee."

"Really? From Dublin to Nashville. How's that move been for you?"

"Difficult at first..." Emmet grows quiet for the first time, before perking right back up. "But it's deadly now! Tennessee is my second home."

"Very cool," Taylor answers, while trying to figure out a tactful way to phrase his next question, but instead blurts it out awkwardly. "So how tall are you?"

"I'm seven feet tall," Emmet proudly responds.

"Cool, a big man," Taylor answers, while pumping his fist in celebration on the other end of the phone, happy they don't play the same position. It's going to be difficult enough to have to learn to live with a stranger, he doesn't want to have to compete with this same stranger for playing time, too. "What kind of hands you got?" Taylor asks in an attempt to take back control of the conversation.

"As you Americans like to say, my hands are as soft as a baby's bottom," Emmet tells him with another laugh. "After looking up Longwood Hills online, I looked up your name. You have one impressive rep, my man."

"Thanks, Bro. I appreciate the props."

"Did the coaches tell you if they're going to play you at shooting forward or power forward next year?" Emmet asks.

"Nah, it's not like that," Taylor replies. "I play both guard and forward positions. Whatever coach needs, I can give it to him. I can also handle some too."

Emmet laughs nervously in response to Taylor's bravado. After two years of playing high school basketball in the States, he's still getting used to the massive egos of Americans. Almost everyone he's met since he arrived seems to think he's a legend-in-the-making, "My bad, roomy. I look forward to seeing your combo game when we get to campus. Do you think we should talk about what we're going to bring to our dorm room to make it our home away from home? Or in my case, my home away from home, away from my home," Emmet laughs out loud again at his own joke.

"Yeah, that's cool," Taylor replies, while taking note that Emmet laughs at his own jokes a lot and hopes this isn't a permanent condition. "I have a small fridge I can bring down from Jersey. Do you think you could find a TV to take with you from Tennessee?"

Ten minutes later, the two strangers who will soon be sharing a 15' x 15' space for the better part of nine months, say goodbye to each other, but not before they promise to friend each other online. Over the course of their conversation, Emmet mentions his girlfriend Emily *a lot*, but other than that, they just cover the basics.

After hanging up the phone, Taylor stares at it for a second, before shaking his head in amazement at what this next year may bring. It seems there's no way to tell what might be right around the corner, "Mooooooommmmmmm!!!" he yells as he walks out of the den. "My roommate next year is going to be a big smelly Irish guy with a high-pitched voice named Emmet!"

CHAPTER 30

On the first Saturday of August, Jimmy rings the doorbell to Taylor's house and instead of letting himself inside like usual, he waits patiently on the front steps with his parents. Holding a white box wrapped in a red cotton string from *Bixel's Cake Place*, a Longwood Hills tradition located in the center of town, Jimmy taps his foot nervously as he waits for the door to open. Freshman orientation starts in a week for both he and Taylor, followed closely by fall classes, which makes today the last time they're going to see each other for months.

Making her way to the front of the house, Deborah opens the door to find Jimmy's anxious, but smiling face waiting for her, "Welcome!" she exclaims with excitement. "It's so nice to see everyone."

"It's so nice to see you too," Rhonda Williams responds from over her son's shoulder. "Thank you again for hosting the party, we really appreciate it."

"Of course, it's my pleasure," Deborah answers, while smiling back warmly. "I'm just glad we could do it before it was too late."

Shifting her eyes, Deborah momentarily looks at Bob Williams, Jimmy's dad, and notices how much thinner and subdued he looks than normal. This is the first time she's seen him since the accident and the change in his appearance is startling.

"Today's going to be such a fun day," Rhonda tells Deborah as she holds her husband's forearm tightly in her hand. "We've been looking forward to it for so long we can't even tell you. And we've received absolutely beautiful weather."

"I couldn't agree more," Deborah answers as she keeps smiling at Rhonda. "But I have to be honest with you, I wasn't so sure it was Jimmy at my door, since he rang the doorbell and waited outside, both things I'm not used to seeing from him. I usually just hear a faint knock on the door, followed by a scream of yo, and then before I know it he's sitting on the couch next to my son with the remote in one hand and a bag of junk food in the other."

"Aww! Come on, Ms. Jones," Jimmy blushes as he responds. "I'm not that bad. Plus, Taylor never lets me touch the remote."

"Ha. You've always been a quick one," Deborah laughs. "The young women at Castleman College better be prepared for you. Otherwise, they're not going to have any idea what hit them."

"Thanks," Jimmy responds as images of hot college girls dance in his head.

"All joking aside," Deborah now looks over at Rhonda and Bob. "I can tell you both without reservation that you've raised an amazing child here. I'm not sure who's going to miss him more, Taylor or me."

"Thank you for the kind words," Rhonda replies. "That means a lot. Especially since we know how much time he spends over here."

"All Williams men are great men," Bob speaks up for the first time from underneath the thick black beard that covers most of his naturally handsome face.

"He always was a chip-off-the-old block," Rhonda adds.

"Agreed," Deborah responds. "Well, don't just stand there, please come inside. After all, that's why we're here."

As Deborah holds open the front door, she focuses her gaze on the deep pain in Bob's normally bright and inquisitive eyes. Keeping her focus still for a second, she watches as Bob slowly makes his way into the house. Leaning hard against the silver titanium cane in his right hand, he clutches Rhonda's wrist firmly with his left hand as he carefully takes one small step at a time. For a man that was a fixture at almost every youth sports game Jimmy played in—from football, to basketball, to baseball—seeing him in this condition was a painful reminder to Deborah of the fragility of life.

At fifty-nine years old, Bob Williams wears the marks of a difficult existence. His hands and arms are nicked and scarred from days lived with a hammer in one hand and a saw in the other. A general contractor by trade, he's worked every type of construction job known to man to help support his family. Naturally warm and inviting, if a crew was being chosen for a job, he was always the first to be asked; a sociability which allowed him to make a steady, if unspectacular, living from a world that's usually filled with constant uncertainty about where the next paycheck is going to come from.

But everything changed sixteen months ago when Bob got hurt on the job. He was kneeling down hammering in some floor boards of a new townhouse when a pile of 2' x 4's that had been placed too close to the edge of a second floor bedroom toppled over and landed squarely on his head and back. The pain was immediate and damaging. 9-1-1 was called and after a few weeks in the Intensive Care Unit, he was released to his waiting family, disability payments and bottles of pain pills. The family has recently resigned itself to the fact that he will more than likely never work again.

Even before the injury, Bob was pushing Jimmy hard to find a way to get to college and use his brain to make a living instead of his body. Repeatedly telling Jimmy, "Don't wait until your body gives out before you start thinking about what else you're going to do with yourself. *Don't be like me.* Your body will give out someday, whether you want it to or not, but the mind...The mind is forever." Since the injury, this prodding has only intensified tenfold.

Instead of being out in the world embracing life, Bob now spends most of his time sitting in the living room in a pair of old Longwood Hills High School sweatpants, watching TV and feeling sorry for himself. His only real company, besides his family, is the physical therapist who comes by twice a week to help him try and regain some of his mobility. But today, today is different. Today, he's a happy man. He's not only getting the chance to wish his son good luck before he leaves for college, but he's also getting the chance to leave the house for a few hours to socialize, something he's been looking forward to for weeks.

Holding tightly onto Rhonda's wrist, Bob takes in his surroundings as he keeps moving slowly into the house, "Deborah, I have to tell you, you really have a lovely home. You've done such a nice job decorating it," he tells her with sincerity.

"Thank you," Deborah replies, while blushing ever so slightly. "Please, come with me. I want to show you to the chair I've set up for you. I think you're going to like it. It's right in the middle of the action."

Two years younger than Bob, Rhonda Williams has been a dental assistant to Thomas Dowley, D.D.S., for the past fifteen years. While not nearly as outgoing as her husband, her job in Dr. Dowley's busy dental practice allows her to not only bring in some much needed money to the family, but also allows her to keep up on all the town gossip. She and Bob have been married for thirty-two mostly happy years and have successfully raised two well-mannered sons. In addition to Jimmy, the Williams have an older son Charlie, who's an officer in the military, currently stationed in Frankfurt, Germany, where he's been assigned for the last year.

Wearing a flowered sun dress and her best pair of summer sandals, Rhonda gently guides Bob to the soft cushioned chair Deborah has placed inside the screened-in porch overlooking the backyard. In Deborah's opinion, this is the perfect location for Bob, allowing him to easily talk to everyone, while only being a few steps from the kitchen and the bathroom. When Rhonda sees the chair, she gives Deborah a reassuring nod that her instincts are once again spot-on.

While their two sons have been as close as brothers since the day they met, Deborah and Rhonda have what can only be considered a casual, yet intimate friendship. They've talked a lot in the last few months planning this party, but haven't seen each other in person since the basketball team's end-of-the-year banquet. While a long break like this is not unusual for them, when they do get together, they have an uncanny way of getting right to the heart of the matter—no question or topic is out of bounds. Maybe it's due to all the years of finding themselves at the same sports game or school activity, but they are often more comfortable talking to each other about personal issues than they are talking to most members of their own family. Yet after they've finished sharing, they rarely make time to spend together outside of these unplanned conversations.

Over the next few hours, the party steps into high gear as extended family, friends and neighbors all stop by to wish Taylor and Jimmy good luck in the next phase of life. Some stay a few hours, some stay only a few minutes, but everyone is all smiles as they send the two friends on their way with hugs and well-meaning words of wisdom. Throughout the entire day, Bob is literally glowing with pride as he washes down his pain and troubles with large quantities of food, drinks and most importantly, laughs.

At every opportunity, Deborah and Rhonda find themselves back in each other's company, huddled close together, talking about hopes and dreams—their own and their sons'—during a day that flies by all too quickly.

Near the end of the party, Taylor and Jimmy stare silently into the distance as they lean up against the old brown fence that marks the small backyard, while their parents remain in the house, laughing, drinking and sharing embarrassing stories about whose kid was worse growing up. Trying hard all day to avoid the conversation they're about to have, with the party winding down, there's no way around it anymore. In less than a week, they'll be apart for the first time since they were five years old and even though they've known this day was coming for a long time, now that it's finally here, the sudden realization that life is pulling them in different directions, weighs heavy on their hearts. Off in the distance, crickets serenade the neighborhood with their songs as the two friends continue to gaze softly into the horizon in front of them.

"So, man," Jimmy cautiously wades in first. "You ready?"

"Yeah, I'm ready. At least, I think I am...You?"

"Yeah, I'm good," Jimmy answers, before taking a big sip from the can of soda in his hand to try and wash down his raw emotions. "I mean, at least I think I am too. All I know is I'm glad I got into a decent school like Castleman, 'cause all spring I was thinking the worst was going to happen. I know I might hide it well, but I was sweating until that financial aid letter came in and I knew for sure I was going to be able to afford to go there. They really bailed me out."

"Yeah, for sure. They came through for you, big time."

"No doubt," Jimmy replies. "They were the only ones who could make it work. It was either Castleman or my choice of community college," he laughs nervously. "The good thing is Castleman seems like a good school. I just hope I like Pennsylvania. But even if I don't, honestly, it doesn't matter. There's nowhere else for me to go."

"It's all good," Taylor reassures him. "That place is all you. You'll see."

"I hope you're right."

"Don't even sweat it. Seriously. Next week is going to be the start of something big for you."

"You think?"

"Yeah, I do. The world has yet to see what Jimmy Williams can do. I've always said you were The Man. Now you've got your opportunity to prove it."

"I definitely like what I'm hearing," Jimmy tells Taylor with a big smile.

"I mean, all likeable people are successful. And who doesn't like you? Name one person."

"Mrs. Rocker from eleventh grade science hates me."

"Yeah, but she's a teacher. She doesn't count. You also told her she looked like she belonged in a morgue. That didn't help your cause any."

"Yeah, good point," Jimmy laughs out loud, almost dropping his can of soda. "Now that I think about it, that was kind of mean, huh?"

"Naaahh, she had it coming," Taylor answers with sideways smile. "But seriously, tell me one person besides Mrs. Rocker who doesn't like you. There's no one."

"I don't know, maybe you're right...But my bigger worry is the school work. College classes are going to be hard, don't you think?"

"Yeah, probably," Taylor responds, although he doesn't seem worried. Naturally smart and curious, he knows he'll be given every chance to succeed academically when he gets to Maryland State University. All college athletes do. Schools can't afford the negative press that comes with a high-profile athlete failing out, so they do everything they can to avoid it. This was repeatedly told to him by all the players he met on his recruiting visits.

"I just hope I'm up to the challenge," Jimmy goes on to tell Taylor. "'Cause classwork has never really come easily to me. But you know that."

"That's true, but you'll find a way to succeed. You always do. Like I said, the world has yet to see what Jimmy Williams can do."

"Thanks, man. I appreciate the love."

"Of course," Taylor responds just as his face turns into a deep frown. "For real, if anyone should be worried, it should be me. I don't think I've ever started a conversation with a girl without you. You've always taken the lead. Even the first time I met Kelly, you talked to her first. What am I going to do without you?"

"Someone needs to do your talking for you, otherwise you'll just stand there like a tall part of the scenery," Jimmy tells him with a laugh. "But don't even worry about it. You're going to be fine. As a matter of fact, you're going to be more than fine. You're Taylor Scott. You're *the* Taylor Scott. Soon to be Taylor Scott, starting small forward of the Maryland State University Revolutionaries. Girls love that guy."

"And what if it turns out I'm not that guy? Then what?"

"Don't even say such a stupid thing!" Jimmy shoots back. "That's never going to happen."

Taylor wants to finally open up and tell Jimmy he's not sure he can make it on the next level. That he knows how strong, quick and naturally talented all the players in the All-American game were. The words are right on the tip of his tongue, but he doesn't say a thing.

"That school fawned over you," Jimmy keeps pumping up Taylor's confidence. "There's no way they're not going to help you become The Man. And once that happens, hell, before that happens, you're not going to need to learn to talk to girls. Like always, they'll just want to talk to you."

"You think?"

"Yeah, I do. Girls love basketball players. Always have."

"What about college ball?" Taylor asks, looking now with purpose into Jimmy's eyes. "You think I can handle those guys?"

"Hell, ya, I do," Jimmy practically shouts "Trust me, you're going to be The Man...Like always."

"Thanks, Bro," Taylor answers as he takes a deep breath and starts to regain his confidence, almost as quickly as it seems as he lost it. "I guess there's going to be a period of adjustment, like in high school. But how much different can it be, it's still just basketball, right?"

"Exactly, it's just basketball and basketball is something you're *great* at. No joke, if you ever need another pep talk after you get down to Maryland, just give me a shout."

"Don't worry, Little Man. You're going to hear from me plenty."

"Anytime, Bro," Jimmy answers and then reaches out and slaps Taylor five.

"Hey, remember when we were twelve and we made plans to meet Gina Pascorelli and Jennifer Howard at the Longwood Hills Arcade?" Taylor suddenly changes the subject. "And instead of asking for a ride, we rode our bikes across the traffic on Route 10, violating every rule our parents ever set up for us."

"Of course, Gina and Jennifer were the hottest girls in school back then," Jimmy responds, his eyes dancing at the memory.

"Then you got a flat tire before we even got there and we had to call your mom at the dentist's office to come pick us up."

"Yeah, that kind of sucked," Jimmy laughs.

"I've still never seen your mom so mad. She came and picked us up, wearing her white lab coat with her name tag still on it. She screamed at the two of us so loudly, I think I can still hear her yelling."

"Yeah, that was one ugly scene," Jimmy keeps laughing.

"Do you know Steven Mason told Gina the reason we didn't show was because I was too poor to own a bike?"

"What?"

"Yeah, he lied to her so she would stay mad at me and then moved in so he could start dating her. Then he came right after Kelly the minute we broke up last year."

"What a *punk*. How do you know that?"

"Kelly and Gina were still best friends when she and I started dating."

"That explains the outburst at Susan Jamison's party."

"Yeah, for real," Taylor answers. "I've hated that kid for years."

"You should've said something sooner. I would've had your back."

"I know, man. I just didn't care that much until I saw them that night."

"I hear ya. Even so, we're a team."

"I know...A great team," Taylor answers with a smile.

"The best," Jimmy responds with a smile of his own.

"Hey, you think you're going to miss this town?" Taylor asks.

"Not really. I'm over this place. I haven't told anyone yet, but I'm never coming back here. After college, I'm heading to a big city, maybe New York or Chicago."

"Really?" Taylor answers, unable to hide the slight disappointment in his voice.

"Yeah, I'm done with this town. What about you? Do you think you'll ever come back here?"

"I don't think I'll have a choice if everything goes according to plan. I'll have to live in the city where I'm playing ball," Taylor scrunches his brow as he shares this realization. "But I'm going to miss this place. Part of me will always love it here. It's where we grew up, you know."

"It's definitely where we grew up…"

With the hazy blue sky in the distance beginning to melt into a calming orange hue, Taylor and Jimmy both instinctively grow quiet as they stare out at the world beyond the small backyard; Taylor dreaming of knocking down jump shots on national television and Jimmy dreaming of running to a meeting in a big city, wearing an expensive suit and tie.

"We'll see each other, right?" Taylor asks, breaking up the silence. "I mean, you'll come down to some home games and when we come up your way, I'll get you some tickets."

"Yeah, of course."

"Very cool. 'Cause you know more than anyone, I'm not that good at making new friends. I have a little trouble trusting people, you know."

"I know," Jimmy answers with a half-smile. "You're not as tough as you want people to think you are. But don't worry about it. Nothing will come between us. Not even a little distance."

"Cool, man…So…Friends, forever?"

"Friends, forever," Jimmy repeats.

With the anxiety of the next week closing in a hurry, the two friends lean in and hug each other like two soldiers going off to war. After letting go of this emotional embrace, they step back and stand in silence one more time as a small tear falls quietly out of the corner of Taylor's eye. He casually wipes it away with the back of his arm, while hoping Jimmy doesn't notice. Jimmy pretends to look away as he does the same.

CHAPTER 31

After signing in on the ground floor of Kent Hall and grabbing the room key to his new home for the next nine months, Taylor jogs back to his mom's car to get the first box of his things from her trunk. Returning moments later, he strides through the dorm's expansive lobby with a brown cardboard box of clothes resting on top of his arms. All summer long, he's listened to stories about how good-looking college girls are going to be, so while he walks through the lobby, his eyes dart back and forth from underneath a well-worn baseball hat, pulled down low just above his eyes. Mildly disappointed by what he sees at first, it seems college is a lot like high school, with a few cute girls here and there, but mostly filled with average girls doing everything they can to make themselves look as attractive as possible.

When he reaches the elevator bank, Taylor stands and waits for what feels like an eternity, before the elevator to his far right chimes open and a large group of students and parents parade off. As he squeezes past them, he can't help but notice every face, including his own, has a look of nervous anxiety plastered on it. It reminds him of the last thirty minutes before a big game, although this time there's

196 / Adam Poe

no game clock and basketball, only moving boxes and a series of long and emotional goodbyes.

Stepping off the elevator on the fourth floor, Taylor walks down to the end of the hall and slides his key into the door marked 408. As he slowly turns the door's copper knob, he mumbles a short prayer under his breath, *"Please, please, let my roommate be more normal than I think he is."*

The answer to his question comes fast and furious. On the other side of the door, staring back at him from the top of Emmet's bed is a 6' x 4' color poster of a plain-looking girl with straight brown hair, sitting on top of a bale of hay. The word E-M-I-L-Y is printed in playful red letters across the top, surrounded by hearts. *"No way! There is simply no way!"* Taylor starts laughing uncontrollably, sending his cardboard box of clothes falling to the floor.

"Roomy! There you are!" Emmet's high-pitched voice greets him with surprise from behind.

Standing in the doorway is a 7'0" wisp of a young man with pointed shoulders and thick dirty blond hair, combed straight back over his head. At no more than 200 lbs., Emmet McShay has a pale complexion, marked by patches of acne, which covers most of his forehead and parts of his cheeks and neck. Wearing a white track suit with royal blue trim, he glimmers from the natural light streaming through the dorm room's two small windows, one above each bed. Temporarily shielding his eyes from the glare, Taylor gets the sense that if a stiff breeze came through those same windows right now, Emmet might blow away for good.

"It's great to finally meet you, my man," Emmet steps forward and awkwardly slaps Taylor five. "Since I didn't see you when I got here yesterday morning, I thought you might've changed your mind. But I have to tell you, last night was RAGING! There were *a lot* of cute 'betties' running around right here in this very room. You would've had a bloody great time!"

Taylor frowns at these remarks, since he knows today is move-in day and he can't imagine why Emmet showed up a day early.

"I see you've met Emily, isn't she a beaut?" Emmet instinctively licks his lips as he points to the poster. "Don't worry, mate. You'll meet her in person soon enough. She'll be visiting us next weekend."

"Next weekend? Where's she going to stay?" Taylor angrily thinks to himself.

After shaking off this uncomfortable thought, he responds by lying through his teeth, "She's definitely nice looking, man. That's for sure."

"Thanks, yo," Emmet squeals with laughter at using his American slang. "Hey, you only have one box?"

"Huh?" Taylor responds as he looks down at the cardboard box of clothes on the floor. "No, I got plenty more. Most are downstairs in my mom's car and the rest are in the back of my dad's SUV."

"You drove down in two cars? How much stuff did you bring?"

"Nah, it's not like that. My parents are divorced. I had to divide up my boxes."

"Let me help you bring them up to our room then. That's what roommates are for, no?" Emmet's thick Irish accent enunciating each word.

"Don't worry about it, man. I got it," Taylor deflects the offer.

"I insist," Emmet responds and then leaves without waiting for an answer.

"Okay, then...Let's go," Taylor sarcastically addresses the now empty room.

As Taylor and Emmet make their way through the dorm's lobby, the two players size up each girl they see like young wolves on the prowl. Athletes are always a lot more alike than they think.

Once outside the lobby, Emmet follows Taylor through the parking lot to where his mom and dad have parked near each other, but not next to each other. They approach his mom first.

"Ma, this is Emmet McShay. My roommate," Taylor states out loud with absolutely no emotion in his voice.

Deborah looks straight up into Emmet's rather unattractive face and decides to concentrate on his soft and kind eyes, "It's nice to meet you."

"Nice to meet you too, Mrs. Scott."

Deborah looks back confused. It's been a long time since anyone has called her by that name, "Actually, my name is not Mrs. Scott. It's Ms. Jones. Mrs. Scott is someone else *entirely*."

"Oh, my bad," Emmet replies, while smiling back awkwardly.

"It's all right, sugar. It's an honest error," Deborah tells him with an understanding voice. "I know Taylor is looking forward to a great year. I take it you feel the same?"

"Oh, yes. I bloody can't wait to get started! And having Taylor as my roommate is going to be deadly! I've read about all of his accomplishments on the court. I can't wait to see his game in person...Are these his boxes?"

"Yes," Deborah answers.

"Should I grab any one?" Emmet asks.

"Any box will do," Taylor sarcastically spits out. "And thanks for the help, Bro."

"Be nice," Deborah whispers to Taylor under her breath. "You're going to have to get along with him, whether you like it or not."

"Sure. Whatever," Taylor grumbles back.

With long thin arms that look like they belong on a cartoon character, Emmet grabs two boxes from the back seat of the car and stacks one on top of the other. He then shuffles away in the direction of room 408.

"Wow, Emmet is tall!" Deborah states in astonishment once he's out of sight. "My whole life I thought you were so tall, but now I know how wrong I was."

"That's how big a college center is supposed to be," Taylor responds, still somewhat annoyed at being told he has to get along with Emmet, no matter what.

"Does he always wear that gold hoop earring in his left ear like that?" Deborah asks.

"What?"

"Emmet, his earring?" she repeats. "And do you know if that boy eats? He really needs to put on some weight."

"I don't know, Ma," Taylor answers, clearly frustrated by the way his mom always seems to ask weird and child-like questions when she finds herself in situations she doesn't understand. "I also just met him today, remember?"

Seeing how visibly upset he's suddenly become, she decides to change the subject, "Thank you again for reconsidering and letting your dad join us for today's move-in. I think it was a really wise decision."

"Thanks. But we'll see…"

Twenty minutes later, after all the boxes have been removed from the back of his mom's car, Taylor leads Emmet over to his dad's SUV, where they find Bill Scott slumped down low in the front seat, listening to a baseball game on the radio. "Dad! This is Emmet McShay! My roommate!" Taylor yells through the glass window.

Looking up, Bill sees his son and a strange looking young man with an acne-filled forehead staring back at him. He immediately lowers the window. "It's nice to meet you, Emmet," he extends his right hand through the window's opening. "And please, call me Bill."

"Thank you, Mr. Scott…I mean, Bill," Emmet corrects himself.

"That's one thick accent you have there. Where are you from again?" Bill asks.

"Dad!" Taylor yells.

"What?" Bill responds with a look of confusion. "It's not an accent I hear every day. I'm just interested in learning more about my son's roommate. What's wrong with that?"

Sensing the sudden tension, Emmet tries to alleviate it the best he can, "I grew up in Dublin, Ireland. But I've spent the last two years in Nashville playing high school basketball. I'm guessing you probably want to know about my Irish accent more than my slight southern drawl," Emmet responds with a smart smile, revealing two oversized front teeth that make him look like a rabbit in heat.

"From Dublin, Ireland, to Nashville, Tennessee, to Washington Springs, Maryland, that's a long way to go to play basketball," Bill tells Emmet with a shake of his head. "You must love the game almost as much as my son does."

"I'm totally mad for it!" Emmet answers with excitement. "I gave up playing football back in primary school. That way I can focus just on basketball. Back home, all my mates thought I was batty. But here in the States, it's totally different. They love their 'round ball' as much as I do," Emmet squeals again at being able to use his American slang to impress his audience.

"Well, it's great to meet you," Bill shakes Emmet's hand one more time. "And I'm counting on you to look after my son this year while I'm not around. But don't worry, you'll be seeing a lot of me."

Taylor rolls his eyes when he hears this and wonders if his dad is even remotely telling the truth.

Satisfied with their short conversation, Bill points Emmet to Taylor's pile of boxes in the back of the SUV, while promising they'll be right behind him in a minute. Once he's out of earshot, Bill turns to Taylor and says, "I know you know this already, but your roommate is *all* skin and bones."

"You're telling me," Taylor agrees. "My man is *thin*."

"The good news for you is I don't think you have to worry about Emmet taking away any of your minutes this season. Not that you two play the same position. He genuinely just looks too weak to survive the college game."

"Dad, don't do that!" Taylor suddenly yells. "He might be skinny, but there's got to be a reason why he was recruited to this school. And how do you know if he can survive the college game? You never played college basketball."

Once more Bill marvels at Taylor's ability to turn an innocent remark into a deep personal insult.

"Taylor, wait...Don't get me wrong," Bill tries to backtrack. "I'm sure Emmet has talent. All I'm saying is I can't imagine he can hold his own in the post."

Even though Taylor knows his dad is probably right, he has no interest in giving him an inch, "I'll let you know after I see him play. Sound good?"

"Please, calm down and listen to your old man, okay? This is a good thing. It's one less person you have to worry about. College is not like high school. Every single one of your teammates will be out for blood. I don't need to have played college basketball to know this. It's just how the world works."

"Sure. If you say so," Taylor dismisses his dad's advice as foolish and uninformed. "I'm going to take the rest of my boxes up to my room. This way we can all go eat lunch and you and Mom can head out before it gets too late."

"Fine..." Bill answers, once again unable to hide his disappointment at not being able to connect with his son. "I'm just trying to help. Believe me, I am. I have your best interest at heart. I always do."

"Whatever...We'll see," Taylor answers as he grabs two boxes from the back of the SUV and starts walking in the direction of his dorm room without so much as saying another word.

CHAPTER 32

Like all Top 25 college basketball programs, Maryland State University has almost half as many coaches as it does players. Add in the support personnel—strength and conditioning coaches, trainers, equipment managers and student managers—and it can seem like a small army has been hired to take care of a privileged few, which, in fact, is exactly what's happened.

With only five basketball players on a court at one time and no face mask to block a fan's view, those college players strong enough to fight their way onto this big stage are treated like campus royalty. Instantly recognizable by students and faculty alike, everyone knows their name, reputation and stats before they even walk into a room. This star-making system can turn even the most humble player into a bona-fide prima donna, so it's up to each team's coaching staff to keep their players' egos in check. If not, the players start believing, in a short period of time, the world owes them something and more often than not, they gladly start taking it.

In addition to Assistant Coach Sean Banks, the Maryland State University men's basketball coaching staff consists of three other full-time assistants. The first of these assistants is Roger Foote. A ten-year veteran of the

Revolutionaries staff, Coach Foote is one of Coach McCallom's most trusted advisors and friends, both inside and outside of basketball. A former small-school college basketball star, Coach Foote spent his first thirteen years after graduation climbing the corporate ladder, rising to become the vice president of a regional supermarket chain, before deciding what he really wanted out of life was to become a college basketball coach. With a long, gaunt face, thin nose, hollow eyes and wavy light brown hair, he has the unfortunate distinction of looking like he's always in pain, even when he's not. A conservative man in his mid-forties, he's constantly searching for acceptance from the players and the rest of the coaching staff. Receiving it, almost as often as it's rejected.

Roger Foote's life changed for good while working for free at a youth basketball camp during one of his vacations from the supermarket chain. During his third year working at the camp, he was asked to chaperone around Coach McCallom, who was hired for the day to make a speech to the campers about "dreaming big" and "working hard to reach your potential." From the minute they met, Roger Foote and Coach McCallom hit it off, agreeing on everything from coaching philosophy, to religion, to politics, to family.

Once Coach McCallom heard Roger's story about his burning desire to coach and his sacrifice of leaving his wife and kids for a week each summer to volunteer at the camp, Coach McCallom decided to check out his story. After finding everything to be true, Coach McCallom offered the then supermarket vice president the opportunity of a lifetime—an hourly paying part-time assistant coach's position on the Maryland State University men's basketball staff. While Roger would have to come in as the low man on the totem pole and it was a huge step down in terms of salary and benefits from his old job, after talking everything over with his wife, he jumped at the chance and never looked back.

This leap of faith paid off four years later, when he was on the Revolutionaries bench as a full-time assistant coach during the school's historic run to capture its only post-season college basketball championship. Not too long after the team hoisted the championship trophy, Coach Foote was offered several different head coaching jobs, but said no to each one of them, remaining loyal to the man who first gave him his start; with a large increase in salary, of course. Over the next five years, Coach Foote steadily climbed his way up to become Coach McCallom's top assistant, before being unceremoniously unseated from this position last year by Coach Banks. Not one to make waves and upset his boss and friend, he's quietly plotted his revenge against Coach Banks ever since.

The two other full-time assistant coaches on Coach McCallom's staff are Gary Dougard and Mike Davis.

After stints as the head coach at several other universities, Coach Dougard joined the Maryland State University men's basketball coaching staff two years ago. Regarded as one of the best offensive minds in the game, he's a husky man with a strong powerful build, bright inquisitive eyes and a large round face that sits on top of a body that seems more suited for an offensive lineman than a basketball coach. Coach Dougard's first head coaching job was at a mid-major university, where he spent eight successful seasons, followed by only a slightly less successful five-year stay as the head coach at one of the biggest universities in the Southeast. After leading this last university on a surprise run deep into college basketball's post-season tournament, he left to take the head coaching job at a university more known for its football tradition than its long-struggling basketball program. In his first full season, his team jumped into the top twenty in almost every offensive statistical category, but unfortunately, couldn't stop anybody on defense.

As anyone who knows basketball will tell you, it's defense that wins games and championships—and not offense—so two days before his fifty-second birthday and only four years after arriving at this football powerhouse with a promise to turn around its struggling basketball program once and for all, Coach Dougard was fired for delivering back-to-back losing seasons and zero post-season college basketball tournament appearances.

With the Revolutionaries' offensive output going down each of the three seasons before Coach Dougard was let go from his last job, Coach McCallom decided to throw a life-line to his old coaching buddy with hopes of reversing his team's offensive woes. As a full time member of the Maryland State University men's basketball coaching staff, Coach Dougard is responsible for the team's offense, as well as recruiting in the Midwest and the Southeast. Since he's already been a successful head coach, Coach Dougard has the respect of half of the current Maryland State University players, while the other half tunes him out for the exact same reason—he's a fired former head coach. In the crystal clear minds of eighteen to twenty-two-year-old young men, if you get fired from a job, you're just not that good at it and you should probably try to do something else with your life.

At thirty-six years old, Assistant Coach Mike Davis has an easy-going personality outside of the gym and intense demeanor inside it. A former college player from California, he led his university to two conference championships and two appearances in college basketball's post-season tournament during his four-year career, including a reputation-making 36-point, eight-rebound performance in a nationally televised loss to that year's eventual tournament champion. After four years of failing to make a living as a professional basketball player, both in the United States and overseas, followed by ten years as an assistant coach at several different schools on the West

Coast, Coach Davis decided to take the same position on Coach McCallom's staff, once it was obvious his marriage was falling apart.

A divorced father of two young boys, the constant moving around from city to city, to first chase his dream of playing professional basketball and then to chase his back-up dream of becoming a college basketball head coach, eventually took a toll on his marriage. A strong and proud man, he doesn't let his personal problems interfere with his job and as a result, he's extremely well-liked by all the Maryland State University players, most of whom blame his ex-wife for their marital problems, even though they've never met her.

As the second of two young African-American assistant coaches on Coach McCallom's staff, Coach Davis has many talents, but is known more as a defensive specialist than anything else. At 6'5" and 230 lbs., he keeps himself in incredible shape and even challenges the Maryland State University players to weight lifting contests in the off-season, winning more often than he loses. In addition to figuring out the most effective way to stop the Revolutionaries' opponents, he's also in charge of recruiting the western half of the United States—from Colorado to California—using these frequent trips to see his kids as much as possible.

The recruiting responsibilities for the East Coast and the Mid-Atlantic states, including the talent-rich cities of New York, Philadelphia and Washington, D.C., belong to Assistant Coach Sean Banks. That is, except for the state of Maryland and those special recruits Coach McCallom has a personal interest in. A former summer basketball coach, Coach Banks put together one of the best All-Star teams in the Northeast by the time he was only twenty-five years old, traveling to tournaments all over the country to battle the other elite All-Star teams for supremacy. After single-handedly convincing one of the major sports apparel companies to sponsor his team from head to toe, he was able to cast an even wider net to recruit the cream of the crop high school players from the entire East Coast, which only made his teams stronger and expanded his growing reputation.

After graduating from the summer All-Star tournament circuit, Coach Banks became the head coach of a large, economically-challenged public high school fifteen minutes outside of Philadelphia. Within no time, he built the Ridge High Hawks into a state power and then a national power—smiling, cajoling and pleading to get what he needed from the administration and the community to compete and excel against the other top-notch high school programs. After winning three state championships in four years and with his reputation on the high school level solidified, Coach Banks next set his sights on an even bigger stage: big-time college basketball.

During his last year as the head coach at Ridge High School, Coach Banks was lucky enough to have national Top 30 recruit Andray Jenkins as his star point guard. Using Andray's talents and his own smarts, he was able to leverage their personal relationship into an assistant coach's position on the Maryland State University men's basketball staff; accepting his job offer on the same day Andray signed his scholarship to play for the Revolutionaries.

Coach Banks' connections run very deep throughout the East Coast and the Mid-Atlantic, and selfishly, this is exactly what Coach McCallom is counting on. He needs Coach Banks to keep funneling recruits from the region's talent-rich urban cities to Maryland State University's suburban campus in order to keep the Revolutionaries succeeding at the height of the college game.

CHAPTER 33

Taylor's cell phone rings loudly at 7:30 a.m., startling him, and waking him from a deep sleep. Freshman orientation has been over for a day already and classes don't start for another few days, but for some reason, the shrill ring of his phone is breaking the peaceful silence of his dorm room. Having no idea where he left his cell phone when he finally climbed under the covers, he blindly reaches in the direction of the piercing sound across the small wood desk next to his bed, accidentally knocking over a pile of empty beer cans left over by Emmet and his new drinking buddies from the night before. The cans skip loudly across the white linoleum floor, snapping him further out of his dream-like trance and propelling him to kick off his covers in anger. On the other side of the room, Emmet barely moves in his bed as he tries to sleep off yet another hangover from the night before.

"Who's this?" Taylor grunts loudly into the phone as he stares at Emmet with hate-filled daggers in his eyes.

"That's how you answer a phone?" Coach Banks' voice playfully barks back at him.

"I do at this hour...Who's this?" Taylor repeats his question.

"It's *Coach Banks*. Who does it sound like?"

"I'm not sure," Taylor answers and then immediately sits up straight in his bed when it sinks in who he's talking to. "But we've never talked too much on the phone before, you know."

"That's a fair point. Although, I can tell you for certain, it's me. How are you settling in so far?"

"Fine, I guess," Taylor answers, while rubbing his eyes in an effort to try and wake up further.

After spending part of the third night in a row on the couch in the resident assistant's room, his head feels heavier than usual. Thankfully, the R.A. on his floor is a kind-hearted senior who happens to love basketball. Without him, these first few days of college would've been even harder than they've already been.

"Don't tell me you're not even up yet?" Coach Banks asks. "I've been awake for a good two hours already. As a matter of fact, Coach Davis and I just got back from an *invigorating* five mile run. We go every morning in the off-season. If you're not doing anything tomorrow, you should join us."

"Sounds like fun. You can count me in," Taylor responds, although he's so tired right now, he's not sure what he just agreed to.

"Is Emmet there?"

"Yeah, but he's still sleeping. Do you need me to wake him?"

"No, as long as I got one of you on the phone, it's okay. I'm calling all of our new guys to let them know the practice gym is open this morning from ten to twelve for pick-up ball. I would recommend going. It's a great way to get to know your teammates without all the pressure of formal practice. Not to mention a real nice opportunity to get loose before the upperclassmen get back to campus."

Taylor can feel the intensity of the oncoming freight train that soon will be his life, but knows there's no way to stop it now.

"Thanks, Coach. Emmet and I will be there at ten."

"Don't you mean nine forty-five?" Coach Banks asks.

"Isn't that what I said?" Taylor replies, full of hesitation.

"I shouldn't have to tell you this, but it's always better to be early than on time. Coach McCallom is also a big believer in this philosophy. It's just something you should keep in mind."

"Thanks...I will."

"And *when* you go to pick-up ball this morning, make sure you have some fun. Try and enjoy it while you can," Coach Banks almost snickers into the phone.

"Sure thing," Taylor responds and then bites his bottom lip. It's as if Coach Banks knows exactly how he's feeling and is playing perfectly into it.

"Taylor, I have a few more phone calls to make, so I have to run. But I will see you tomorrow morning at five-thirty in front of the Liberty Arena. You remember how to get there?"

"Yeah, no problem."

"Great. And by five-thirty, you know I mean five-fifteen, correct?"

"Five-fifteen. Got it, Coach."

"Also, make sure you come ready to go tomorrow morning. Coach Davis and I only warm up for a few minutes and then we get right into it. Time is always ticking and we don't like to waste a second of it."

"Sounds good."

"And Taylor?"

"Yes, Coach."

"Make sure you wake up that roommate of yours and bring him with you to the gym for pick-up ball. Also, tell him to stop drinking so much. In this country, he's underage and your dorm room is not a pub."

"How in the world does he know that?" Taylor thinks to himself.

"Uhm...No problem, Coach. I'll let Emmet know."

"I've got to run now. I'll see you tomorrow morning."

"Okay. Bye, Coach."

After pressing the red call end button on his cell phone, Taylor stares straight ahead in disbelief at the conversation he just had with Coach Banks. Shaking his head from side to side—as if it was all a dream—he asks himself for the hundredth time since he arrived on Maryland State University's campus, what he's gotten himself into.

At the end of this ongoing conversation, he always comes back to same thing...*He loves the game of basketball and will do anything for it.*

CHAPTER 34

At exactly 9:45 a.m., Taylor and Emmet stroll casually into the Rosenberg Center and find their way over to one of the two empty basketball courts inside the practice facility. They are the first ones to arrive this morning, and seeing this, Taylor can't help but laugh out loud at how much pressure he put on Emmet to make sure they arrived "on time," especially now that they are standing alone inside the large empty building.

"What's so funny?" Emmet asks, looking over at Taylor.

"Nothing."

"I thought you said Coach Banks told us to get here at a quarter to ten?"

"He did."

"Where is the bloke then?"

"I don't know."

"Are coaches even allowed to be here? I thought we got a free pass until practice starts on October fifteenth?"

"I'm not sure, man. I just know what Coach Banks told me. He also told me to tell you to stop drinking so much. How he knows about that is beyond me. But he's right about one thing, you do smell like a stale beer can. Did you even bother to put deodorant on this morning, after you decided *not* to shower?"

"Very funny, mate. But why do I need to smell good for pick up ball?"

"It's not for you. It's for me *and* everyone else."

"Smelling badly is one of my secrets to playing in the post," Emmet answers with a grin, putting his oversized rabbit teeth out on full display. "It keeps the other guys at a distance. And how do you think Coach Banks knows about my drinking?"

"Don't know, man…Really, I don't."

"I can see how my European lifestyle might rub the coaches the wrong way. But I've been drinking since I was thirteen years old and it hasn't held me back yet."

"Whatever, man. I'm just saying you should be careful. Coach Banks is obviously on to you."

"No worries, mate. It's 'all good' as you American ballers like to say."

"You can be such a clown sometimes," Taylor replies with a shake of his head.

"What'd you say?"

"Nothing, Bro. Let's just get loose before everyone else gets here. Okay?"

"Whatever you say. You're the boss," Emmet responds with a shrug of his shoulders.

A few minutes later, the Revolutionaries' other two freshman recruits, James Knight and Daquan Mayes, walk through the Rosenberg Center doors with purpose. Roommates and fast friends since move-in day, Coach Banks obviously got a hold of them this morning too, since they both are already dripping with sweat, looking like they are ready to play.

A native of suburban Washington, DC, James Knight is a 6' 7" ultra-smooth athletic small forward that was not only a Top 100 basketball recruit, but also one of the most highly recruited football tight ends in the country. Before committing to play basketball only at Maryland State University, the betting man's opinion was James was going to play both basketball and football at the school he signed with. He wound up surprising everyone, except his parents and Coach Banks, when he decided to concentrate on just basketball in college.

James carries himself with a swagger that tells the world he's loaded with confidence, knows where he's going and is not afraid to show it. Bursting with natural talent, he's an explosive leaper with surprisingly long arms, which allows him to block shots at an alarming rate for someone of his height. Even though he can't hit a jump shot consistently right now beyond ten to twelve feet, he has what is known in basketball circles as a huge "upside." He also has a very coachable attitude—a direct result of all his years of playing football, where being "heard" meant delivering a crunching hit on an opponent and not using your mouth. The Maryland State University coaches are extremely excited to start working with James and feel it's only a matter of time before his great work ethic helps him develop into a player to be reckoned with.

James' roommate and friend is Daquan Mayes, a 6' 6" mountain of a power forward from inner-city Baltimore. Even though Daquan grew up in the dangerous projects, he carries himself with a seemingly unaffected lightness; the complete opposite of the difficult environment in which he was raised. Known more as a "bruiser" with a big heart than anything else, he dominated on the high school level due to the massive size of his backside and thighs, becoming the best rebounding forward recruiters from the region had seen in years. Lower on the talent scale than Taylor and James, the one thing Daquan knows how to do better than most is compete and *compete with toughness*.

One of only a handful of inner-city kids to come to Maryland State University in the last ten years, the big knock on Daquan right now is he can only play with his back to the basket from eight feet in. In order to overcome this limited range, he's developed a variety of crafty moves in the post, moves that allow him to get his shot off over taller opponents when he needs to. While not a great student, he's naturally smart and curious, and the Maryland State University coaches are hoping that once he's exposed to the school's nurturing academic environment, it will light a fire under him. Out of the four freshman recruits in this year's class, Daquan was the closest one to not qualifying academically; with his borderline grades leading to a fight between the coaches and the university's admissions board over whether or not he should be accepted. In the end, it's a fight the coaches are very happy they won.

When the four freshman players—Taylor, Emmet, James and Daquan—see each other from across the gym for the first time, they don't say anything. Like lost boys of a displaced tribe, the soon-to-be-teammates stare at one another to determine if they're looking at friend or enemy. With nothing more than this sideways glance, James and Daquan decide they're not sure what to make of the other two players in the gym right now and head over to the empty practice court, leaving Taylor and Emmet to keep warming up for their first informal college work-out on their own.

As the clock inches closer to 10 a.m., the other players who were either called by Coach Banks or heard about today's open gym start streaming inside the Rosenberg Center. Made up of mostly would-be walk-ons and maintenance men from the buildings and grounds department, included in this group is a determined player that spent all of last season practicing with the Revolutionaries, but was ineligible to play in games due to transfer rules.

At 6' 0", Damon Michaels is a twenty-one-year-old junior who spent his first two years after high school as the starting point guard for a mid-major university in Northern California, before deciding to chase his dream of playing in a "power conference" and of one day hopefully going pro. A tremendous ball handler and capable outside shooter, he's been at a disadvantage since he arrived on Maryland State University's campus, because he hasn't been able to fully show off his natural leadership abilities to the coaches in game competition yet.

Originally from the state of Delaware, Damon is glad to be back on the East Coast again and wants nothing more than to prove to everyone who thought he was a step too slow to be a big-time recruit coming out of high school, they were dead wrong about him. With only two years of eligibility remaining and Andray Jenkins in front of him at the point guard position, Damon knows this season is going to bring about its own unique set of trials, as many of the friendships he made on the team last year will be severely tested once practice starts and he begins challenging these same friends for the most precious commodity there is on a basketball team—*playing time*. All of this has been weighing heavy on Damon's mind, so he came back to school early to get a jump on the season and keep working on his weaknesses before practice officially starts on October 15th.

After watching everyone in the gym warm up in a disorganized fashion, complete with scores of missed dunks by the walk-ons trying to impress the new recruits, Damon waves at James, signaling for him to meet at center court.

When two players reach the center court circle, they slap each other five.

"What's up, man. Name's Damon, you?"

"Hey, man. I'm James."

"You one of the freshman recruits?"

"Yeah, you?"

"Nah, I'm a junior. Transferred in last year."

"Cool."

"You know any of these guys?" Damon sweeps his hand across the gym.

"Only the big guy down there. The one that looks like a truck. He's my roommate."

"What's his name?"

"Daquan."

"Freshman?"

"Yeah."

"I like it, the *Mac Man* has been busy this offseason."

"Who?" James asks.

"The *Mac Man*," Damon repeats. "Yo, sorry. My bad. *Coach McCallom.*"

"Right," James replies as if this was the obvious answer.

"What about those two other tall guys?"

"Don't know. They were here when me and Daquan walked into the gym, but they never said anything. So we just ignored them."

"Not the most mature approach, but I hear ya. They look legit to me and we need to pick some teams and get this going. I've got other stuff I need to get done today."

"I'm with you on that one," James replies.

"Hey, you!" Damon shouts at Taylor.

At the sound of Damon's voice, Taylor looks up to see a stocky player calling over in his direction and except for the players from the buildings and grounds department, who could easily be mistaken for holdovers from a local thirty-five plus recreational league, the shouting player looks to be a lot older than everyone else in the gym.

"Yeah, you! The tall guy with the black shirt on that has a cat on it or something! Over here!" Damon shouts again at Taylor.

With a confused look, Taylor bounces the basketball he's holding over to Emmet and casually strolls in the direction of Damon at center court, still thinking the world will always wait for him.

"Let's go, man!" Damon yells one more time at Taylor. "We don't have all day!"

Taylor now looks over angrily at Damon.

"Come on, big man!" Damon ignores Taylor's facial expression and keeps shouting. "Put a little pop in your step, will ya?"

When Taylor finally reaches center court, he eyes up both Damon and James with reserved caution.

"You another one of the freshman recruits?" Damon asks Taylor.

"Yeah, why?"

"Just asking, big man."

"Who's asking?"

"Settle down. I'm on your side."

"What side is that?" Taylor asks.

"*Easy*," Damon tells Taylor with a laugh. "I'm just trying to pick some teams and I need to keep the legit players on the court and the pretenders off it. Pretenders like those guys down there," he points to the players from the buildings and grounds department.

"Okay, cool," Taylor responds with a casual nod.

Standing to the side of the conversation, James is mesmerized by the tension Taylor seems to be carrying around with him. He's like a bag of cinders looking for a flame.

"Let's try this again, okay? I'm Damon and this here is James. What do your friends call you?"

"I'm Taylor. Taylor Scott."

Both Damon and James' eyes grow a little wider when they hear Taylor's name. *They've heard all the hype.*

After a short pause, Damon reaches out and slaps Taylor five. James does the same.

"The good news for you, Taylor, is James here is also a freshman and just like you, he'll soon be a member of this year's *Bag Crew*. I think you two are going to be good friends."

"*Bag Crew*?" Taylor asks.

"Yeah, *Bag Crew*," Damon answers. "Don't worry, you'll know all about it soon enough. I did my time last season, now I'm happy to pass along the torch to you new guys."

"You played on the team last year?" Taylor asks. "I thought upperclassmen don't arrive for a couple of more days?"

"Yeah, I was on the team last year. But I couldn't play in games, because I was a transfer...But not this year."

"That's cool," Taylor replies as he swallows down hard. Even though Damon is a point guard, no one told him when he was being recruited the team would have any transfers on it. There is only so much potential playing time to go around and every available minute counts.

"The other tall guy down there," Damon asks Taylor. "The one who looks like a live stick figure. Do you know him?"

"Yeah, that's my roommate, Emmet. Another future member of the *Bag Crew*, I guess."

"Ha...ha...exactly," Damon responds with a laugh. "If that's the case, I say we split up the roommates and go from there. What do you say?"

Taylor and James both nod back their approval.

"All right, I'll take James and the skinny kid, Emmet. Taylor, you take Daquan and then pick up three more."

"Sounds cool," Taylor answers, happy a level of respect has been injected back into the conversation.

"Once you're done picking your three, I'll take my last two from what's left," Damon gives Taylor final directions.

In no time, the two teams are on the court ready to play, with the players not selected pushed to the side to form their own game on the gym's second court.

As soon as Taylor bounces the ball to James to be checked in, Damon announces the rules to everyone—

games are 15 straight by 1's and 2's, call your own fouls, And 1's count, best three out of five games takes it. Everyone grunts their approval as James bounces the ball back to Taylor at the top of the key. Immediately passing it to the wing, Taylor cuts down the middle of the lane to start the action.

Over the next hour, the two teams battle each other as if the post-season college basketball championship is on the line. With nothing to lose and everything to prove, Damon and the four freshmen use every ounce of talent and skill they have to try and impress each other. Unfortunately for Emmet, the general observation about him seems to be spot-on—he's too thin and weak to play on the college level right now. While he has a nice shooting touch and surprisingly soft hands, when he's matched up one-on-one with Daquan, Daquan takes him to school every time.

Sometime during this first game, it becomes crystal clear that Damon is the most polished guard on the court. Whether he's running his team's offense, passing the ball with timing and accuracy or hitting his open shots, he seems to be in complete control of every move he makes. If the freshman could tell the Revolutionaries' other point guards to watch their backs right now, they would do so in a heartbeat.

Nervous at first, Taylor settles into a groove once he starts to sweat. Doing everything he can to show the rest of the players the skills that made him such a highly recruited talent, his feet barely touch the ground as he glides up and down the court. In one memorable offensive stretch alone, he completes a spinning right-handed tomahawk dunk over a surprised-looking Emmet, followed by back-to-back three pointers, the last of which hits nothing but net from several feet behind the three-point line. Even though they are on opposite teams, Damon smiles when he watches Taylor play the game, instantly recognizing talent when he sees it. Now if he could only understand their strange and uncomfortable interaction when they first met, he would feel much better about becoming his teammate.

Throughout the full hour, Taylor and James battle each other in a memorable match-up. Raw, strong and extremely athletic, James is without a doubt a young man in a grown man's body, and the only way Taylor is able to get the best of him is by using his highly developed basketball IQ, learned through a lifetime of playing and watching the sport. Although Taylor is sure James will catch up to him in no time once the Maryland State University coaches are able to start working with him.

After Damon leads his team to victory three games to two, the four freshman players sit in a semi-circle off to the side, resting and casually talk to each other. With sports drinks in hand, they share basketball stories from their past, while letting the nervous anxiety from their first college pick-up games slowly drift away. A few minutes later, with the gym completely empty, including Damon, who left without even saying goodbye, Emmet apparently decides he's had enough of their conversation and collapses onto the floor in exhaustion, throwing a towel over his head. Taylor, James and Daquan look over in amusement and then keep on talking as if he's not even there.

"So you're the double-A recruit?" James asks Taylor.

"Double-A?" Taylor responds.

"The All-American."

"Yeah...That's me."

"That game must've been crazy mad!" Daquan shouts.

"It was cool, I guess," Taylor answers with a shrug.

"Cool, you guess? Damn, son! You don't have to be so modest, 'least not around me," Daquan loudly tells Taylor.

"It's not my style to brag to my teammates."

"Man, if I'd played in that game, I'd tell everyone! I'd wear my All-American game gear *everywhere*. Let 'em all know who they're messing with," Daquan keeps after Taylor.

"It was just an exhibition game. It didn't mean a thing," Taylor answers with another shrug.

"Fine, give me your All-American game shorts. I'll wear 'em and tell everyone I was an alternate. We're in college now. You need every edge you can get."

"C'mon, D'," James chides Daquan. "Leave him be, will ya? You just met him."

"Whatever, man. I'm just saying a man's got to brag when he can."

"I let my game do my talking for me," Taylor tells Daquan with a serious expression. "No need to advertise past accomplishments. Besides, none of that's going to help me now anyway. We're all starting over and Coach McCallom is going to play who he wants."

"Don't you mean the *Mac Man*?" James replies.

"The *Mac Man*?" Taylor asks.

"Yeah, *Coach McCallom*. That's what the players call him when he's not around. At least, that's what Damon called him when we were talking before we hooped."

"Fine, the *Mac Man* is going to play who he wants," Taylor answers with a look of indifference. "Either way, we're all starting from scratch and no All-American game gear is going to help me get on the court any faster."

"Just think about it. That's all I'm saying," Daquan responds, saddened that his enthusiasm was shot down so easily.

"Hey, how did you get stuck with your dead looking roommate over there?" James asks Taylor.

Upon hearing this question, all three players look down at Emmet, who hasn't moved in the last few minutes. If it wasn't for the towel over his head, moving up and down with each new breath, they wouldn't even know he's still alive.

"Don't know. Luck of the draw, I guess," Taylor answers.

"Don't you mean unlucky of the draw?" James sarcastically laughs.

"Tell me about it," Taylor replies.

"Hey, me and D' are heading up to the weight room to lift. You want to come with?" James asks.

The intense and anxious pit in Taylor's stomach that usually stops him from opening himself up and making new friends pushes him to say no. Fighting hard against this natural impulse, he nervously taps his thumb in an unending rhythm on the gym floor as he thinks, "Yeah…That sounds cool," Taylor finally answers, deciding to let James and Daquan into his world, if only temporarily.

"What about him?" Daquan asks, pointing to Emmet on the floor.

"Just leave him. He'll make it back to our room, eventually," Taylor answers.

"You sure?" Daquan asks.

"Yeah, it's all good," Taylor responds as he gets up and throws his gym bag over his shoulder.

"If you say so. It's your call," Daquan replies as he follows Taylor to his feet.

Moments later, as the three players leave the Rosenberg Center practice courts to head up to the weight room on the third floor, Taylor yells over his shoulder to Emmet that he'll catch up with him later. Right before the gym's steel door slams shut, Emmet starts to grunt something unrecognizable back in Taylor's direction, only to be drowned out by the sound of the door closing.

CHAPTER 35

At 5:15 a.m. the next morning, Taylor stands alone in front of the Liberty Arena wearing a black hooded Longwood Hills sweatshirt, grey basketball shorts and an old pair of orange and white running sneakers. Even though it's late August, there's a slight chill in the early morning air left over from the night before, letting him know fall is just around the corner. Barely awake, he dances in place to stay loose, while fixating his tired gaze on the quiet stillness of the beautiful campus all around him. Once again captivated by his surroundings, he turns to the horizon to watch the last remaining moments of darkness change from a dark blue to a majestic purple, a surefire sign that today is going to be another picture-perfect day in Washington Springs, Maryland.

A few minutes later, Coach Banks and Coach Davis arrive at the exact same moment, looking like giddy teenagers in their matching red, white and blue Maryland State University sweat suits. As they move swiftly in Taylor's direction, they smile and laugh with one another as if it was the middle of the afternoon and not the ungodly hour of 5:00 a.m. When Coach Banks sees Taylor standing on the cobbled walkway leading to the arena's large glass doorways, he can't help but smile to himself that his young freshman actually showed up. If nothing else, it seems Taylor is a man of his word. *Now if only he could find out what makes him tick?*

"There you are!" Coach Banks starts in before he even reaches Taylor. "I was telling Coach Davis that one of our motivated freshmen was going to join us this morning, but he didn't believe me. So thank you for not making a liar out of me."

"No problem, Coach," Taylor responds with a half-smile from underneath tired eyes. "I said I'd be here...So here I am."

"I like it a lot!" Coach Banks responds loudly as he claps his hands, sending a wave of noise echoing across the empty campus. "Taylor, you remember Coach Davis from your recruiting visit. And Coach Davis, you, of course, remember Taylor Scott."

"Nice to meet you again," Coach Davis addresses Taylor with a warm gentle smile.

"Same here, Coach," Taylor replies as he shakes Coach Davis' sizeable right hand.

"Taylor, I keep hearing such great things about you from Coach McCallom and Coach Banks, so I'm glad we can go on this run together and get to know each other a little bit outside of the gym."

Taylor instantly likes Coach Davis and feels like he's someone he might be able to open up to, but since this doesn't happen too often, he proceeds, like always, with caution.

Moments later, their small group of three begins to stretch in front of the Liberty Arena, using the grey stone benches that line the cobbled walkway every few feet for support. As Coach Banks and Coach Davis banter back and forth with each other, Taylor hangs off to the side, listening to their conversation. Since Coach Banks and Coach Davis are the only two African-American coaches on the Maryland State University men's basketball staff, it's only natural for the two of them to gravitate toward each other. But as far as Taylor can tell, there's something more to it than that. Their friendship appears to be genuine.

This morning's five-mile run has been honed to perfection by Coach Banks and Coach Davis through trial and error over the last year and half, and includes just the right amount of on-campus and off-campus running to keep things interesting. The run starts by heading west along Washington Avenue, past the university's main student center and the bed Taylor reluctantly left this morning inside Kent Hall, before moving past the large open quad that captured his attention during his recruiting visit and the main buildings of the business department, to exit the campus near the "Arch on Arm." After making a left at the corner of Washington Avenue, they run directly underneath the "Arch on Arm" and parallel the campus, heading south down Armstrong Avenue, past its many restaurants, shops and bars, before making another left at the corner of Chester Road and re-entering the campus near the landscaped mansions of Fraternity Row. Once back on campus, they run past the newly-built Science Center to finish up back in front of the Liberty Arena. This five-mile loop usually takes the coaches no more than forty minutes on a bad day and just under thirty-five minutes on a good day. Today, they hope to show Taylor what a good day's run feels like.

After silently saying goodbye to the giant Revolutionaries mascot banner hanging off the face of the Liberty Arena, Taylor follows Coach Banks' and Coach Davis' lead as they leave the arena behind at a brisk pace almost from step one. Running three across, Taylor is sandwiched uncomfortably in between Coach Banks and Coach Davis.

"So how was pick-up ball yesterday?" Coach Davis opens up the conversation after only a few steps.

"It was cool, I guess," Taylor answers, just above the sound of their group's heavy footsteps hitting the pavement.

Thump-Thump-Thump.

"Must've felt good to get your first college pick-up games out of the way," Coach Davis keeps up the conversation.

Thump-Thump-Thump.

"Yeah, not too bad," Taylor plays it close to the vest.

"I remember my first college pick-up games like they were yesterday," Coach Davis tells Taylor as his eyes momentarily drift off into distance. "I can't believe it's been eighteen years already...Wow, I feel old!"

"That's because you *are* old," Coach Banks leans forward and laughs at Coach Davis.

"What are you talking about? You're two years older than me," Coach Davis fires back with a smile.

"But you've got to *feel* a lot older. Seeing as you have two kids already and I have none."

"That's nothing to brag about," Coach Davis answers in a serious tone. "You're the one who's missing out. I can't imagine my life without my two boys."

"You have two sons?" Taylor asks. For some reason he's surprised by this.

"Yes," Coach Davis answers with a vigorous nod of his head. "My oldest, Jamal, is six-years-old and my youngest, Benjamin, is three. They live back in California with their mother."

"How often do you see your wife and kids?" Taylor asks.

"My kids, I try to see as often as I can. My ex-wife, I try to see as little as possible," Coach Davis laughs.

When Coach Banks and Taylor hear Coach Davis' joke, they laugh out loud right along with him, although Taylor isn't sure why, since being an ex-wife almost killed his mom.

After a few more steps, Taylor decides to keep asking Coach Davis personal questions, "Why do your kids live in California? Couldn't they live in Maryland with you?"

"Those are good questions, Taylor," Coach Davis responds and then grows quiet for a moment.

Thump-Thump-Thump.

"To be honest, it's just easier to have my boys live with their mother. My ex-wife and I are both from the same town in Southern California and we still have a lot of family there. So on top of the much needed help it gives my ex, having family nearby gives the boys some additional stability...I also don't want to have to uproot them every time I switch coaching jobs. Not that I'm going anywhere, anytime soon," Coach Davis awkwardly smiles as he says this last line.

"I guess that makes sense. But aren't you their family?"

"I definitely am. That much is for certain. I will tell you this, it *hurts* me not being around them every day. I love my two boys with all my heart. But a man has to make sacrifices sometimes. It's the hardest part about getting older. I only hope one day you're not forced to make a similar decision."

This is a lot for Taylor to take in any time of the day, let alone this early in the morning.

"But enough about that," Coach Davis snaps out of his funk. "Right now you're a freshman. You have your whole life ahead of you. Don't let what I just said even cross your mind."

"Thanks, Coach," Taylor politely responds, while taking the hint to stop asking so many questions.

Thump-Thump-Thump.

"Do you have any brothers or sisters?" Coach Davis asks a few seconds later.

"No, I'm an only child," Taylor responds in a chopped voice, his breathing now matching the pace of the run.

"Only children can be tough," Coach Davis falls right back into his own trap. "I remember how selfish Jamal behaved until Benjamin was born. I can't imagine how he would've turned out if he wasn't forced to learn to share with his younger brother. Although, I'm sure you were an easy child," Coach Davis grins at Taylor as he says this.

"The easiest," Taylor responds with a large smile. "Truthfully, I do have a half-sister and a half-brother, but I don't see them too much. They're a lot younger and my dad's second wife isn't so into me."

"Really? That's a shame. How old were you when your parents got divorced?"

"Seven."

"Wow, seven is a tough age to go through something like that. How do you feel you handled it?"

"Okay, I guess," Taylor answers with a shrug. "Not much I could do, you know."

"That's a very healthy attitude to have," Coach Davis responds, impressed with Taylor's appearance of emotional strength. "I only hope one day my boys feel the same way as you do. Jamal was four and Benjamin was only a year old when my ex and I called it quits. I think the whole thing has been easier on Benjamin, since he never knew anything different. But as you know, it's never easy. Are you and your father close?"

"We were...But not anymore," Taylor answers, then immediately wants to take back this comment. He always feels guilty sharing personal family information, especially with someone he just met.

"Hey, enough of this personal chit-chat!" Coach Banks suddenly jumps back into the conversation. "I think it's time we talked a little basketball!"

Even though he was pretending not to listen, Coach Banks was hanging on every word shared between Taylor and Coach Davis, not wanting to miss a single detail. While he knows everything he needs to about his friend Mike

Davis, each response by Taylor was another glimpse into the personality behind his seemingly unflinching mask.

"Since we can't watch you freshmen play in person until October fifteenth, what did you think of the rest of your recruiting class?" Coach Banks asks Taylor. At the same time, he and Coach Davis share a sideways glance, their wordless exchange saying so much more than they were letting on.

"Huh?" Taylor grunts back.

"How do you feel we coaches did pulling your recruiting class together?" Coach Banks presses Taylor.

Suddenly uncomfortable and also confused by the silent exchange between Coach Banks and Coach Davis, Taylor does his best to search for the right words—words to let the coaches know he was paying attention during yesterday's pick-up games, while also being careful not to say anything that can be judged too harshly. *These are the exact kinds of questions he hates answering from adults!*

"It was only a few games of pick-up, but I think our recruiting class is loaded with talent," Taylor finally tells Coach Banks. "Everyone can play and everyone can also do something a little better than the next guy, you know. And we seem to complement each other pretty well too."

"I like what I'm hearing," Coach Banks enthusiastically responds. "Anything else?"

"I D'ed up James all five games and he can definitely get out and run," Taylor looks Coach Banks in the eyes as he says this. "He also has some serious hops. Especially when he attacks the boards. To be honest, I can't wait to play with him and not against him."

"Believe it or not, James has only been playing basketball since eighth grade. Before that, it was *all* football. I recruited James most of this past year and I can tell you, without a doubt, I used to love watching his high school games. Once a game, he always did something on the court to make you stop and take notice."

"I can definitely see that," Taylor answers with a slight trace of jealousy.

"And what did you think of Daquan?" Coach Banks asks.

"I think Daquan is a serious beast down low. He's a little short to play with his back to the basket so much, but he's strong as a bull. I've never played with someone who has that type of pure strength. It's kind of *awesome*."

"I couldn't agree more. If we can keep Daquan academically eligible, I think we have a future all-conference power forward on our hands."

"Totally."

"And what about your roommate?"

"What about him?"

"You think he can help the team this season?"

"Yeah, I do. He might be insanely skinny right now, but he has a nice jumper and really soft hands."

"Hopefully you're right," Coach Banks counters. "Emmet is one of Coach McCallom's finds. And Coach is very high on him right now. Once he fills out, who knows? Maybe he'll surprise even me."

"Didn't you forget to mention Damon?"

"What about Damon?" Coach Davis intercepts the question.

"We all thought Damon was beyond legit," Taylor glows. "How did he get to Maryland State?"

"I found him, or rather, I should say he found me," Coach Davis answers. "He was playing for one of my coaching buddies in Northern California, when I found out he wanted to transfer back east to be closer to his family. During one of my first recruiting trips out west after being hired on by Coach McCallom, I went to see if Damon might be a good fit for us. After hearing I'd scouted one of his games, and after getting permission to talk to us, Damon called me every day for what seemed like three straight months, until we officially offered him a scholarship. If nothing else, he's a determined young man."

"I don't know who's officially in front of Damon, but if I were him I'd watch my back," Taylor warns.

"Whoa!...Whoa!" Coach Banks jumps back in as he puts up his hands. "I'll tell you exactly who's in front of Damon. It's Andray Jenkins."

Taylor instinctively flinches from Coach Banks' sudden outburst.

"The starting point guard spot belongs to Andray," Coach Banks repeats. "Andray had a great year last year and is a projected future first round draft pick. Damon would have to play like a lottery pick to take away Andray's minutes. Just wait until you see Andray play, then you will *really* be impressed. Damon is a quality ball player, but he's no Andray."

Coach Davis looks over at Taylor with a raised eyebrow, before breaking up the sudden silence, "Don't mind him," he tells Taylor. "Coach Banks has a soft spot in his heart for Andray. He was Andray's high school coach. Between you and me, Damon is a very skilled player and I'm looking forward to seeing how he plays in practice this year, now that he's competing for real minutes."

Coach Davis cocks his head sideways to get a full view of Coach Banks' face as his eyes scream, *"Quit it!"*

Coach Banks purposefully ignores Coach Davis as he continues to tell Taylor his thoughts, "It's not just Andray. Wait until you see our other returning starters play. Corey Lawrence and Maurice Barnes will show you what a starting forward looks like on this level. And once we get Tim Daulton playing the center position the way we know he can, we're going to be tough to beat. All we have to do is get you and the rest of your recruiting class up to speed and I think we have a real shot at playing deep into March this season. I know Coach McCallom feels the same way. Otherwise, what's the point?"

What Taylor envisioned when he got up this morning as a casual jog to get more acquainted with two of his coaches has quickly spiraled into a conversation he no longer wants to have. With his black Longwood Hills sweatshirt now pooled with sweat, he begins to count footsteps until he can go back to his dorm room and crawl into bed. With each passing step, his mind drifts further and further away from the present, filling his head with unavoidable questions that explode like fireworks on the 4th of July...

"Why was I the only player to show up this morning?"
"Was I the only one who was asked?"
"Or was I the only one dumb enough to accept?"
Thump-Thump-Thump.
"How can Coach Davis not be with his sons each day?"
"Can his career matter more to him than his kids?"
Thump-Thump-Thump.
"What about my own dad?"
"Does he have any conflicted feelings about me?"
Thump-Thump-Thump.
"And what is it between Coach Banks and Andray?"
Thump-Thump-Thump.

CHAPTER 36

"Roomy! There you are! The party's just getting started!" Emmet yells to Taylor above the music pumping out of the stereo in their room.

"Son of a bitch!...Not again!" Taylor shouts under his breath through clenched teeth. It's only been a week since they arrived on campus, yet Emmet's nightly party routine was already driving him crazy.

"My man! Come here! I want you to meet Emily!" Emmet yells to Taylor again, waving for him to come over to his side of the room.

After a slight hesitation and with his top two teeth almost puncturing his bottom lip in frustration, Taylor starts weaving his way through the ridiculous number of bodies packed into their small room, noticing for the first time as he gets closer there's a girl sitting on Emmet's lap.

The live version of Emily is naturally thick with a big chest, pale skin and straight brown hair resting just above her shoulders. Wearing faded blue jeans, ripped below the left knee, a white button down shirt pushed wide open at the neck, clearly visible from a few feet away at her neckline is an ornate gold cross dangling from a thin gold necklace. Emily seems happy and content sitting on Emmet's lap as her feet sway high in the air above the floor.

As Taylor approaches Emmet and Emily, Emmet rises off his bed without telling Emily first, sending her crashing to the floor in a heap. Emily's face instantly changes from love, to horror and then back again to love as she stands up and brushes herself off. A shy girl by nature, she blushes bright red as Emmet practically thrusts her hand into Taylor's, "It's nice to meet you," she tells Taylor in an unmistakable southern drawl, her soft voice barely audible above the pounding music in the background. "Thank you for letting me spend the weekend in your room. We all know how tiny these rooms are," she blushes again as she says this.

"No problem," Taylor answers, while managing to crack a small smile. *He wants to hate her, but her politeness is disarming.*

"I want you to know, we plan on staying out of your way as much as we can this weekend. Hopefully, you won't even notice I'm here," Emily tells Taylor, while wondering yet again how she and Emmet were going to find some alone time before she leaves on Sunday afternoon.

"Like I said, no problem," Taylor replies, quickly realizing it's better to make friends with her than stew in anger about his personal space being invaded one more time without his consent.

"I'm so happy you could meet my Emily!" Emmet suddenly shouts out of nowhere, making their awkward conversation, now even more awkward. "Isn't she beautiful, mate?" he eagerly asks.

"Stop it, Emmet! You're embarrassing me!" Emily giggles as she leans in and rests her head on Emmet's shoulder.

"You're definitely one lucky man," Taylor tells Emmet, his lying eyes darting back and forth between Emmet and Emily.

"Don't I know it, mate! I'm just glad she likes tall Irishmen, because without her, I wouldn't have made it through my first two years in the States. She saved this tall good looking Bloke from a serious case of homesickness. Isn't that right?"

"Guilty," Emily responds with a light laugh, raising her right hand. "I just couldn't let Emmet give up on his dream before he gave it a chance. I also didn't want to see him go back to Ireland so soon. I would've missed him too much," she impulsively grabs Emmet's forearm even tighter as she says this.

"I guess we're both glad Emily came along then," Taylor replies, forcing one last smile.

"Thanks, mate! See Emily, didn't I tell you how great my roomy is? Now when I talk about him, you'll know it too!"

"Thanks, man," Taylor answers, unsure once again of how to handle an unprovoked compliment thrown his way.

"I hope you don't mind, mate, but we borrowed some of your music while you were out. But don't worry, I'm watching it myself...I'll make sure it doesn't walk out of here," Emmet tells Taylor with a silly grin.

Ignoring this last comment so he doesn't get too upset, Taylor scans the room closely for the first time and sees Emmet's usual crowd of hard drinking foreign buddies and its ever expanding circle of female groupies.

"It's Saturday night, yo! It's time to party!" Emmet suddenly shouts once again out of nowhere as he thrusts a drink into Taylor's hand. Laughing at his own joke, Emmet looks to Emily for approval—Emily giggles right back at him.

After reluctantly accepting Emmet's drink, Taylor moves to the corner of the room as Emmet and Emily leave him alone to make their rounds. With forced and awkward first week college conversations taking place all around him in a meld of American and foreign accents, Taylor nurses his drink and fixates his eyes on the faint lights outside the small window above Emmet's bed. As he stares out into this semi-darkness, he starts rifling through different scenarios in his head which can free him from this situation as soon as possible—*there's no way he can stand here all night in the discomfort of his own room!* He just hopes that when he comes back later, there isn't anyone randomly sleeping in his bed. Even Emmet has to know by now not to mess with certain things—*no matter what*—like his bed and his clothes. He likes his things exactly how he left them, in the exact place he left them, and even though Emmet has been unintentionally pushing his buttons since they arrived on campus, he has to believe Emmet is aware enough not to cross this line.

With this last thought lingering and before he can finalize his plan to sneak away, his front pocket vibrates, breaking the stranglehold of awkwardness floating around inside his head, "Hello!" he yells, putting the phone to his ear. "What? Jimmy? Is that you? I can't hear you! My roommate is having a party! Stay where you are! I'll call you back in five!"

After hitting the red call end button on his cell phone, Taylor shouts in Emmet's direction, "Hey, man! I gotta jump! That was my boy, Jimmy! I need to hit him back and I can't hear him from inside our room! I'm going to the end of the hall!"

"Whatever you need, my man!" Emmet shouts back. "But don't be too long! We're leaving soon for a party at Carl's dorm! They're hosting a *rager* in their basement common room!" Emmet points at one of his new drinking buddies, who gives Taylor a casual head nod. "If you're not back in time, Emily and I are going to have to leave with my other mates...We can't slow down the pack!"

"No worries, Bro!" Taylor returns the shouting. "Do what you have to do!"

At the end of the hallway on the fourth floor of Kent Hall is a small laundry room crammed with three washing machines and three dryers that were in constant use during the first week of school, but are now not being used, on account that it's Saturday night. Grabbing the only chair inside this small laundry room, Taylor pulls it up to one of the dryers and sits down.

In addition to its partially cracked seat and two slightly dented silver legs, the old blue plastic chair has an oval-shaped hole cut out of its seatback, which is supposed to provide additional comfort to a person of regular height. But since Taylor is so tall, the oval-shaped hole digs strangely into his back, causing him further discomfort on a night already filled with pointed discomfort. Doing what he can to ignore this dull pain, he props his feet on top of the dryer, takes his cell phone out of his front pocket and dials Jimmy's phone number, looking forward to hearing his best friend's voice on the other end.

Sitting inside his own dorm room on the Castleman College campus—deep in the heart of central Pennsylvania—Jimmy picks up his cell phone on the first ring, greeting Taylor with his usual level of excitement.

Within seconds, the two friends continue from where their last conversation left off and as they feed off each other's energy, they pin-ball back and forth between laughing, talking seriously and poking fun at each other during a conversation that is all comfort food and no distractions. When Jimmy talks about his new surroundings, his happiness practically bursts through the phone with every detail and it's obvious he thinks the freshman at Castleman College are a lot cooler than he ever thought they would be.

After ending the thirty-minute call, Taylor briefly reflects on their conversation, before scrolling down to his home number in Longwood Hills and calling his mom. Just like old times, Deborah only picks up the phone after the answering machine screens the call first and while she's happy to hear her son's voice, at the time he called, she was sitting alone on the couch in her favorite robe and slippers, watching a romantic comedy on TV and sipping a glass of red wine from an $8 bottle she bought herself as a present earlier in the week. Minutes later, after saying goodbye with her usual string of "I love you's" and words of encouragement, she goes right back to her movie and the golden silence of her planned night of selfish indulgence.

Taylor next calls his dad's house, but hangs up the phone before it can even connect through. He does this two more times, before deciding that calling his dad isn't a good idea. While he knows he needs to check in with him, he doesn't have the strength to go through with another forced and difficult conversation right now.

After putting his cell phone back into his front pocket, he stares at the grey painted wall behind the dryer and thinks intently about what he should do next. With a sad and confused heart, he stands up and heads back down the hallway, but instead of rejoining the U.N. party happening in his own cramped room, he stops halfway down the hall and knocks lightly on the R.A.'s door.

Once again, he's greeted with a soft and understanding smile by the small senior R.A. with black bushy hair and matching black glasses that's in charge of his hall. Tonight, the R.A. is wearing a red Maryland State University sweatshirt, light brown khaki pants and red and green striped socks, which if Taylor had to take a guess, were probably once an unwanted Christmas present.

As he walks into the R.A.'s room with his head tilted downward, Taylor returns the R.A.'s soft smile, before methodically kicking off his shoes and making a beeline for the ugly brown couch pushed up under the room's only window. Flopping down hard on the couch, he reaches for the old comforter the R.A. leaves out for wayward freshmen like himself who are having a hard time adjusting to their new surroundings and pulls it tightly up to his chest. With his feet hanging off the end of the couch, he props his head up on a small handmade pillow that somehow matches the hideous color of the couch, noticing since the last time he was in the room the R.A. has draped an old white bed sheet over the ugly and mismatched plastic milk cartons he's using as his TV stand. While the bed sheet is an improvement to the room's décor, it's not necessarily a great one.

When the R.A. is completely satisfied Taylor is settled in, he turns the volume of the TV back up, so he can enjoy what's left of his own Saturday night, while wondering silently to himself if Taylor will be able to get him better tickets to Revolutionaries' home games this season. He makes a mental note to wait a few weeks until Taylor is over the hump and feeling better about his standing at the school, before innocently asking this question.

As Taylor fixates his eyes on the small TV screen in front of him, he lets his mind drift back to Longwood Hills; a place he misses right now more than he ever thought could be possible.

CHAPTER 37

On Monday morning, Taylor wakes at 7:00 a.m. and stares straight into the concrete ceiling of his dorm room, trying to focus his attention on the significance of the day. It's the first day of college classes and while he feels no different than he did the day before, things couldn't be more different. He went to bed last night as a high school graduate and woke up this morning as a college freshman—this life-changing transformation taking place over six hours of fitful sleep.

After slowly getting out of bed, he stretches his arms skyward toward the ceiling, before exhaling deeply and letting his arms fall once again down to his side. Moving his hands to his spine, he arches backward toward the floor and grunts loudly as he tries to ease the remaining tension from last night's sleep out of his body. Not satisfied with the results, he stands up straight again and violently twists from side to side, until he happily hears his spine crack loudly in a chorus of alternating pops. Biting his bottom lip in satisfaction, he looks over to make sure Emmet is still fast asleep—he is, like usual—before pulling off the basketball shorts he sleeps in.

With a flick of his wrist, he throws his basketball shorts onto his bed and walks over to the towel rack behind the door to grab the light green towel his mom bought for him the week before school started. After wrapping this towel tightly around his waist, he leans down and picks up the white plastic shower caddy—bought by his mom during the same shopping trip as the towel—from the bottom shelf of the bookcase, located to the left of the door, and heads for the communal bathroom down the hall. His shower caddy is filled with soap, shampoo, conditioner, a toothbrush, toothpaste, deodorant and the one thing he can't live without: Vitamin E skin lotion. He's been using this lotion religiously since he was thirteen years old and not a day goes by that he doesn't bathe himself in it, sometimes rubbing it on two or three times per day.

Twenty minutes later, with his shower finished and the Vitamin E skin lotion successfully rubbed on his body from head to toe, he walks back to his dorm room and puts on the clothes he picked out while lying awake in bed last night—a solid light grey T-shirt, a black zipper hooded sweatshirt, dark blue jeans and white low top sneakers. After looking at his image in the long mirror secured to the wall between the two closets in the room, and satisfied that he looks "collegiate" enough, he grabs his new black backpack with red trim from the floor and looks inside to make sure he has the right textbooks and colored spiral notebooks for today's classes. Satisfied that he does, he throws his backpack over his shoulder, with only one strap and not two—as wearing the backpack the way it was intended would look too dorky in his opinion—before double-checking the front pocket of his jeans to make sure he has his student ID card. With everything in its proper place, he closes the door behind him and steps out into the next chapter of his life, without as much as an attempt to say goodbye to Emmet.

On the ground floor of Kent Hall is a dining hall that covers two expansive rooms, connected by a smaller room in the middle, where students wait in line to pay for their food. The first large room is dedicated to the preparation and plating of food at either self-serve buffet-style tables, divided by food type, or served to students by dining services staff from behind made-to-order counters. The second large room is dedicated to eating, with tables and chairs set up in varying shapes and sizes—from square 4-tops, to round 8-tops, to rectangle 12-tops—with all three rooms matching Kent Hall lobby's design scheme of beige painted walls with black trim and bone white linoleum tiles. Every night Taylor is required to eat dinner with the basketball team at a player's only area set up inside Heritage Hall—the dining hall closest to the Liberty Arena—but just like this morning, he gets to eat breakfast and lunch at any campus location he chooses.

On the back of each student's ID card is a magnetic strip that allows students to use their card around campus for gaining access to different buildings including the dorms, the fitness center and the aquatic center. This magnetic strip also acts as a debit card at the dining halls and snack bars spread throughout campus. Every meal plan is tied to this magnetic strip and covers a tremendous variety of food, albeit not always great tasting food, but don't tell that to the hard working dining services staff that does everything it can to put out the best food possible to an ever-increasing choosy Maryland State University student population of 25,000, 10,000 of whom live on campus.

Since this morning is the first breakfast of a new semester, the Maryland State University administration and the dining services staff have pulled out all the stops. From the hot breakfast bar that includes waffles, pancakes, French toast and scrambled eggs, to the sides bar that includes bacon, sausage, cold cereals, bagels, breads, juices, coffees and muffins, to the made-to-order counters offering egg white-only omelets, poached eggs and breakfast burritos. If you want it, they have it, and if they don't have it, today they'll make it for you. The goal is for every student to feel good on his or her first day of classes and nothing puts a smile on a student's face like a meal to call their own. This food experience is a long way off from what most students ever receive at home, but then again, going to college at Maryland State University is a privileged life and its dining halls are a direct reflection of this.

As Taylor sits alone at one of the square 4-top tables running along the back wall of the dining room, he inhales three scrambled eggs, a side order of bacon, four pieces of whole wheat toast with butter, a blueberry muffin, a banana and two large glasses of orange juice. After placing his last empty glass down on the table, he pauses briefly to catch his breath and look up at the large black and white clock above his head. Satisfied that he's still running on time, he grabs the only piece of uneaten food off his tray—a Red Delicious apple—and puts it into the side pouch of his backpack for later. Getting up from the table, he walks his tray of dirty dishes, used silverware and garbage over to the large conveyer belt by the door, where he watches the tray move safely out of sight. With his backpack once again slung over only one shoulder, he leaves the dining hall behind and starts heading over to his 9:30 a.m. Biology 101 class, located in the Science Center, clear across campus, near Fraternity Row.

Even though he's heard all the rumors by now of how the coaches check each player's daily class attendance, he chooses not to jump on one of the blue buses offered for free by the university to get him to class on time. Instead, he decides to take the long walk in solitude, hoping to burn off some of the anxious energy that's been slowly building up inside him since he got out of bed this morning.

As he walks swiftly toward the Science Center with his head down and his eyes fixated on the front of his sneakers, he barely notices the rest of the world happening around him—the only thing that's registering right now is what's going on inside his mind, a space that is filled with conflicting thoughts, fantastical ideas and doomsday scenarios. Moving at a rapid pace, he covers a tremendous amount of ground with his giant steps and while it's still early in the day, the bright blue sky overhead is already helping to welcome students back to the Maryland State University campus for one more semester of higher learning.

By the time Taylor arrives at his Biology 101 class at 9:20 a.m., his black zipper hooded sweatshirt is completely wide open and small droplets of sweat are trickling down the side of his face. With ten minutes to spare—Coach Banks would be proud—he pulls off his sweatshirt, wipes his face clean and ambles inside the classroom to find a seat in the back, away from the rest of the students who've also arrived early. After dropping his backpack on the floor next to his feet, he pulls out a blue ballpoint pen and a yellow spiral notebook with the word BIOLOGY written in black marker on the cover. Placing both items on the long table in front of him, he stares straight ahead at the large green chalkboard at the front of the room, his face once again projecting no readable emotion.

While he's not sure what to expect from his first college class, it turns out he finds the subject of biology boring and uninspiring. It doesn't help any that his ancient-looking professor, who's been teaching this same class for longer than all of his freshman students have been alive, speaks in a droll and disconnected voice that makes the subject matter seem even duller than it already is. The first half of this hour and fifteen minute class is spent reviewing the semester's syllabus in meticulous detail, while the second half is spent going over cell mitosis and other mundane general biology processes. Since Biology 101 is a requirement for all freshmen, Taylor unfortunately has no choice but to take the class and do well in it.

The only good news is that unlike high school, where teachers are required to keep students in class until the next bell rings, when his seemingly disinterested professor finishes his lecture early, he lets everyone leave at 10:30 a.m.; fifteen minutes before class is scheduled to end. With his next class not until 12:30 p.m., Taylor suddenly finds himself with a larger break than he'd expected.

Walking aimlessly out of Biology 101, Taylor follows what seems to be a relatively unused red brick pathway that twists and turns away from the Science Center, until it wraps around the backside of the Rosenberg Center, coming to an end under a patch of overgrown elm trees. To his surprise, the pathway opens up to a small student center that looks to be completely empty, even though all of its lights are on. It's *exactly* the type of refuge he's looking for.

After cautiously entering the building's double glass doors, he looks around to make sure he isn't doing anything wrong before taking the stairs to the right of the entranceway one floor down. What he finds next is nothing short of miraculous!

At the bottom of the stairs is a furnished basement, filled with all types of recreational activities—table tennis, air hockey, pool, board games and a 50" flat screen TV wired for cable. With no real plan in mind, he plops himself down on one of the jumbo-sized leather couches in front of the TV and flicks the power on with the remote. A few minutes later, after mindlessly flipping through the channels, he stops his search and smiles in total satisfaction when he sees his favorite game show flash onto the screen. Excited beyond words, he stares in wonder at the TV, while thinking to himself how much better college is than high school—he's watching a game show in the middle of a school day and he's not doing anything wrong! He also has nowhere to be right now and no one is looking for him. *Life is perfect.*

After a gleeful hour spent staring at the TV screen and imaging how he'd use his own strategy to win all the prizes and cash offered by the game show host, Taylor sighs softly when the credits roll and he knows he has to leave his private oasis. Stepping out once again into a day filled with bright blue skies, he makes a promise to himself to visit this student center three times per week from now until the end of the semester, or each day his Biology 101 class meets. Unfortunately, he won't be able to keep this promise, not even for one more day. As a matter of fact, he won't make it back to this student center for months.

Things pick up with his next class, American History 101: The American Revolution. The class is taught by a small and passionate man with a tiny mustache that sits just underneath eyes that seem to jump out of his head with excitement when he talks. From 12:30 p.m.-1:45 p.m., Taylor listens with fascination to the real-life stories of the Founding Fathers of the United States and not the watered-down version of the truth it's now apparent he was spoon-fed in high school.

During this lecture, he learns Maryland State University is located right below the Mason-Dixon Line, strategically positioned close to the Chesapeake Bay and its many waterways and seaports. A fact that helped Washington Springs, Maryland, play an important role during the American Revolution and the subsequent Revolutionary War. Throughout this hour-and-fifteen-minute class, Taylor finds he's enthralled by the professor's stories from the time period, not to mention his pen can't scribble notes fast enough into his red spiral notebook marked HISTORY. It's the complete opposite of his biology class from this morning.

After American History 101 lets out and with his political science class not starting until 3:30 p.m., Taylor decides to walk out of his way and eat a late lunch at Heritage Hall—this way he can scout out the location of the basketball team's dinner table and mentally prepare for meeting his new teammates later that night. With two of his three classes already finished, he thinks back to the phone call he received from Coach McCallom right before he left for Washington Springs; a phone call that started with all pleasantries and ended with Coach McCallom trying to convince him to take some physical education classes during his first semester, rather than the full slate of traditional liberal arts classes he'd signed up for. After his mom got wind of what Coach McCallom had suggested, the conversation ended right there and while he knows his current class load is more of a challenge than it needs to be for a freshman basketball player, he wants to make sure he takes full advantage of his time on Maryland State University's campus, however long or short it may be.

The professor for his Political Science 102 class: American Government and Politics is a stiff and buttoned-up woman who happens to be a former career professional from the U.S. State Department. Because of this, Taylor can't decide after the hour and fifteen minutes they spend together whether he's going to like this class or not. Although he can safely say after it's over, he has no idea why this is the major most students choose who go on to attend law school. With one great class, one mediocre class and one dud under his belt, he comes to the conclusion these results are as good as he could have hoped for from his first day of college classes.

After walking out of Political Science 102, Taylor looks around at the surrounding buildings and realizes he's not too far from Essex Hall, James' and Daquan's dorm. Feeling energized at successfully navigating his first day of college classes, he makes the decision to step outside of his comfort zone and text James to see if he and Daquan are around.

After getting a return text of "Y. We're here. C U in a few," Taylor enters the lobby of Essex Hall, where the guard on duty calls upstairs to James' and Daquan's dorm room to make sure they agree to accept their visitor before asking Taylor to sign in by swiping his student ID card through the credit card-looking machine on the desk in front of him. Moments later, when he walks into James' and Daquan's second floor dorm room, both players look extremely happy to see his friendly face—and for the next hour, the three of them hang out talking music, basketball and, of course, girls, as their burgeoning friendship slowly grows one conversation at a time.

Before they head out for dinner at Heritage Hall, James and Daquan ask Taylor whether they should call Emmet to see if he wants to meet them. Taylor responds by letting them know he hasn't seen or heard from Emmet all day; and when pressed further, he goes on to tell them, he actually has no idea if Emmet even got out of bed this morning.

The section inside Heritage Hall's dining room reserved for the Revolutionaries men's basketball team is made up of two long rectangle 12-top tables pushed together and is open only to players, coaches, team managers, trainers, strength and conditioning coaches, sports information employees and the occasional athletic department representative that's decided to drop by.

The team's first dinner, on this Monday night of the first day of classes, is not at all what Taylor thought it would be. The four freshmen and Damon arrive when the dining room's doors open at 6:30 p.m., but the eight upperclassmen don't show up until much later, at 8:15 p.m.—less than fifteen minutes before dinner is scheduled to end. But instead of being a problem for the dining services staff, they all appear genuinely happy to see their local campus celebrities again after the long summer break.

When the upperclassmen finally migrate over to the team's designated eating section, they're not nearly as friendly to the four freshmen and Damon as they were just a few moments ago to the dining services staff. They barely even say hello as they sit down at the other end of the second 12-top table, as far away from the four freshmen and Damon as they possibly can get. It's a deliberate act of solidarity intended to hammer home to the new guys and the transfer—this is their team and they're already one tight-knit unit.

Even though the four freshmen and Damon finished eating a long time ago, they've waited around, thinking they would be spending some time together as a team. But instead of being rewarded for this loyalty, they're now being forced to watch from afar as the upperclassmen catch up with each other, laugh about their summers and mercilessly make fun of the coaches, including Coach McCallom.

The one thing that's obvious from this first team dinner is Andray Jenkins is the upperclassmen's self-appointed leader, which subsequently makes him the team's leader. All of the upperclassmen constantly look to Andray for acceptance and approval—and if you weren't sure who Andray is, all you would have to do is listen for his incredibly distinct laugh—a high-pitched cackling sound as piercing as a fire alarm—to find out.

A few minutes before 8:40 p.m., the four freshmen and Damon finally decide they've had enough of the upperclassmen's cold shoulder and get up to leave the table. Before they can even stand up, Andray officially acknowledges them for the first time—shouting loudly from his seat—they need to be inside the Rosenberg Center tomorrow night at 5:00 p.m. for team-only pick-up ball. No excuses allowed.

CHAPTER 38

On Tuesday morning, Taylor returns to his dorm room from his English class to find a voicemail on his cell phone from Coach McCallom, telling him he needs to see Frank Gilchrest in the Liberty Arena equipment room whenever he can. Given this is the first time Coach McCallom has called his cell phone directly since he arrived on campus, he instinctively knows this message is not a request, but a direct order. Looking at the clock on his phone, he works backward from his 12:30 p.m. macroeconomics class and calculates that if he leaves right now, he can safely make it to the Liberty Arena before lunch and the start of class. Opening up his backpack, he swaps out his English textbook and colored spiral notebook for his macroeconomics materials and then carefully pulls out from the dresser at the end of his bed a T-shirt, matching basketball shorts, compression shorts and low-cut socks— all the clothes he will need to meet James and Daquan to lift weights after macroeconomics and play pick-up ball with the team later this afternoon.

Grabbing his gym bag from underneath the foot of his bed, he neatly places all the clothes into the bag's main compartment, laying each item perfectly on top of the other, in the exact order he'll be putting them on later in the day.

Turning around, he opens up the small closet located to the left of the bookcase by the door and selects a pair of black high-top sneakers from the row of shoes at the bottom of the closet, organized left to right, by color and style—the darker colors starting on the left. After zipping these high-tops into the shoes-only compartment of the bag, he checks out his image in the mirror between the two closets and notices the creases running along the thighs of his jeans are sticking up more than he'd like them to be. Pressing down hard with the palm of his hand, he forcefully flattens out these creases to his satisfaction, before throwing both his gym bag and his backpack over his right shoulder and leaving his dorm room behind.

Deep within the bowels of the Liberty Arena, just down the hall from the mechanical room that houses the building's heating, ventilation and air-conditioning system, is the equipment room for the men's and women's basketball teams. Like everything else in the Liberty Arena, this equipment room is brand new, even though the room itself amounts to nothing more than one large open space with a concrete floor, long rows of permanent metal storage shelves that stretch from the floor to the ceiling, scores of silver rolling racks and a laundry room full of commercial-sized washing machines and dryers. Other than Maryland State University's bright and colorful school crest, which has been prominently painted on the back wall, there are no other markings on the equipment room's white walls, giving the entire space the distinct feel of a warehouse.

Designated as a top-tier school by the major sports apparel company that sponsors Maryland State University's men's and women's basketball teams, the equipment room is filled at all times with expensive clothing, sneakers, uniforms and accessories. Whatever

Maryland State University's basketball teams need to succeed on the court—and some things they don't—this sports apparel company sends to fulfill its annual multi-million dollar contract with the school.

Since Revolutionaries branded basketball apparel is in such constant demand—and not just from the players—the athletic department had to install surveillance cameras at the entrance of the equipment room and sporadically throughout the space to insure nothing leaves its four walls that's not supposed to. But even with this security system in place, Frank Gilchrest, the full-time equipment manager for the men's and women's basketball teams, or one of the part-time managers, is required to stand guard at all times—this way there isn't a repeat of a few years ago when a large number of sneakers and practice jerseys went missing, never to return.

A native of Washington Springs, Maryland, Frank Gilchrest has spent the last forty years of his life in the role of full-time equipment manager for the Maryland State University men's and women's basketball teams. Married for fifty-two years to his grade school sweetheart, he and his wife Ginny returned to their hometown of Washington Springs after Frank hurt his shoulder playing semi-professional baseball and could no longer work the line at a factory located just outside of downtown Philadelphia for a company that supplied electrical switchboards to large high-rise buildings in the Northeast. An old man of seventy-three now, Frank is the only employee of the school who's been associated with Maryland State University basketball longer than Coach McCallom.

When Frank first started working as the Revolutionaries' equipment manager all those years ago, he could've never imagined how television would change college sports. The first equipment room he was stationed in was nothing more than a re-purposed supply closet, in the back of the Rosenberg Center, near the public bathrooms. This is also during the time when Maryland State University not only had to pay for all its uniforms, sneakers, warm-ups and practice gear, but had to beg the few sports apparel companies that were around then to give them the best deal possible. At the end of this annual negotiation, Frank would win the privilege of driving a small truck to the selected company's plant to personally pick up a year's supply of athletic equipment from its loading docks—paying for everything in cash.

Fast forward to two years ago when Maryland State University's ten-year sports apparel contract was up, which the current company won by outbidding three other global companies for the business. The day the contract's eight figure total was announced in the media, Frank marveled over dinner that night with Ginny about how far things had come since he'd first stepped foot on Maryland State University's campus.

Striding with purpose down the grey carpeted hallway leading to the equipment room for the men's and women's basketball teams, Taylor approaches the outsized brown wood door that marks the room's entrance. The door itself has been cut in half, so the top half can be opened, while the bottom half remains locked, allowing Frank and the part-time managers to stand guard over the equipment room, yet still giving them the opportunity to talk to passersby at their leisure. When Taylor steps into the archway of the door, he finds Frank sitting in a chair on the opposite side, his feet propped up on an empty box.

"Hi, I'm looking for Frank," Taylor asks the old man.

"I might be Frank, who's asking?"

"Uhm, Coach McCallom asked me to come to the equipment room and ask for Frank," Taylor answers with some hesitation.

"Coach McCallom, huh? And you are?"

"I'm Taylor," his voice suddenly soft and quiet.

"I take it you're one of Coach McCallom's new guys," Frank looks Taylor up and down. "I'm sure Coach McCallom told you, you were destined for greatness, but never the bench."

"Excuse me?"

"Easy, young man. Just trying to catch your attention. It gets slow down here sometimes. You have a last name, Taylor?"

"Yes, it's Scott."

"You're definitely tall, Taylor Scott. I'll give you that. Well, it's nice to meet you. My name is Frank Gilchrest and I run this here equipment room. Where you from?"

"New Jersey."

"Okay, Taylor Scott from New Jersey. Now that we've been formally introduced, let me grab my sheet and see what we can do for you," Frank slowly gets out of his chair and reaches for a clipboard hanging off a nail next to the door. "Let me see here...Ahh, there you are. Taylor Scott, freshman scholarship player from Longwood Hills, New Jersey. It says right here in this note Coach McCallom penciled to treat you nicely, so I guess I'll just have to listen," Frank smiles smartly at Taylor, hoping he gets the joke. "Lucky for you and the rest of the guys, the newest shipment of gear arrived last week. God forbid we should have any of you ballplayers walking around in last year's gear."

"Sounds good to me," Taylor responds, excited by the treasure-trove of athletic apparel and equipment he'll soon be receiving.

Unlocking the bottom half of the door, Frank intentionally points his thumb upward to the security camera hanging above the door—just in case his young new friend has any misinformed ideas. Taylor momentarily stares at the camera, before stepping into the equipment room.

"I will tell you this, I never know where Coach McCallom is going to get his guys from these days. Do you know there was a young man in here earlier this morning all the way from Ireland? You believe that? I remember when I first started here and we landed our first recruit from outside the state of Maryland. You would've thought he'd come all the way from Mars and not just from Virginia. Now you have to come from another country to catch someone's attention. By the way, what's in the gym bag?"

"Huh?"

"The large bag hanging off your shoulder," Frank repeats.

"Oh, just my stuff for lifting and playing ball later. Why?"

"Do me a favor, put both your bags down here for a second," Frank points to the concrete floor.

"Okay. Why?"

"You're not going to need your own gear anymore. That's why. You're a part of the Revolutionaries now and if nothing else, Coach McCallom takes care of his guys. But you have to do me another favor."

"Sure. Anything."

"You have to make this quick, okay? I don't know how much longer I have on this earth and I don't want to waste any of my precious seconds watching you agonize over whether you should choose red, white or blue."

"Whatever you say. You're in charge," Taylor responds with a smile.

"That's right, I am. Now let's get going here. I need you to first grab yourself one of those blue Maryland State University men's basketball gym bags from that shelf down there and bring it back this way," Frank orders.

As Frank watches Taylor walk away, he's struck by how much he instantly likes the young man, even though there is a softness about him he can't quite put his finger on.

In less than thirty seconds, Taylor is back in front of Frank with his brand new gym bag open in his arms, waiting for his next set of directions.

"Good. It's nice to see your ears work properly," Frank tells him. "As far as I'm concerned, I'd say we're off to a great start. You'd be surprised how many players get distracted just by walking down to that shelf and coming back to this here spot we're standing in. I think there's a drug or something they put into these products to make you young people lose your minds when you're around it."

"Hey, you're kind of funny, man," Taylor tells Frank with a light laugh.

"Thanks...I think. But let's keep this thing moving, okay? Like I mentioned earlier, I don't have all day. Now take that bag in your hands and go choose these next items. And make sure you choose these items in the exact amounts I tell you. Some of you players don't think I'm going to check your bag when you're done. *Stupid. Very stupid.* Just because I'm not following you around, don't think for a second I don't have to personally sign out every item you choose on this here handy sheet attached to this clipboard. Got it?"

"Got it, Frank."

"Now I need you to head down that way and get yourself three practice shirts. Doesn't matter to me what color shirts you choose, or if the shirts have sleeves. Once you're done picking your shirts, go find yourself two pairs of practice shorts. Not the old ones, but the ones that just came in that have the Revolutionaries logo on the left side. Got it, so far?"

"Got it, Frank."

"Good. After you've selected some shorts you're happy with, make sure you take two pairs of compression shorts from the shelf next to it. Again, the color doesn't matter to me. If we have your size, just grab it."

"Still with you," Taylor responds with a wide smile.

"Please stay focused, son. I'm not done yet," Frank responds with a shake of his head.

"Sorry, I can't help it. I'm just excited."

"I knew you would be. I haven't met a player who isn't. But you have to stay with me, okay?"

"Okay, Frank. My bad."

"Once you have your shorts and compression shorts picked out, I need you to choose three pairs of socks for yourself. All we have right now are the ankle-high kind. But that's okay, because Coach McCallom doesn't allow you guys to wear those low cut tennis-looking socks in games anyway. So you might as well get used to the high ones. Still with me?"

"Uh, huh."

"Great. After you have your shorts, compression shorts and socks safely in your bag, you need to choose for yourself one sweatshirt and one pair of sweatpants. For the sweatshirt, it doesn't matter to me if it has a hood or not. It's up to you. You can also take one small towel if you want. The small towels are stacked on the shelf next to the sweatpants. Larger towels for showering belong to the school and are already upstairs in the Liberty Arena locker room or over at the Rosenberg Center locker room. We wash those daily, so you don't have to worry about keeping those. Same goes for the basketballs, those belong to the school. But if you want to sign one out for the preseason, all you need to do is choose one from the rack down there and let me know the number on the side. Unlike the clothes, which are yours to keep, any basketball you sign out has to be returned to me before practice starts. But not everyone signs one out, since there are plenty of basketballs to use upstairs in the Liberty Arena and over at the Rosenberg Center. Also, if you lose the basketball you sign out, you have to pay for it."

"How much does a basketball cost?" Taylor asks.

"Fifty-five dollars."

"Whoa! I think I'll leave the rocks alone," Taylor responds loudly.

"Okay, then. You think you can handle the list I just gave you?"

"No problem," Taylor reassures him.

"If you have any questions, just ask. I'll be right in this here chair waiting for you. This way I can inspect your bag, sign you out and get you on your way as soon as possible."

"Cool."

"Cool indeed, young man," Frank answers with a grin. "Oh, I almost forgot, darn old age. I tell you, I used to be sharp as a tack. Make sure you also choose two pairs of sneakers. One pair should be for basketball and one pair should be for running. For running, take either a pair of traditional running sneakers or those cross-trainers that seem to be so popular these days. But whatever you choose, make sure you can run in them. You'll be out on the track soon enough. For your basketball sneakers, don't worry if you scuff them up, you'll get another pair as soon as practice starts and other pairs throughout the season."

"Got it, Frank."

"You sure?"

"No worries," Taylor responds.

Fifteen minutes later, with his free shopping spree now over and his new bag open and ready for inspection, Taylor stands over Frank, who has found his way, as promised, into the chair Taylor first found him in when he arrived this morning. And while Taylor moved quickly to get through his checklist, none of the players ever move fast enough for Frank.

With a look of impatience, Frank thoroughly inspects Taylor's bag, writing down all the sizes and colors he selected on the sheet attached to the clipboard, before asking Taylor to initial each entry for posterity. Frank next hands Taylor a large clothes pin with a number on it, a mesh laundry bag and a padlock for his locker upstairs—

along with a request for Taylor to flip over the padlock and repeat out loud the combination written in masking tape on the back—this way he can check the combination against his master inventory sheet.

With the deliberate movements of a master sage, Frank shows Taylor how the pin for the mesh laundry bag works, while also letting him know that just like the large towels he mentioned earlier, Taylor can throw his mesh laundry bag filled with dirty clothes into one of the designated slots located either upstairs in the Liberty Arena locker room or over at the Rosenberg Center's locker room. It doesn't matter where, since all the mesh laundry bags make their way back to the equipment room on a daily basis, with the contents of every bag washed, folded and neatly placed inside each player's locker by the next morning.

After saying goodbye to Frank with a firm handshake, Taylor takes the long flight of stairs at the end of the grey carpeted hallway, one floor up, to the Liberty Arena locker room; the official locker room for the men's basketball team. Once again moving with purpose, Taylor walks up to the dark brown wood door that marks the locker room's entrance and slowly steps into the quiet of the empty room as chills once again run down his spine.

The locker room is exactly as he remembered it from his recruiting visit...and as impressive as ever. A large 100' x 50' rectangle space, it's decorated identical to the office of the men's basketball team three floors up; with matching blue carpet running from wall-to-wall, the words *Maryland State University Men's Basketball* etched into carpet in the center of the room and the same dark wood used to construct the players' lockers. Above every locker is a small gold plate, displaying each player's full name, along with his jersey number. At the same time, a few gold plates have been intentionally left blank for the walk-ons who'll successfully play their way onto the team between the start of practice and the first game. On one of the locker room's back walls is a brand new 60" flat screen TV—with three leather chairs in front of it—while a black chalkboard that looks to be held up by two old wobbly wood legs stands in front of the other back wall. Cracked from years of use, the chalkboard is the only unimpressive thing in the locker room. The last holdover from the team's old downtown Baltimore arena locker room, the chalkboard played a key role in too many important victories for Coach McCallom to ever consider leaving it behind or replacing it with something new.

After finding his locker in the back right corner, next to Daquan and two down from James, Taylor immediately places a few items from his new blue bag into the locker and secures it closed using the padlock Frank just gave him. With the realization that he's now one step closer to becoming a college basketball player, his excitement runs almost unchecked as he stands in front of his locker staring at his name plate, then over to the school name etched into the carpet in the center of the room and then back again to his nameplate in an unending circle. He only goes to leave when he realizes he's been standing in the same spot for over ten minutes.

"What are you still doing here?" a familiar voice calls out to him from behind, momentarily catching him off guard.

Turning around, Taylor sees a confused-looking Frank with a brown paper bag in his hand.

"I guess you could say I'm visualizing my future filled with a lot of playing time and not a lot of sitting on the bench," Taylor answers with a sarcastic laugh. "Better question is what are *you* doing here?"

"Don't tell anyone, but I like to come up here on my lunch hour and watch my soaps on the big screen TV. You guys also have the nicest bathrooms in the place. There's nothing like a little piece and quiet when you need it. You have to remember, I've been married for fifty-two years. What'd you say we keep this between us?" Frank asks.

"It's all good," Taylor replies with a small smile. "I gotta run anyway. I need to grab some lunch before class. The place is all yours."

As Taylor heads for the door, Frank calls out to him one last time, "Hey, Taylor."

"Yeah, Frank," Taylor momentarily turns back around.

"Remember something. They're *always* watching. Even when you think they're not. You're part of the Revolutionaries now and Coach McCallom likes things the way he likes them. You didn't hear it from me, but every time you swipe your student ID card on campus, they're watching. It doesn't matter whether it's at the gym, the weight room or just eating lunch. They even check which players drop off laundry bags for cleaning."

"Thanks for the heads up, Frank. I'll keep it in mind."

"Please do. And good luck, son. I'm pulling for you."

"I appreciate the love," Taylor answers as he heads for the door with a wave.

Later that afternoon, after an hour of lifting, Taylor, James and Daquan leave the Rosenberg Center's weight room and take the elevator three floors down to the basketball courts to meet Emmet, Damon, the eight upperclassmen and two walk-ons to play pick-up ball. With fifteen guys even, three teams are selected by Andray, Chase—the projected starting two-guard—and Damon. The game rules are the same as the first time Taylor played, with only one difference: Today's winning team stays on the court, while the losing team gets banished to wait out the next game on the sidelines.

Without his baggy clothes on, Andray appears a lot different than he did at dinner the night before. At 6' 1", he has chiseled muscles sitting on top of a naturally strong frame and looks more like a running back playing the point guard position than a basketball player. As far as Taylor can tell, all the upperclassmen are as big and strong as he was afraid they might be when he tried to imagine this day sitting alone in his bedroom in New Jersey. The one thing he never thought about—but should have—is the level of intensity at which the upperclassmen play. Over the course of two hours, they never seem to take *any* plays off. With only forty minutes of game time available each time the Revolutionaries step on the court during the season, minutes are the one thing all players *desperately* need. No one wants to watch from the bench and while today isn't an officially sanctioned practice, each player's march toward securing precious game minutes starts from this moment on.

About halfway through the two hours of pick-up ball, at the end of a tie-game—a game that feels even more intense than the rest—Andray and Taylor get into a heated argument over a ball that Andray felt went out of bounds off Taylor's fingertips. Fully expecting Taylor to back down, Andray is *blown away* when he doesn't. This unexpected bold stand triggers alarm bells inside Andray's head that maybe the freshman simply doesn't know his place on the team.

After pick-up ball is over and the freshmen and walk-ons have long left the gym, the upperclassmen hang around to evaluate their new teammates. It's an informal tradition that's been passed down from year to year. Almost to a man, they decide they like James and Daquan, and also have no real opinion of Emmet; and as for Taylor, they unanimously agree he has an attitude and sense of entitlement that needs to be knocked out of him.

As the team's fearless leader, Andray volunteers to be the one to slowly grind away at Taylor's attitude and then violently knock this sense of entitlement out of him for good when the time is right.

CHAPTER 39

After Taylor's biology class lets out on Wednesday morning, he decides to head over to the Rosenberg Center to lift weights alone, instead of watching his favorite game show in the empty student center. While he knows he's breaking a promise to himself that's not even two days old, he wants to make sure he has enough downtime in between lifting this morning and training with the basketball team on the track later in the afternoon. Never one to voluntarily run for exercise, he now has no choice but to run his guts out each time the team trains on the track—to prove to the upperclassmen—and to himself—that he belongs.

Later that afternoon, Andray manages the team's training session on the track the same way he leads the team's pick-up games and the upperclassmen's half of the dinner table; with a lot of jokes and laughter, followed by harrowing intensity when it comes time to perform or deliver an important message. With an air of invincibility and unwavering confidence, Andray pushes, prods and challenges everyone to work their hardest—yet still somehow manages to come across as "just one of the guys."

As for the freshman basketball players, Andray mostly ignores them and talks around them. Because of this—and even though he's a natural leader and brilliant player on the court—every time he opens up his mouth and talks about something other than basketball, Taylor can't help but wonder how low Andray's grade point average must be.

In addition to classes, studying, eating and lifting weights, the team "unofficially" plays pick-up basketball on Tuesdays and Thursdays in the Rosenberg Center and on Fridays in the Liberty Arena. The team also "unofficially" runs on the track on Mondays and Wednesdays. Hour by hour, day by day, week by week, the Revolutionaries basketball program begins to methodically take over the player's lives and before Taylor knows it, every minute of every day seems to be accounted for. The only free time he finds himself with is late at night and on the weekends. But after hearing Frank's warning the day he picked up his athletic gear in the equipment room, he makes sure to show up at the gym, the weight room or both, every chance he gets. Sometimes he asks James and Daquan to join these extra work-out sessions, other times he goes by himself and if he gets lonely enough, he even convinces Emmet to use his free time to work out instead of party.

By the end of September, Taylor feels physically and emotionally exhausted. He's been training harder and longer than he ever did in high school and practice hasn't officially started yet, let alone the season.

On the last Thursday of September, Taylor finds himself inside the Rosenberg Center, warming up for pick-up ball, next to Andray and Corey Lawrence—the team's starting senior forward. While Andray and Corey play a casual game of one-on-one in the corner, Taylor practices foul shots and short jump shots a few feet away. As the two upperclassmen go about their game, they make every effort to ignore Taylor's presence and interact with him only when they have to.

A few minutes later, Taylor watches as Andray makes a step-back jump shot over Corey's outstretched arm. As soon as the ball falls through the rim, Andray looks up into the air and laughingly tells the "fishbowl" to go shove it! When Taylor hears Andray yell this, a look of confusion washes across his face. He's repeatedly heard the upperclassmen use this phrase since he's arrived on campus, yet he still has no idea what it means—none of the freshmen do. And with Damon migrating, after that first night, over to the upperclassmen's half of the dinner table, there's no one to casually ask this question to anymore.

With all of this in mind—and even though he knows this question is most likely going to cost him dearly—he decides now is as good of a time as any to find out what the upperclassmen mean by the "fishbowl." Looking around cautiously to make sure no one else on the team is within ear shot, he takes a deep breath and opens up his mouth, "Hey, Andray."

When Andray and Corey hear Taylor's voice, they both look over in amusement.

"Did *you* say something to me, freshman?" Andray asks.

"Yeah," Taylor answers, swallowing down hard. "You older guys always seem to talk about the fishbowl. What does it mean?"

"Are you for real?" Andray responds with a laugh, his signature cackle practically bouncing off Taylor's face. "Silly freshmen, don't any of you know nothing? We're standing in the fishbowl right now."

"This is the fishbowl?"

"Yeah, man. This is the fishbowl," Andray mocks Taylor's voice.

"How long have you been here already?" Corey asks, looking over at Taylor with concern.

"Six weeks."

"In six weeks, you telling me you've never seen a coach 'round here?"

"Yeah, I've seen plenty of coaches...So what?"

"Man, are you for real?" Andray asks again.

"The coaches' offices are in the Liberty Arena," Corey tells Taylor. "They got no business over here this time of year. What'd you think they're doing in this building?"

"I don't know, working out?"

"C'mon, man! You can't be that naïve!" Andray practically falls over Corey laughing. "You think the coaches need to come over here to work out at the same time we happen to be playing ball?"

"Yeah, why not?" Taylor answers red-faced.

"C'mon, man! Didn't the fishbowl come up during your morning jog with Coach Banks and Coach Davis?" Andray keeps making fun of Taylor. "What were you thinking saying yes to that anyway? Are you really that big of a suck up?"

Dying to respond in anger, Taylor bites his bottom lip, knowing any negative reaction will only make things worse, "Seriously, why do you guys call it the fishbowl?" he stands his ground and asks his question one more time.

"Because they're watching, man!" Corey responds in frustration. "You think the coaches are going to make their decisions about whose going to play from only a few weeks of practice? There's too much at stake. Just like they do at every school, they bend the rules like crazy here."

"It's against the rules for the coaches to be watching us now," Taylor states with confidence.

"It don't matter what the rules are," Andray responds loudly. "The *Mac Man* owns this place. Revolutionaries ball is about winning games and winning games *only*."

"Hold up, hold up. The coaches don't break the rules as much as bend 'em to their advantage," Corey clarifies what Andray just said.

"So if they're really watching, where are they?" Taylor asks.

"Look up," Corey replies.

"Look where?" Taylor asks.

"Up, man. You know the weight room equipment pushed up against the windows?"

"Yeah."

"Take one guess who's working out on that equipment right now."

"The coaches?" Taylor answers.

"That's right, the coaches," Andray sarcastically responds with a soft clap of his hands.

"They've been working out every day we've been in here," Corey tells Taylor.

"How do they get away with it?" Taylor asks.

"Don't know. Don't care," Andray responds. "There ain't nothing we can do about it anyways."

"What about the track?"

"Nah, the track is the one place we're safe," Andray answers.

"It's even worse on Fridays," Corey shakes his head in disgust. "When we play pick-up in the Liberty Arena, the *Mac Man* doesn't even bother to leave his office. He just sits up there in the dark, looking down on us, like we don't know he's there."

"Really?" Taylor asks in astonishment.

"Yeah, man. Really. Wow, you're one innocent dude," Andray tells Taylor with pity in his voice.

"You have to understand, the *Mac Man* has more power at this school than the Athletic Director," Corey goes on. "Every couple of years we get a new A.D. and none of 'em ever want to mess with the money train the *Mac Man* has built. So they just look the other way."

"Once we step foot on this campus, this place owns us until we leave," Andray states as a matter of fact. "It ain't even worth trying to fight."

Feeling violated and angry and somehow stupid, Taylor shakes his head in disbelief at what Andray and Corey just told him. He wants to run and tell James, or Daquan, or Emmet, or all of them at the same time what he just found out, but all he can muster is, "Thanks, man. I appreciate you letting me know."

"Silly freshman. None of you know nothing," Andray responds as he laughs out loud one more time. "Now that we've educated you, why don't you go down to the other basket? This way we can warm-up in peace," he flicks Taylor away with his hand.

Once again angered by Andray's put-downs, Taylor's instincts tell him to fight back. But instead of taking the bait, he simply stares back with a look of calculated coolness, before walking away toward the other end of the court.

After only a few steps, he sees James walk into the gym from across the way. With no sign of any of his raw emotions bubbling just underneath the surface, he heads straight for James to share the news about the fishbowl, while trying to forget Andray's actions.

CHAPTER 40

Later that night, instead of going straight back to his dorm room after eating dinner with the team in the Heritage Hall dining room, Taylor decides to head over to the library to use one of its computers to see if he can find out any more information on the "fishbowl." He doubts there's much to be found, but he's still shocked at what Andray and Corey told him earlier and he needs to satisfy his gnawing curiosity, otherwise he won't be able to sleep tonight.

After entering the red brick library located to the north of Kent Hall, he takes the stairs to the third floor and searches for an open computer station as far away from the other students as he can get. Finding an unused desktop in the back, near a window overlooking the partially lit campus below, he places his backpack underneath the chair and uses the mouse to wake the computer from its sleep. Double-clicking the web browser icon, he goes straight to the search engine and types the words "fishbowl" + "Maryland State University" into the search box.

In less than a second, the search engine returns its results—a marketing software agency in Virginia, followed by several online fish aquarium companies and underneath those results, a nightclub. Only at the way bottom of the page does he find something that might be worthwhile. It's a blog written by someone called *#1RevFanOnEarth*.

Clicking on the *#1RevFanOnEarth* link, he's taken to a die-hard fan's view of all things Maryland State University men's basketball. At first glance, this anonymous blog is mostly a series of rants and unconfirmed rumors about the team and its players; the exact kind of information Taylor usually does everything he can to avoid. But instead of closing the site, he uses the navigation bar to scan through the blog's entries to find what was highlighted in the search results. While he was hoping for more, what he does learn from the blog is...

"Even though the Rosenberg Center was last renovated in 1996, rumor has it the "fishbowl" nickname was first invented in the late 1990's by the men's basketball players and has stuck ever since. While no one outside of the Revolutionaries program knows where this nickname came from, this #1 fan has heard unconfirmed whispers it has something to do with the coaches exploiting an unspecified loophole in the rule book..."

Unfortunately, the rest of the blog entry doesn't touch upon the "fishbowl" again and while Taylor should be shocked by the ridiculousness of the entry right below it— he isn't. The blog entry in question is dedicated to the rumor that one of Maryland State University's cheerleaders is dating a basketball player from the Revolutionaries' in-state rival, with this cheerleader recently being overheard at dinner telling this rival player the meanings of all the hand calls Coach McCallom uses during games. Since it's clearly obvious this die-hard fan has too much time on his hands and not nearly enough friends, Taylor decides to leave *#1RevFanOnEarth*'s blog for good, navigating back to the search engine; where he types the words "fishbowl" + "Maryland State University" + "Rosenberg Center Renovation" into the search box. This new search happily returns better results, including an online encyclopedia entry for the Rosenberg Center. Clicking on this link, he begins reading the summation paragraph at the top of the page...

"The Rosenberg Center was the original on-campus home gym for the Maryland State University men's and women's basketball teams and while it hasn't been used in this capacity for many years, it now serves primarily as the practice facility for these same teams and for Maryland State University's intramural sports programs..."

Immediately bored by whoever wrote this entry, Taylor hits the back arrow button at the top left corner of the web browser and starts scanning through the search results again. About three-quarters of the way down the page, he finds a link to an old interview in something called *Inside Washington Springs Magazine*. The interview is with a man named Michael Baker; the lead architect in charge of the Rosenberg Center renovation, and at the time, a majority partner in the Washington, D.C. architectural firm of Baker & Lane. The article reads...

"The design for the Rosenberg Center's weight room came from Michael's personal experience. He hated watching TV when running on the treadmill or riding the stationary bike in his home gym, since he found it impossible to concentrate on both the exercises and what was being shown on TV at the same time. So when it came time to draw up the final plans to renovate the Rosenberg Center, Michael changed the back wall of the weight room to glass windows. This way Maryland State University's students could mindlessly watch the different sports being played on the Rosenberg Center's courts below, rather than trying to focus their attention on a small TV screen..."

The rest of the *Inside Washington Springs Magazine* article covers Michael's professional experience and his passion for hunting, both things that immediately make Taylor's eyes glaze over in boredom. And even though he didn't find the exact information on the "fishbowl" he was looking for, based on what he did find, he's now satisfied that Andray and Corey were at least telling him the truth.

Using the mouse to once again navigate back to the search engine, he now types the words, "Maryland State University Men's Basketball" into the search box. When the results flash onto the screen, he clicks on the link he was looking for and waits another half-of-a-second to be directed to the homepage of the Maryland State University men's basketball team. While he's already spent a great deal of time on this website, when the page loads and he first sees the same captivating picture he always sees—the Revolutionaries' rabid fans cheering on the team inside the Liberty Arena—excitement courses through his veins. Every few seconds after that a new picture rotates before his eyes—most being action shots of the team's returning players doing battle against the Revolutionaries' opponents. These pictures do what they always do; make Taylor extremely jealous, since he wants nothing more than for his own picture to be flashing onto the screen, instead of these other players.

Once these pictures rotate completely through, Taylor turns his attention to the large photo of Coach McCallom on the right side of the screen, just above a "call to action," telling Revolutionaries fans, "Now is the perfect time to order game tickets for the upcoming season!" Shrugging off this overt commercialism, Taylor uses the mouse to open up the drop down menu at the top of the page, selecting the word "Team" and then the word "Roster." While he's already studied the Revolutionaries' roster extensively for the upcoming season, with the start of practice approaching fast, he's now determined, more than ever, to figure out who he has to beat out for playing time.

After a good twenty minutes spent staring at the team's roster on the screen and cycling through every imaginable scenario where he gets to play ahead of almost everyone else who plays his same position, Taylor once again clicks the back arrow button at the top left corner of the web browser and heads to the homepage of the Maryland State University men's basketball team. While he's not sure what he's looking for next, he selects the word "History" from the drop down menu and starts scanning through the information on the screen. A few paragraphs down, he finds a highlighted link for the "Rosenberg Center" embedded into a sentence and decides maybe he's not done with searching for information on the building after all. Clicking on this link, he's taken to a brief history of the Rosenberg Center, written by Maryland State University's Sports Information Department...

"Built in 1967 through a generous donation from Arthur Rosenberg, the Rosenberg Center served as the home gym for the Maryland State University men's and women's basketball teams until the end of the 1991 season. A graduate of Maryland State University's class of 1925, Arthur made most of his fortune building war ships for the U.S. Government through his company Chesapeake Bay Iron. At the height of its production, Chesapeake Bay Iron was building ships out of Baltimore's Inner Harbor, twenty-four hours a day, seven days a week, and only slowed down when the Government's demand for new ships dwindled. But instead of sitting idly by counting his money, Arthur retooled his company to build ships for the emerging vacation cruise ship industry..."

Bored again in no time, Taylor sees Arthur's name also appears as a highlighted link embedded into a sentence. Clicking on this link, he's taken to a new webpage. With a speedy inspection of the screen, he realizes he's been directed to a biography of Arthur Rosenberg, written many years ago by a local business reporter from Washington, D.C....

"After Arthur's wife died, he first donated a large sum of money to Maryland State University's School of

Engineering, the school from which he graduated to help complete the final phase of construction for a new hall of classrooms that were being built. Rosenberg Hall, which still stands, is home today to the engineering department's faculty offices and its computer labs.

"Only slightly satisfied by this contribution, Arthur next set his sights on making a much bigger impact at the school—with something even dearer to his heart—the men's basketball team. At 5' 8", Arthur was neither big enough, nor talented enough to ever play for the Maryland State University Revolutionaries, but he did serve as the team's student manager his last three years on campus. Even after he struck it rich, Arthur was quoted many times as saying, 'The happiest years of my life were those I spent as the Revolutionaries' student manager.' Telling anyone who would listen, 'There's just nothing else like being part of a team.'

"Unfortunately, by the time Arthur decided to donate his money to help Maryland State University build its new on-campus home gym, he'd already been diagnosed with leukemia. The doctors gave him only a few short years to live, so to combat this, he helped push along a building schedule that was an engineering marvel for the time, completing the 4,500 seat Rosenberg Center in just under a year.

"Once the Rosenberg Center was finished, Arthur attended every home game, sitting court side in the same brown suit and red tie, until his death in 1973. The only thing that changed each game were his companions: doling out his prized court side seats to the cream-of-the-crop of Maryland's social society in an ongoing game of Show and Tell that kept the media and fans constantly guessing who his guests might be. After Arthur passed away, the school left his court side seat empty as a memorial, which is exactly how it remained until 1991 when the Rosenberg Center was deemed too small and old to continue to serve as the home gym for the growing Revolutionaries men's and women's basketball programs..."

By the time Taylor gets to this last sentence, he's once again bored by what he's reading; especially by what he considers to be ancient history. Using the mouse, he goes back to what was written by Maryland State University's Sports Information Department. At the bottom of this page, he sees that Coach McCallom's name is also highlighted as a link. He picks up his reading from there...

"The end of the Rosenberg Center coincided with the arrival of Coach Rory McCallom from a little-known university in the heart of Baltimore, Maryland. During a time of unparalleled growth for the game of college basketball and its fans, Coach McCallom ushered in a new era of success for the Revolutionaries' men's basketball program. Banking on the continued growth of what is now modern day college basketball and looking to capitalize on the success of Coach McCallom's early years, Maryland State University's Athletic Department decided five years after his arrival to move both the men's and women's basketball team's home games from the small on-campus Rosenberg Center to a much larger arena in downtown Baltimore. In addition to providing the Revolutionaries' growing fan base with extra seats and greater food choices, this move also allowed Maryland State University's Athletic Department to offer its fans corporate luxury boxes for the first time.

"Many years later, after watching this downtown Baltimore arena become outdated in its own right, the athletic department, the school administration, Coach McCallom and a group of prominent alumni helped lead a fundraising drive called, 'Taking It Back to Campus!' The end result of this successful campaign was the old science building in the center of Maryland State University's campus was razed to make way for the Revolutionaries' new 15,000 seat on-campus home gym, the Liberty Arena..."

After reading this last paragraph, Taylor stares at the screen for a few moments, trying to digest everything he just read. While he always knew there was a lot of history and expectations that came along with the scholarship he'd accepted, the weight of it all was only now beginning to sink in.

CHAPTER 41

Since Coach Banks called his cell phone, sent him a text, emailed him and also went as far as to put a memo in his student mailbox, Taylor knows, beyond a shadow of a doubt, that today's first official team meeting inside the Liberty Arena at 4:30 p.m. is an important one. And while he's relieved to get the day off from running on the track, he has no clue what Coach McCallom is going to cover in today's meeting, which makes him both nervous and excited. Despite the fact he's starting to get more comfortable with the idea that real excitement can only come from new beginnings, starting over as a freshman and being new to everything can sometimes feel like blindly walking into a busy intersection.

Later that afternoon, on this first Monday of October, Taylor makes his way over to the Liberty Arena with innocence and idealism pulsating through his veins. With a bounce in his step, he walks at a fast pace, while images of all the great college basketball players he watched on TV growing up—along with the words to the song they play after the post-season college basketball championship game is over—shuffling joyfully through his mind on repeat.

A few minutes later, he finally snaps out of his walking daydream and looks at the clock on his cell phone to see he's running early. Since he doesn't want to be the first one to arrive, he slows his pace down to a casual walk, while occupying his brain with guesses of what Coach McCallom might go over in today's meeting.

"Taylor! Over here!" a familiar voice shouts to him from a distance.

Looking up, Taylor sees Coach Banks bounding toward him wearing his usual red, white and blue Maryland State University sweat suit. "How are you doing?" Coach Banks asks with a broad smile, once again displaying his perfectly straight white teeth as he gets closer.

"Fine, Coach. And you?"

"Doing great! The season is right around the corner. Can you feel it?" Coach Banks inhales deeply as if he can smell the season lying hidden in between the blades of grass.

"Yeah, I can feel it," Taylor responds, displaying a smile of his own. "This season is going to be a lot of fun."

As optimism fills their hearts, each for a different reason, Taylor and Coach Banks begin walking across the campus' perfectly manicured landscape in the direction of the Liberty Arena.

"Do you know what the *Mac Man* is going to be talking about today?" Taylor asks after a few steps.

"Excuse me?" Coach Banks suddenly stops dead in his tracks. "What did you just call Coach McCallom?"

Swallowing hard, Taylor answers, "The *Mac Man*. Why?"

"Why?" Coach Banks repeats as he stares straight up into Taylor's face. "Let me tell you something. I know you haven't been here that long, but let's get something *perfectly* clear. Coach McCallom's name is not the *Mac Man* or any other nickname. His name is Coach McCallom or just Coach. At least as far as you're concerned. He has two hundred and seventy-three career wins, seven conference titles and one post-season college basketball championship. I think he's earned your respect. Don't ever make that mistake again. Are we clear?"

"Yes," Taylor answers as his face turns red hot with embarrassment.

"And you're lucky Coach McCallom isn't here right now. If he heard you call him that name, you'd be running bricks until your arms fall off."

"Running bricks?"

"Yes, running bricks. You'll know what it means soon enough."

"Sorry, Coach. It won't happen again," Taylor responds as his eyes sink down to the front of his sneakers.

"No, it won't," Coach Banks replies and then tilts his head up so he can look directly into Taylor's face. "But no good is going to come from you dwelling on a past mistake. So pick your head up. We have a meeting we need to get to."

As Taylor nods back that he understands, the two of them begin walking again in the direction of the Liberty Arena, but this time, in complete silence. With each passing step, the campus' manicured landscape which seemed so alive to Taylor only a few minutes ago, now seems almost sad in a way. At the same time, he's suddenly unable to recall in his head any of the images of his favorite college basketball players growing up or the words to that special song.

CHAPTER 42

Once they enter the meeting room inside the Liberty Arena, Taylor and Coach Banks part ways as Taylor finds an empty chair in the second to last row by himself and Coach Banks takes his place along the right wall, next to the other assistant coaches. This is the first time Taylor has been inside this specific meeting room and he can't help but notice the room itself is relatively plain, with no pictures or slogans hanging off its beige painted walls, and only a few rows of hard plastic desks and chairs facing a large white dry erase board that's been secured to the front wall.

From his vantage point, Taylor stares at Coach McCallom as he studies a pile of blue note cards in his hands from behind a small wood podium at the front of the room, before turning his attention to the large pyramid drawn in black marker on the white dry erase board just over Coach McCallom's shoulder. This large pyramid has horizontal lines running across it to show levels or layers, and above the tip of the pyramid, two words have been written in big capital letters. They read, "PHILOSOPHER KING!"

Completely confused by what he's looking at, Taylor's eyes dart around the room for help, but with James and

Daquan sitting two rows in front of him and Emmet nowhere to be found, he decides to leave this question alone. Instead, he watches as the upperclassmen, who are occupying most of the room's front rows, mess around with each other, without it seems a care in the world— displaying a level of confidence and comfort in the situation that he can only hope to one day achieve. Taking his eyes off the upperclassmen, he scans the rest of the room and notices there are four players sitting behind him in the last row of seats that he's never seen before. He can only assume these are some more of the team's walk-on candidates.

"Close the door!" Coach McCallom suddenly bellows to Coach Davis, who moves swiftly to do as he's told.

The second the meeting room door closes, Coach McCallom turns his now steely gaze onto the players in front of him, "It's four twenty-five p.m.!" he thunders. "This meeting was called for four-thirty. If someone isn't here by now, they're *late*. Men, this is the first lesson of the year and it's an especially important one for you freshman and walk-on candidates to learn. If you're five minutes early to one of my meetings, you're on time. If you're on time to one of my meetings, you're late. I shouldn't have to tell you this, but don't *ever* be late to one of my meetings."

Taylor's heart sticks in his throat from the back of the room. The warm and fuzzy Coach McCallom he spoke to on the phone all of last year, the same one he met on his recruiting visit, seems to be long gone, replaced by the real Coach McCallom standing behind the podium at the front of the room. As Taylor looks around again, he notices the upperclassmen are no longer messing around with each other and are now sitting up straight in their seats. It's 4:26 p.m.

"Welcome to a new season of Maryland State University men's basketball," Coach McCallom tells the players. "Every new season begins fresh and holds so much promise for the future and this season is no different…"

Before he can even finish this sentence, Emmet opens the door to the meeting room and casually walks inside with a happy grin stretched across his unpleasant-looking face. Immediately, Emmet's facial expression changes from happiness to panic, when he sees the rest of the players are already sitting in their seats and Coach McCallom is standing alone at the front of the room.

"Welcome, Emmet," Coach McCallom barks from underneath laser-focused eyes. "Since you're new, I'm going to repeat myself this one time only. You're now less than five minutes early to one of my meetings, so you're *officially* late. Don't ever be late to one of my meetings again. If you are, I promise you, you'll never see the light of day on court this season."

Startled by Coach McCallom's words, Emmet's acne-filled face turns redder than the red in Coach Banks' sweat suit at the front of the room, "Yes, Coach," Emmet softly answers. "It won't happen again."

"No, it *won't*," Coach McCallom sneers back with authority. "You get one free pass. This is it. Don't ever forget it. Now go find yourself a seat."

Emmet picks up his eyes and looks like he wants to say something back to Coach McCallom, but then thinks better of it.

"Before I hand out a few forms for all of you to sign and Coach Banks goes over the responsibilities for this year's *Bag Crew*, there are a few things I need to say," Coach McCallom once again addresses the team. "Upperclassmen, you've heard most of this speech before, so please bear with me. But with that said, before you tune me out, I suggest you pay close attention to what I'm about to say as these may be the most important words I share with everyone all season. If you ignore these words, thinking you're above it all, the next time we'll talk like this is the day I take back your uniform and hand you a one-way ticket out of here."

Pausing for a second to adjust his reading glasses, Coach McCallom now leans forward and tightly grips the sides of the podium, "For those of you lucky enough to wear a Maryland State University uniform this year, you're now about to become part of the Revolutionaries. So first of all, welcome," a wide smile spreads across his face, before disappearing in an instant. "And second of all, don't do *anything* to screw it up. This is my life's work. For twenty-five years, I've been building what you see here today and just in case your math skills are poor, that's a very long time before any of you ever arrived on this campus. But make no mistake about it, each one of you in this room is the keeper of my legacy. Your job is to work hard and leave things better than you found it. The Revolutionaries men's basketball program is also much bigger than any one individual, so please don't ever think your own accomplishments are greater than those of the whole, because I can assure you, *they're not*. If it wasn't for the success of the players that came before you, none of you would be in the position you're in to receive the attention from our fans this season. So keep it all in perspective. And just in case you don't, I can *guarantee* you someone from this coaching staff will help you do so. *No* individual is above the team and *no* team is above the program."

Coach McCallom now turns half-way around and points to the pyramid drawn in black marker on the dry erase board.

"To be even clearer, you're now also playing for the students of this university and your parents." Using the black marker, he writes the words "Students" and "Parents" into the bottom level of the pyramid...

"In addition, you're now also playing for the faculty of this school, our fans, the alumni and the people of the state of Maryland whose taxes built this university and help keep it running and looking beautiful," he now writes all of these words into the second row of the pyramid...

"And just in case you weren't paying attention a minute ago, as you can already see from this board, it's no longer just about *you*. But make no mistake, you're also playing for yourselves. So take pride in everything you do, both on and off the court. Everyone in this room is a highly visible representative of the Revolutionaries. That means twenty four hours a day, seven days a week, from now until the day you leave this campus. Please respect this responsibility and take it seriously," Coach McCallom holds the black marker extremely tight in his right hand as he writes the word "You" into the top layer of the pyramid...

"I began this speech with this same statement, but I want to say it out loud one more time, because I feel it's *that* important. You're now most importantly playing for *me*. For *my* reputation. For what *I've* built. And what *I've* built is not a democracy. I repeat *it's not* a democracy. I make all the decisions when it comes to this team. That's right, the Revolutionaries men's basketball program is a theocracy and I am the Philosopher King!" holding the marker in a stranglehold, Coach McCallom first points and then repeatedly underlines the words "PHILOSOPHER KING!" at the top of the pyramid.

Turning back around, he now stares into the players' eyes as the vein in his forehead flexes and bulges with each heartbeat, "All preseason long I've heard the rumors about what you think I should be doing with this year's team," he angrily states. "About who you think I should start and what kind of offense we should be running and what I consider to be other rather inconsequential and amusing side conversations. Let me say this: You can discuss anything you want with each other ad nauseam. You can also discuss it with your friends, your family, your girlfriends and even the assistant coaches. But know this, if you're coming to talk to me about something, it *better* be serious. My door is always open, but open doesn't mean open for *anything*. My time is valuable and my decisions are final. And if you think I'm being unfair, well...*too bad*. So if you're coming to me to complain about your lack of playing time, or gripe about another player on this team, or something else I might consider to be trivial, I'm telling you right now that's not why my office door is open. Basketball is a tough sport. It's not for the weak. If you think you're not cut out for this, the door is right over there. Feel free to leave."

All the players instinctively look around the room to see if anyone is going to make a move for the door. No one does.

"But just so there is no confusion, if you have a family matter, or school matter that you need to talk to me about, please come find me. I want to know about it. I *need* to know about it. It's my job. You're my team and besides turning you into great basketball players, my job is to help turn you into great men. This way when you leave this campus, you'll make a positive impression on the world. But make no mistake about it, life is a battle and that battle *starts* here today."

After waiting a few seconds to let everything sink in, Coach McCallom now calms his voice, "Once this meeting is over, I don't want anyone in this room touching a basketball between now and Saturday night's midnight practice. If you want to lift weights, or run on the track, you can, but please go easy. We don't need anyone getting hurt before the start of practice. And while I'm mentioning school work last, it's definitely not the least important. With mid-terms starting tomorrow, I want everyone to study hard and do your best. We can't afford to lose anyone to academics this year. If you need to schedule some time with the team's tutors, all you have to do is see Coach Foote and he will take care of it from there. To finish up, welcome again to a new season of Maryland State University men's basketball. We're happy to have you. Any questions?"

None of the players raise their hands.

"Sean, will you please come up here now and go over this year's *Bag Crew* duties with our freshman class," Coach McCallom waves Coach Banks over to the podium. "We'll fill out all the paperwork from the athletic department after Coach Banks speaks," Coach McCallom addresses the team one last time, before stepping away.

Bounding up to the podium wearing his usual broad smile, Coach Banks first thanks Coach McCallom for his inspiring words and then asks James, Daquan, Taylor and Emmet to raise their hands. "Everyone, please turn and look at the four freshmen with their hands in the air," Coach Banks begins. "These players are this year's *Bag Crew*. Take a close look at each one of them and if you haven't done so already, please get to know them. Just like each freshmen class before them, this new group will be responsible for 1) Filling up the water buckets in the equipment room before practice starts, carrying the water buckets up to the practice floor and then back down again after practice is over, 2) Carrying the trainers' kits up to the practice floor and then back down again after practice is over and 3) Taking the team's extra equipment bags when we travel for away games, making sure these bags get on the bus, plane or whatever mode of transportation we use. Upperclassmen, during these away games, if you see anyone on the *Bag Crew* without an extra bag in his hands, feel free to give them your own bag to carry. You've earned the right to not carry your own bag. But don't overdo it. Use your judgment and don't get caught abusing this privilege. Walk-ons, if any of you make the team this year, you'll be added to the *Bag Crew* once you're officially on the roster. After this meeting is over, *Bag Crew* members please stay seated so I can hand each one of you a schedule of assigned responsibilities."

Sitting in his chair in the back of the room, Taylor's heart once again sticks squarely in his throat when he hears everything Coach Banks just said. Upset and angry at not being told he'd have to perform these extra chores when he was being recruited, he can't help but shudder at what else they didn't tell him.

CHAPTER 43

By the time Taylor wakes up the next morning, mid-terms are in full swing across Maryland State University's campus. With a feeling of muted anxiety coursing through the entire student body, everyone tries to manage the pressure they feel to deliver on what they should have learned during the first half of the semester. Since he's diligently kept up on all of his school work, Taylor feels nothing but confidence heading into mid-terms, although he still plans on studying hard—since he can't leave anything to chance.

With his biology mid-term scheduled for first thing Wednesday morning, Taylor sits alone in the basement of the library late on Tuesday night, staring at the same open page in his textbook for what feels like an eternity. When he finally snaps back to reality, he decides to take a break and clear his head. Throwing his biology textbook into his backpack, he turns off the small lamp secured to his work station and heads outside into the cool night air.

The clock on his cell phone reads 11:08 p.m.—way too late to his call his mom—so he scrolls down to "JW" in his contact list and hits the green call button. While he and Jimmy have texted a lot lately, they haven't spoken in a few weeks.

On the other end of the call, Jimmy's pocket rings loudly with the special ring dedicated to Taylor, "Hey, man!" he shouts into the phone, grabbing it after the second ring.

"Hey!" Taylor responds with excitement, the sound of Jimmy's voice immediately putting him at ease.

"What's going on?"

"Nada," Taylor answers. "Just studying for mid-terms, you?"

"Nada, myself. Just got back from closing down the weight room."

"That's cool. What about your guys' midterms?"

"Our exams don't start until next week."

"Lucky for you, man. This studying is a beast. So what's the word?"

"Can't complain," Jimmy answers, while making sure to downplay the tone of his voice. Everything in his life seemed to finally be falling into place—he couldn't imagine being anywhere else right now. Besides working part-time at the weight room to make some extra money, Castleman College's small class sizes were helping him adjust to the academic demands of higher education, he was just voted president of his fraternity's pledge class and the girls, well, there seemed to be no shortage of cute ones who wanted to get to know him, "So, what's the word at Maryland State?" he finally asks Taylor.

"Nothing too much. I just needed a little break from the books. Oh, yeah, practice starts on Saturday night. Besides that, same old, same old." He wants to tell Jimmy about Coach McCallom's "Philosopher King" speech, but for some reason he doesn't think he can do it justice.

"That's cool. When you're done on Saturday night, make sure you let me know how it went. Doesn't matter how late it is. Hit me up, okay?"

"Yeah, man. No worries. You'll be the first to know."

"Cool...Very cool...Hey, I haven't asked you in a while, what's up with that crazy roommate of yours?"

"Emmet. He's all right, I guess. We've got completely different schedules, so we really don't see each other all that much. Besides when we're sleeping, I can't even tell you the last time we were in the room together. He also leaves to go visit his girlfriend every chance he gets."

"That's good for you. I mean, that guy seems like a total joker."

"For real."

"Hey, speaking of jokers, did you see Smitty's recent social media posts?"

"Yeah, man," Taylor answers with a laugh. "What's wrong with that kid?"

"No idea," Jimmy responds with his own laugh. "But I can't believe he keeps posting all those ridiculous photos of himself partying like that. I don't think he ever wants a job someday."

"Totally. But you have to remember, Smitty has always been a little loose in the head."

"I almost forgot...High school sometimes feels like it was a lifetime ago."

Over the next fifteen minutes, with the phone pushed hard up to his ear, Taylor begins to learn how well Jimmy has settled into his new life and for some reason, he's both happy and sad Jimmy is doing so well without him. He also wishes he could say the same thing back, but knows he can't. Even though he hand-picked Maryland State University from all the other schools that came calling after him and Jimmy had to choose Castleman College for financial reasons, Jimmy's transition seems to be going flawlessly, while he can't shake the feeling that he keeps stumbling every step along the way.

CHAPTER 44

At 12:01 a.m. on Saturday night, October 15th, Taylor and the rest of Maryland State University men's basketball team enter the sold-out Liberty Arena for the team's annual midnight practice. While all the players are dressed in full gear for this first official practice, tonight is much more of a staged show for the team's faithful fans than anything else. With painted faces and man-made Revolutionaries costumes dominating the stands, students sing and chant right alongside season ticket holders, during a night of dreaming big for the Revolutionaries basketball season just around the corner.

With the Maryland State University student band blasting the school's fight song from the stands just beyond the main basket, the players go through lay-up lines, only a few feet away, smiling and joking around with each other. Unlike a real game, where dunking during warm-ups is illegal and three-point shots are looked down upon by the coaches, *tonight is different.* In order to give the fans their money's worth, the coaches have given the players free rein to dunk as often as they want and shoot three pointers from as far away from the basket as their bodies will let them.

When the team's energized lay-up lines come to an end ten minutes later, the players move to the sideline and watch along with the crowd as the arena grows dark and a high-end light show any professional team would be proud of fills the arena. At the end of this light show, the four-sided LED screen hanging above center court roars to life as a highlight video from last season is projected into the crowd. The last frame of this video leads right into the P.A. announcer introducing Coach McCallom, who's now standing alone at center court underneath several bright spotlights.

Opening up his speech, Coach McCallom first thanks the crowd for coming out tonight and also for welcoming the team back with such energy and enthusiasm. *The crowd erupts into a deafening cheer when they hear this.* Coach McCallom then calls for Andray and Corey to join him at center court, where he tells the crowd how much he appreciates the dedication of the two young men standing beside him and how much they mean to the Revolutionaries men's basketball program. With this last sentiment complete, he announces Andray and Corey have officially been selected as this year's team captains. When the crowd's applause finally dies down, Coach McCallom hands the microphone to Andray and steps to the side to give him the floor.

With the microphone resting loosely in his hand, Andray states in his clearest voice possible that he speaks for everyone when he says the team wouldn't be nearly as successful as they are without the support they get each time they step onto the court for a home game. That it's them—the crowd—and not the players that make the Liberty Arena one of the toughest places to play in all of college basketball. *Upon hearing this, the crowd erupts into its loudest cheer of the night.*

As Taylor listens to the rest of Andray's speech from the sideline, he's awed by his public speaking abilities and overall poise, especially since he comes across as so coarse and demonstrative when he's in private. Throughout this speech, Corey stands over Andray's shoulder, pumping his fist at all the right times, but never taking the microphone himself. While Andray and Corey are co-captains in name, it's once again obvious this year's team belongs solely to Andray.

The night's much-anticipated slam dunk contest takes place about halfway through the midnight practice. Flying through the air to slam the ball through the rim with style and strength, Taylor generates some extraordinarily loud *oooohh*'s and *aaaahh*'s from the crowd—eventually finishing third in this spectacle behind Maurice Barnes and Corey—a finish which doesn't disappoint.

In general, tonight's practice includes a lot of standing around and waiting for something to happen, which reminds Taylor of most of his high school practices; and makes him think he might have allowed his overactive imagination to once again get the best of him—that maybe college practices aren't going to be that hard after all.

Standing in the players' tunnel, next to a duffle bag filled with extra equipment, Frank sees Taylor smiling a great deal throughout the night and as if he can read his mind, he hopes his young friend doesn't think all of Coach McCallom's practices are run like this.

After showering and changing back into his street clothes, Taylor walks with Emmet to their dorm room at 2:30 a.m., simultaneously excited and relieved his first college practice is over.

Even though it's extremely late, he texts both Jimmy and his mom to let them know how everything went. The text to each of them is the same, "Midnight practice = Amazing! Can't wait 4practice 2morrow - T."

CHAPTER 45

The alarm on Taylor's cell phone rings loudly at 9:00 a.m. the next morning—arriving way too quickly in his opinion. While today's practice doesn't start until 12 noon, he set his alarm early to make sure he has plenty of time to get out of bed, eat a full breakfast and still get to the gym with enough time to warm up properly. After shaking out the kinks from his sleep, he walks across the room to wake Emmet; Emmet responds by pulling the blanket over his head and turning to the wall with a low grunt. Instead of fighting the situation, Taylor decides to leave Emmet alone to his dreams, heading out of their dorm room a half hour later, practically skipping with excitement down to the dining room and then over to the Liberty Arena.

When he enters the men's basketball team locker room a little before 11:00 a.m., he immediately changes out of his street clothes and back into his practice gear. While it seems he can still feel the positive energy from last night's practice dancing on his skin, when he ties up his brand new red, white and blue high tops, *it suddenly feels like he never left.*

A few minutes later, after getting both ankles taped in the training room, he takes the stairs at the end of the hallway, one floor down, and reports to the equipment room where he casually asks Frank if he needs to fulfill his *Bag Crew* water duties. Fully expecting Frank to laugh and tell him it was all one big joke, Frank instead uses his thumb to point to two large empty white buckets in the back, next to the commercial-sized ice machine and sink. As a wave of anger washes over Taylor—*he can't believe he's being subjected to this menial labor*—he nonetheless does as he's told, heading in the direction of the empty buckets sitting on the concrete floor.

With both buckets filled to the rim, Taylor heaves them onto the flatbed dolly next to the ice machine. It takes all of his strength, but he somehow manages to push the dolly over to the elevator and hit the up button to the Liberty Arena floor. When the elevator doors open, he's shocked to find he's not one of the first players to arrive. While it's only 11:35 a.m., it seems almost all of the players, including the walk-ons, are already in the gym. He didn't see most of these players in the locker room, so he can only assume they arrived when he was in the training room or when he was filling up the water buckets. As he looks even closer, he sees both Andray and Damon are already sweating heavily, which means they've been on the floor a lot longer than the rest of the players.

Once the water buckets are safely positioned on top of the small folding table near the players' tunnel, Taylor walks over to one of the metal ball racks and grabs a basketball to his liking. Dribbling casually, he takes in the rest of the scene as he heads to an empty side basket to get loose by himself—the same way he's done his whole life. After all, basketball is still just basketball.

At exactly 12:00 noon, Coach McCallom blows his whistle and instructs the players to put all of the basketballs back onto the racks and come together at center court to stretch. With Andray and Corey positioned in front of the rest of the players, Coach McCallom reminds his two captains they have precisely twelve minutes to get the team stretched out and ready to go, *and not a minute more.* He also tells everyone to concentrate on getting very loose today since the next few hours are going to be a far cry from last night's midnight practice. Taylor's heart momentarily skips a beat when he hears this and he can't help but notice none of the assistant coaches are smiling.

When Coach McCallom blows his whistle again at 12:12 p.m., he tells the players to line up along the baseline *so they can warm-up for real.* Not sure what to do, Taylor moves to the back of the line, near the walk-ons, and watches the upperclassmen closely for direction. At the sound of Coach McCallom's whistle, Andray—who has taken his place at the front of the line—starts sliding in a defensive stance diagonally from the baseline to the sideline. When Andray reaches the far sideline, he alternates his feet and repeats this diagonal slide. Followed closely by Damon and Corey, Andray completes two more diagonal slides before finishing up on the far baseline.

As the players in front of Taylor push themselves through this drill, Coach McCallom stands at center court, watching like a hawk and screaming for everyone to "Stay down low!"..."Get your ass to the ground!"..."Don't cross your feet!" Every once in a while, he also sees a player who he thinks is cheating the drill and yells at him using words Taylor would have a hard time repeating to his mom.

After the team completes one more of these diagonal slide drills, finishing up on the same baseline where they first started, Andray immediately leads everyone through a similar drill, but this time, instead of sliding diagonally across the court, the players now slide around it. At the end of this second drill, the players move back to the baseline and are told to pair up in twos. As each pair of players now shuffles up and down the court, they pass a basketball back and forth to each other—first chest passes, then bounce passes and finally, one-handed passes. By the time this last drill is finished, Taylor's lungs, thighs and calves are all burning with a fiery intensity, *yet* it's only 12:30 p.m.

With only twenty hours of practice time allowed each week during the season or a little over three hours per day, based on a six-day practice schedule, there's little doubt in anyone's mind after the first few minutes of today's practice that Coach McCallom plans on using every single second he's been allotted.

Over the next hour, Taylor moves around the gym in tightly timed increments, visiting different stations that have been set up to help improve each player's skills. With Coach McCallom or one of the assistant coaches running each station, Taylor works either by himself or as part of a small group on his foot work, the release of his jump shot, dribbling, passing, how to get free on the wing against a defender, where to set up in the post when he's on offense, how to call for the ball in the post and finally, what's the best way to box-out and rebound. The only thing the coaches don't try to teach him is how to tie his sneakers, although he suspects that's probably coming next.

As Taylor moves from station to station throughout this first hour, he shakes his head at the sheer intensity and hands-on approach of the coaches. In high school, Coach Waters primarily left him alone to do what he wanted, with a little bit of instruction and encouragement here and there, but that was it. Never has he experienced this type of in-your-face coaching and overall scrutiny.

The last hour and a half of practice brings more of the same, only now the players work five-on-five, with the starters in white and the reserves in blue. *Taylor wears blue.* As the players run through drill after drill, Taylor is made highly aware there are no easy minutes during a college basketball practice, which immediately makes his mind hurt at the thought of the next years of his life unfolding in the exact same way.

"Let's go!" Coach McCallom screams in Taylor's face during one of the team's five-on-five drills. "This isn't high school any more and I'm not Coach Waters! I'm not going to sit idly by while you pick and choose when you want to play hard!" Taylor's bones ache as he shoots Coach McCallom hate-filled daggers with his eyes. "I'm your Coach now! These are your teammates! When I tell you to do something, you do it! End of story! And no looks of incrimination! I know what I'm doing! I'll coach, you play! Got it?"

"Yes, Coach," Taylor softly responds, while still looking at Coach McCallom with hate-filled eyes.

"Good. Now get back into your defensive stance, but position your feet wider apart this time. Loosen up your knees and relax your lower body. I know it might feel weird, but it will give you better balance."

The only thing that keeps Taylor sane during this three hour practice is Coach McCallom seems to be an equal-opportunity yeller. No one appears to be safe. Not even the captains.

Before the team shoots its free throws to mercifully end practice, Coach McCallom tells the players to hustle up and grab two bricks wrapped in gym socks from the plastic crates near the water buckets and line up on the baseline. As Taylor grabs his two bricks, he catches Coach Banks' eyes from across the gym, *Told you!* they scream back at him. Based on the size and weight of the bricks, Taylor guesses these are the same red bricks used to lay the foundation of the beautiful campus he finds himself on each day.

After telling the players they shouldn't under any circumstances drop these bricks, because if they do, besides getting a bill from the university for the hole in the court, the punishment for the whole team is something *no one* wants to find out about, Coach McCallom blows his whistle again. On his whistle, the players start running suicide sprints with the bricks in their hands from the baseline to the baseline, touching the foul lines and the half court line with their feet in between. While the players run their hardest, the coaches stand on the sideline yelling at the players to pump their arms and use the bricks for momentum—believing this will help build up the players' forearm strength and increase their free throw accuracy during games, especially when they're tired. *None of the players buy into this belief.*

In between the second and third suicide sprint, Taylor begins to wonder for the first time what Coach Horner is doing right now with his Central New York University team at practice today.

CHAPTER 46

The next several days fly by in neatly scheduled blocks of time—practice, classes, schoolwork, eating and sleeping. Sleeping for Taylor comes in either "dead to the world" stretches that make seven hours feel like five minutes or the complete opposite, unending hours spent staring at the ceiling unable to sleep because he can't get that day's practice out of his head. On these restless nights, it feels as if he can remember exactly how the coaches look as they yell seemingly endless instructions at him or the expression of intense determination on each player's face as they push, grab and fight him for every inch on the court.

After another long practice, Taylor walks back to his dorm room feeling exhausted and frustrated. Even though there is a slight chill in the night air, he stops on the outer edge of one the campus' well-manicured quads and takes out his cell phone. With his emotions running high, he scrolls through his contact list and finds Jimmy's number again; but this time, the call goes straight to voicemail. Rather than leave a long-winded message, he hangs up and texts Jimmy to call him back as soon as he can.

While he desperately wants to call his mom next, he knows he can't. There is just no way as a single mom she can understand what he's going through right now. She never played a competitive sport in her life, let alone one in arguably college basketball's most competitive conference. So against his better judgment, he scrolls back through his contact list and finds his dad's cell phone number.

After hitting the green call button, he listens to four empty rings, before hanging up without leaving a message. Thinking long and hard about what he should do next, he finally decides to go ahead with something he's hated to do for as long as he can remember—he calls his dad's house number. This time the call gets picked up on the third ring.

"Hello," Bill's voice answers on the other end.

"Dad."

"Taylor?...Is that you?"

"Yeah, it's me."

"I can hardly hear you. Is everything okay?"

"Yeah, everything is..."

"Bill, who is it?" Cindy's voice squawks in the background.

"It's Taylor, Hon! I got it!" Bill shouts back.

Cindy jumps on the phone anyway, "Bill, who's on the phone?"

"It's Taylor, Hon. I have it."

"Oh...Hi, Taylor," Cindy states with total indifference.

"Hi, Cindy," Taylor responds as politely as his voice will let him.

"Bill, please don't be too long. I need your help getting the kids to bed real soon," their conversation hadn't even started, yet Cindy was already putting a time limit on it.

"Fine, dear. I'll be up as soon as I'm done. Can I please talk to my son now?"

"Absolutely...Have a nice conversation," Cindy replies and then hangs up without saying goodbye to Taylor.

"Sorry about that," Bill apologizes.

"It's fine, Dad. It is what it is."

"Well, it's good to hear your voice. What's going on?"

"Not much," Taylor responds, still speaking softly into the phone.

"What's wrong?" Bill asks.

"Nothing."

"Come on, Taylor. I can hear it in your voice. What's wrong?"

"It's just...I...I just finished the fifth day of practice."

"I know. How's it going so far?"

"It's going...Well, it's going *hard*. Really *hard*," Taylor responds.

"I'm not sure what to tell you," Bill answers. "Except, I think it's supposed to be hard. It's big-time college basketball."

"I know. It's just...It's so intense, *all* the time. Everyone is at each other's throats. They also make me carry the water up to practice and pick up after the upperclassmen. Didn't I work as hard as I did in high school so I wouldn't have to do all of that?"

"Please take a breath and relax for a second. All of that is just part of being a freshman. You'll adjust soon enough."

Taylor doesn't hear a word his dad just said and continues to ramble, "And the coaches are always yelling at me and telling me what I'm doing wrong. I thought they wanted me to come here and play basketball. All they seem to want to do is yell at me."

On the other end of the phone, Bill tries not to smile. While he feels bad for his son, he knows the coaches are forcing him to work hard to accomplish things that up until now have always come so easy to him, "College basketball is a tough game," Bill tells Taylor. "I'm sure every single guy on your team was told by the same coaches that recruited you, how great they were also coming out of high school. Everyone wants to play. No one wants to sit."

"Maybe," Taylor answers. "But I just feel right now like *no one* wants me here. I feel so stupid, you know."

"That's ridiculous. You have nothing to feel stupid about. Coaches say what they have to in order to get players to commit to their schools. You're going to do great there. Just give it some time. It's only been five days."

"Honestly, I'm not sure if I'm cut out for this," Taylor finally says out loud.

"What do you mean?"

"I mean, I think I might want to quit."

Shocked at what Taylor just said, Bill almost drops the phone in disbelief.

"And on top of everything else," Taylor continues to ramble. "The upperclassmen push me around and make me feel *worthless*. I feel like I can't do anything right. Basketball used to be fun. It's not fun anymore."

"Maybe basketball isn't supposed to be fun right now," Bill does his best to calm Taylor down. "Maybe you just have to get through these first few weeks of practice so you can get to the fun stuff, the games."

"I guess."

"And don't let any of those other players push you around like that," Bill now talks loudly into the phone. "Fight back if they do that to you! Don't be afraid to get into someone's face if you have to!"

"You think?" Taylor asks. "Aren't we supposed to be teammates?"

"It doesn't sound like they're treating you like a teammate right now. College basketball is a man's game and there are certain things only a man understands."

"BIIILLLLL!!!" Cindy's voice squawks again in the background. "I need your help with Jack! He's acting up and I told him you're coming upstairs right now to talk to him!"

"You know what, Dad. Forget it. You're busy. It's no big deal, really."

"I'm not busy," Bill responds. "Cindy can handle Jack by herself. She'll be fine."

"BIIILLLLL!!!" Cindy squawks again. "Did you hear me?"

"Hold on!" Bill yells back with irritation. "I'm still on the phone with Taylor!"

"Dad, go help Cindy. It's fine. I'll figure it out on my own. Whatever Cindy needs seems to be more important than what I've got going on."

"How can you say that? You just told me you don't think you're cut out for college basketball and you're thinking of quitting the team after only five days of practice. College basketball has been your dream for as long as I can remember. Come on, Taylor. Even I don't believe what you just said."

"It's fine, Dad. Really. Do what you have to do. Go help Cindy."

"BIIILLLLL!!!" Cindy squawks again. "I need your help! Now!"

"I gotta go, Dad. Sorry I called."

"No!...Wait!" Bill shouts into the phone, just as the line goes dead.

Looking out into the dark quad in front of him, Taylor leans back and throws his cell phone in frustration as far as he can. The cell phone lands in the distance, ricocheting off something hard.

Minutes later, still visibly upset and shaken, Taylor crawls on his hands and knees to find his cell phone buried at the root of an elm tree and luckily not in someone's head. The phone is scratched and nicked from its aerial journey, but still in good working condition.

CHAPTER 47

The next day at practice, Taylor once again finds himself in the middle of a grueling and intense three hours of basketball. With the starters facing off against the reserves in a drill of offense versus defense—running through all of the sets they've been working on since the day after midnight practice—Coach McCallom stands a few feet above the three-point line looking angrier than usual as he watches what looks to him to be a group of lethargic and uninterested players going through the motions.

For the first time Taylor can remember, Andray seems to be struggling during this drill in his match-up against Damon. After calling out play #1, Andray passes the ball to his left and cuts down the center of the lane, before popping out to the wing to receive a return pass, a step above the three-point line. Instead of dumping the ball into the low post like he's supposed to, Andray tries to take Damon off the dribble by going baseline. Attacking the rim with two incredibly quick power dribbles, Andray explodes off the floor to shoot the ball, only to see Damon recover and cut him off. Damon's alert defense forces Andray to turn his body awkwardly in the air and blindly pass the ball into the middle of the lane, where it's easily stolen by James.

The second James steals the ball, Coach McCallom blows his whistle in utter disgust, unleashing his pent-up rage on Andray, "God damn it, Andray! You called play number one! Why are you going baseline?" Filled with self-hatred for letting his frustration get the best of him, Andray wants to explain his thinking, but knows there's no right answer. "I need you to run the plays exactly as I draw them up!" Coach McCallom keeps yelling at Andray. "Baseline? Come on! You think you're going to play in the pros someday? You keep playing like that you better forget it and start learning Mandarin, because China is the only place you'll be playing in the future! Let's go! Be a leader on this team and start making better decisions!"

When the guards and big men split up thirty minutes later to work on individual skills in smaller groups, Taylor is told to go with the guards so he can practice his one-on-one half court moves. Working at the basket at the far end of the court, Coach Banks goes over the rules of the drill, telling the players what he wants to see from them on offense and defense, reminding the players on offense they only get one dribble to get their shot off, just like in a real game.

The instant Coach Banks finishes his instructions, Taylor steps to the front of the line on offense, where he's picked up on defense by Troy Hopkins. When Andray sees Taylor standing at the front of the line, his frustration from earlier boils over into an intense rage—*just from looking at Taylor*. Tapping Troy on the shoulder, Andray dismisses Troy to the passing line and steps right up into Taylor's chest, staring at him with a scary glint in his eye.

When Coach Banks sees Andray voluntarily pick Taylor up on defense, a big toothy smile once again spreads across his face. Taking a few steps forward—so now only the two players can hear him—Coach Banks' hot breath lands squarely on the back of Taylor's neck as he growls, "You think you're so good, don't you? But let's see what you can do against a real defender. Andray is no high school kid from the 'burbs. That I can guarantee you," he practically laughs at Taylor. "You're lucky if you can even get open."

Turning to Andray, Coach Banks now commands him, "Don't let him get the damn ball! And if he does, you better not let him score!"

As soon as Taylor hears Coach Banks' whistle, he takes a step in Andray's direction, pushing off to try and get open. Andray counters this move by grabbing Taylor around the waist, locking him down with his hands. Unable to break free from Andray's defensive foul, Taylor looks for Coach Banks to blow his whistle—but Coach Banks simply ignores him and allows Andray to hold, bump and foul him as much as he wants.

This sudden defensive pressure from Andray feels almost surreal to Taylor. He's never experienced anything like this before—not from all the city schools he faced in high school or even during his summer All-Star basketball tournaments—at the same time, he can hear his dad's voice inside his head, telling him to, *"Fight back! Get right into someone's face if they try and push you around!"*

Managing to get free from Andray's grip by spinning his body so his backside is up against Andray's chest, Taylor extends his long arms and receives the pass from Troy Hopkins. Immediately, he turns and squares-up on Andray, noticing that if he attacks Andray's top foot, he can go baseline. Before he can even react to this opening, Andray jumps back in front of him and slaps at his wrists, trying to knock the ball out of his hands. With the sound of his skin being repeatedly slapped echoing across the court, Taylor once again looks for Coach Banks to call a defensive foul, but just like before, Coach Banks doesn't even bother to raise his whistle to his lips.

Not sure what to do next and with panic setting in, Taylor makes the fateful decision to listen to his dad's advice and send Andray a message. Lowering his shoulders, he violently swings his elbows across Andray's face, landing his left elbow squarely into Andray's jaw with a loud crack. Momentarily caught off guard, Andray takes a half of a step backward, before pursing his lips with blistering hatred and stepping right back up into Taylor's chest.

In less than a split second, Coach Banks jumps forward and grabs Taylor by the wrist, yanking him forcefully away from Andray, "What the hell is wrong with you?" he shouts into Taylor's face. "Are you trying to get yourself killed?" Taylor stares back at him without saying a word. "You're lucky I'm here and you and Andray aren't playing in some schoolyard right now, because if you were, your ass would be in a sling! We don't tolerate that kind of cheap crap around here!"

After taking a minute to let the situation cool off, Coach Banks sends Taylor to the back of the offensive line, as far away from Andray as he can get him.

As Taylor stands patiently at the end of this line, all he can think about is how he shouldn't have once again listened to his dad.

Moments later, when Taylor reaches the front of the line on offense, he's picked up on defense by Chase Johnson. But just like when the drill first started, Andray walks up behind Chase and taps him on the shoulder so he can play defense on Taylor. While Coach Banks knows he probably should put a stop to this, he decides to let Andray do what he wants; this way he can see how the young freshman reacts to what Andray is about to do.

With the glazed look of a murderer, Andray gets right back up into Taylor's face as the rest of the guards working the drill stare in anticipation at what might happen next. It seems to Taylor as if Andray's skin is *literally* burning with raw intensity as he whispers under his breath, "You throw your elbow at me like that again and I will break you in two! You hear me freshman? I will destroy you!"

Taylor pretends not to hear as he stares over Andray's shoulder, waiting for Coach Banks to blow his whistle again to start the drill.

"I know you can hear me!" Andray snarls. "Don't pretend like you can't! Why don't you just quit? You don't got what it takes to play ball here! You're too soft!"

Taylor keeps ignoring Andray's taunts as he waits for Coach Banks' whistle—which seems never to be coming.

"Let's go, baby!" Andray claps his hands inches from the front of Taylor's nose and then jumps down into his defensive stance. "Let's see what you're made of," Andray cackles, his unmistakable high-pitched laugh touching a spot of discomfort in Taylor's gut he didn't even know he had.

Standing three feet away, watching the situation unfold, Coach Banks talks loud enough again so only Taylor and Andray can hear him, "Freshmen, you're all so weak...What are we going to do with you?"

CHAPTER 48

Life continues to unfold for Taylor over the next few weeks in the same pattern—practice, classes, schoolwork, eating and sleeping—but instead of each three hour practice getting easier, each one only seems to get harder and more intense, leaving him feeling like a hollowed-out version of himself. To counter this body-numbing fatigue and to make sure he doesn't fall behind on his schoolwork, he becomes a master at organizing his time away from the basketball court, carving out a few minutes each day to nap, hang out and for his favorite past time of all: daydreaming.

During these daydreams, he often lets his mind wander back to that first day of classes when he watched his favorite game show in the student union. He thinks about how happy and content he was that day without all the prying eyes that have followed him around since eighth grade keeping track of his every move; yet he wants to yell at that version of himself, to tell him, *"Stay in that room! Each day is only going to get more difficult! And don't trust the upperclassmen! They aren't going to let you into their inner circle anyway!"*

Even though it doesn't make him feel any better, James, Daquan and Emmet are also struggling to adjust to the speed and intensity of the college game. But the thing that has really turned Taylor's world upside down is the mental strain of constantly being belittled by the coaches and ignored by the upperclassmen. For eighteen years, everyone he knew—and a lot of people he didn't—went out of their way to build him up and make him feel like he couldn't do anything wrong. But now it seems everyone is going just as far out of their way to tear him down. Never before has he felt so unsure of himself and out-of-sorts. He also doesn't understand how carrying buckets of water, or lugging the trainers' kits, or hauling a bunch of extra equipment bags like a bell-hop is going to turn him into a better college basketball player.

Amidst the pain and difficulty of adjusting to this new life, the magic of Maryland State University's campus continues to empower him. Each time he walks across its beautifully landscaped grounds, his chest swells with pride, feeling lucky to be part of such a special place filled with smart, sophisticated and driven people pursuing their dreams.

Inspired by his own dreams—along with his unquenchable desire to succeed and prove people wrong—he decides during this time, from a place deep within him, a place he didn't even know he had, that he's *never* going to let the coaches and the upperclassmen break him down for good. Try as they might, they're not going to take away his sense of self. Not now. Not ever.

CHAPTER 49

To get ready for the season, the Maryland State University Revolutionaries have scheduled one intra-squad scrimmage and two preseason games against outside competition. The team's intra-squad scrimmage is an annual event that pits the white team starters versus the blue team reserves, and is treated as an official game by the coaches in every way. Held inside the Liberty Arena, this game includes warm-ups, the announcement of team starters, three game referees, piped-in crowd noise, timed halves and score kept on the oversized LED screen hanging above center court; the only things missing to make it a real game are the fans, the ticket ushers, the student band and the cheerleaders. Of the previous twenty-four years Coach McCallom has been the Revolutionaries' head coach, the white team starters have won twenty-three of these intra-squad scrimmages.

After a slow and sluggish start, fueled mostly by overconfidence, the white team starters eventually assert their dominance over the blue team reserves late in the first half of this year's game, winning handily by a score of 85-63. While Damon did what he could to try and lead the *Bag Crew* and the rest of the blue team reserves to victory, the blue team's inexperience simply couldn't match the white team's strength and court savvy.

The Revolutionaries' two other preseason games are both at home and both purposefully scheduled against much weaker opponents. The team's first test from the outside comes against a group of former college players who aren't ready to give the game up yet and enter the real world, so they travel around the country in the preseason playing as many exhibition games as they can in exchange for a small appearance fee, food and lodging. While this team of ex-collegians is full of talent, they no longer play with the same sense of urgency they once did and their lack of hunger is obvious. Because of this, Taylor and the rest of the *Bag Crew* play for long stretches of time during this victory.

The Revolutionaries' second and final preseason game is against a small historically black college from the area. Even though all of this team's players are on full scholarship, the school doesn't have much of a winning basketball tradition and the talent on its roster reflects this. As a result, the Revolutionaries easily beat this team going away—but unlike the first preseason game, Taylor doesn't play very much, a development which dredges up his deep-seated fears that once the games start counting for real, he's going to be doing a lot more watching than playing.

While Taylor tries not to read into the little amount of court time he received during this second preseason game, *he can't help it.* He desperately feels the need to find Coach McCallom and ask him about it, but remembering his "Philosopher King" speech all too clearly, he instead seeks out Coach Davis, who tells him, "Not to worry. It's a long season and you'll have more than your fair share of opportunities to prove yourself." Still not one hundred percent convinced this is true, he decides to ask Coach Foote and Coach Dougard this same question—just to make sure Coach Davis isn't just telling him what he wants to hear. But after thinking everything through, he changes his mind and decides this isn't a good idea, as he can't let all of the coaches see his inner fears at the same time.

The first game of the new season for the Maryland State University Revolutionaries is at home against the Semaphore University Jackrabbits. While the Jackrabbits have made a few appearances in college basketball's post-season tournament over the years, like many mid-major programs, its teams are up and down from season to season. With not a lot expected from the Jackrabbits this season, the Revolutionaries are favored to run away from them in no time for their first victory of the year.

With a little over an hour before tip-off, Taylor sits in front of his locker listening to his music as an almost indescribable feeling of exhilaration flows through his body. Knowing that his lifelong dream is about to become a reality, his heart pounds rapidly inside his chest, making his breath choppy and difficult to catch. Doing what he can to remain as still as possible and not let his emotions completely overtake him, he inhales long deep breaths, holding the air inside his lungs for as long as he can, before letting each breath out slowly through his nose.

After gaining complete control of his bodily functions, Taylor gradually rises from the red, white and blue chair in front of his locker and deliberately starts putting on his uniform—piece by piece—just like he imagined it a thousand times before in his head. With the unrestrained adrenaline and excitement of young men in the prime of their lives engulfing the locker room around him, Taylor watches as the rest of his teammates get ready for tonight's game—some stretch out on the floor, others dance to the music being pumped out of the locker room's loud speakers, a few scurry to the bathroom to throw up their anxiety and one or two even relax on the leather chairs in front of the team's 60" flat screen TV. As usual, Taylor watches this big moment of transition in his life unfold from a safe distance, allowing the enormity of it all to wash over him in quiet solitude.

After leaving the locker room to get his ankles taped in the training room, Taylor returns to find a quiet spot to stretch out alone on the blue carpet and keep listening to his music. A few minutes later, with the clock above the door reading 6:57 p.m.—a little over thirty minutes before tip-off—he sees Coach McCallom and the assistant coaches enter the locker room and make their way over to the old black chalkboard.

Unlike Coach Waters in high school, Coach McCallom is *all* business when he enters the team's locker room. He doesn't smile, he doesn't find players to offer words of encouragement and he doesn't pat anyone on the back. He simply clears his throat and asks everyone to stop what they're doing and gather around him. With even less fanfare, he picks up a piece of white chalk and writes down the names of the starting five for tonight's game. There are no surprises. The starters are the same players that took the floor for the white team during the intra-squad scrimmage: Andray Jenkins-PG, Chase Johnson-G, Maurice Barnes-SF, Corey Lawrence-PF, Tim Daulton-C.

After writing down Tim Daulton's name, Coach McCallom tells each of the starters which Semaphore University starter they'll be covering on defense. As he goes over these match-ups, he reviews the strengths and weaknesses of each Jackrabbits starter, writing these down in shorthand on the right half of the chalkboard. These are the same strengths and weaknesses that were covered during yesterday's film session.

After placing what is now a half of a piece of white chalk back on the small wood ledge extending from the front of the old black chalkboard, Coach McCallom rids himself of any leftover chalk dust by violently clapping his hands together with a few well-directed slaps. He then finishes up his pregame speech by telling the Revolutionaries starters to do their job like he expects them to or he will just find players who will.

Coach McCallom next does a few things that Taylor finds strange, all of which remind him he's no longer playing for Coach Waters and Longwood Hills. Looking at Andray, Coach McCallom tells Andray the first five plays he wants him to run when the Revolutionaries have the ball on offense; as if he could predict the defense Semaphore University will be playing on each possession, going so far as to tell Andray how much time on the shot clock he wants there to be left when these shots are taken. It seems to Taylor as if Coach McCallom is trying to control the first few minutes of the game from the sideline, all by himself.

After finishing up these instructions to Andray, Coach McCallom walks to the center of the locker room and asks the assistant coaches and the players to make a circle around him. Standing in the middle of this circle, with his heels resting on top of the *U* in the words *Maryland State University Men's Basketball*, Coach McCallom instructs everyone to bow their heads and remain silent. He then asks the Lord, "To watch over the Revolutionaries tonight and help them play with passion and tenacity, so they can bring home a victory."

As soon as Taylor hears the word Lord come out of Coach McCallom's mouth, he instinctively pulls his hand down from Tim's shoulder in front of him. While he has no idea what the Lord is doing tonight, he doubts he has the time to watch over a regular season college basketball game between the Maryland State University Revolutionaries and the Semaphore University Jackrabbits.

With his head now up, Taylor looks around the circle, only to find he's the one player not following along with the rest of Coach McCallom's prayer; which makes him wonder, for the first time in a while, what's going on inside everyone else's mind and not his own. But since he doesn't want to draw any unnecessary attention to himself, he spends the rest of this pregame prayer staring absent-mindedly at the clock above the door, while anxiously waiting to take the court.

When Taylor finally checks into the game against the Semaphore University Jackrabbits, with a little over eight minutes to go in the first half, the sold-out crowd of 15,000 greets him with hushed applause. Never in his life has he felt more alive than those first few steps onto the Liberty Arena floor—but unfortunately, the game doesn't go like he envisioned it in his head. Playing in front of the largest crowd of his life, everything on the court moves *way* too fast for him—the players, the shot clock, the offensive play calls, the defensive rotations and the referees' whistles—not to mention the knowledge that every step, dribble, shot, rebound, foul and turnover he commits is being watched, remembered and recorded by the fans and the media—makes him hesitate a split second each time he touches the ball and overthink everything he does. Without warning, it seems as if he's looking down on himself on the court. He can see his body reacting to everything that's happening in the game, but it's as if he's not in control of his own movements. It feels like he's in a dream. He wants to yell at himself to snap out of it, but he can't! He has no voice!

Taylor plays a total of eleven minutes against Semaphore University, finishing up with 3 points, two rebounds, one block, two turnovers and zero assists. As predicted, the Revolutionaries easily beat the Jackrabbits by a score of 79-61.

CHAPTER 50

Even though his heart isn't completely in it, Taylor closes the door to his dorm room and heads out to meet James and Daquan. It's been a few weeks since the team last had a Saturday night off and with no more empty Saturday nights on their schedule for months, he reluctantly agreed after their road win earlier in the week to go with his two new friends to a fraternity party. But with Emmet once again out of town visiting Emily, all he really wants to do is stay in and watch a movie alone, or possibly spend a few more hours shooting a basketball toward the ceiling feeling sorry for himself.

As Taylor steps out into the cold night air, he's amazed at the clarity of the sky above him. He can't ever remember the nighttime sky in New Jersey looking like this. Instead of finding a blanket of complete darkness, he finds the entire sky is filled with bright and effervescent white stars that provide him cover and illuminate his path no matter where he walks.

Once inside the lobby of Essex Hall, Taylor shows his student I.D. card to the guard on duty and waits for the call up to James' and Daquan's room. After getting the okay from the other end of the phone, the guard instructs Taylor to finish signing in by swiping his student I.D. card through the same credit card-looking machine as always. With a casual head nod goodbye, Taylor takes the stairs to the second floor, where he knocks loudly on the door of his friends' dorm room.

"Yo! Who's dat?" James' voice booms.

"Just me," Taylor responds as the door opens.

"Hey, man!" James shouts as he slaps Taylor five and gives him a fast hug. "C'mon on in."

"Double-A! What's up?" Daquan screams from the old beaten-up love seat in the center of the room that serves as his and James' couch.

"D', when are you going to lay off the double-A jokes?" James asks.

"Never, man. I gotta call him something. Taylor is just too boring," Daquan gives Taylor a silly smile before returning his eyes to the TV and his video game.

"No worries, man. It's all good," Taylor answers. "I'm happy to take a little heat from my friends. Strangers are the ones that bother me."

Not sure how to respond, James asks what he thinks is the obvious question, "You want a drink?"

Looking around the room, Taylor doesn't see James or Daquan drinking anything, but before he can even ask, James cuts him off, "They're underneath D's bed. We're pouring 'em into these plastic cups they gave us during freshman orientation. We don't want to be fined by our R.A. for drinking in our room, or worse, have the coaches find out about it."

"That's smooth, man," Taylor answers with a half-smile. "But I think I'm good for now. I'll just wait until we get to the party."

"Boo, ya! Take that!" Daquan shouts out of nowhere.

"Seriously, just ignore him," James tells Taylor. "He's playing that basketball video game again. That's all he does besides read comic books."

By the time Taylor reaches half court, he already feels like a different person. The Great Scott—much criticized and much misunderstood—*has arrived!*

With the noise of the arena continuing to overpower the Red Demons, their head coach has no choice but to call another timeout. At the sound of the referee's whistle, Taylor hops over to the Revolutionaries bench, still pumping his fists and absorbing every magical moment. He's first greeted by Daquan, then James, before the rest of the team high fives him and slaps him on the back. The assistant coaches also reach out to him, including Coach Banks, whose congratulatory tap doesn't go unnoticed.

Once the five players that came off the court are seated, Coach McCallom leans in and gives Taylor a vigorous nod of approval, but doesn't say anything out loud to him. A second later, a hand touches Taylor's knee cap and when he looks up, he sees Andray tell him with a laugh, "Nice dunk, freshman...Real nice dunk."

The Revolutionaries next try to focus their attention on Coach McCallom's detailed instructions, but it's impossible. *The arena is just too loud.* Seeing the situation for what it is, Coach McCallom stops what he's doing and tells the players with a smile, at least the ones who can hear him, "It seems Taylor has turned this place on its head. Let's keep doing what we've been doing and finish this game out strong."

When the horn sounds three and a half minutes later, the Revolutionaries have taken down the vaunted Red Demons by a score of 81-74. Enormously impressed by Taylor's career-making performance of 21 points, nine rebounds and four steals, the TV broadcasters unanimously name him the Player of the Game.

Back in Northern New Jersey, his mom and dad beam proudly inside their own homes when they hear this announcement; and up in central Pennsylvania, inside his fraternity house, Jimmy high fives his new house brothers, his old life and new life continuing to meld perfectly together into one.

An hour after the game ends and less than ten minutes after he's done talking to the media, Taylor slides out of the back of the Liberty Arena unnoticed even by the security guards. With the cold winter air swirling all around him, he pulls down hard on his wool hat to try and block out the surrounding elements, but sadly knows that's impossible. Placing one foot in front of the other, he starts walking toward his dorm room alone so he can celebrate tonight's amazing turn of events in the newfound quiet of his room.

As he forges ahead, his feet seem lighter than they did only a few short hours ago and even in the darkness, he can feel a sense of satisfaction and purpose he's never known before fill his body and spirit. A feeling he now knows can only come from hard work, dedication and a belief in what has yet to come.

With the night's events coursing through his heart, and most importantly his soul, his walk slowly breaks into a jog as he looks out to the horizon and his future. Keeping his eyes focused straight ahead, he starts rushing forward into tomorrow and the rest of his journey. A tomorrow he can't wait to see.

THE END

"It's not my fault," Daquan pipes in, without taking his eyes off the TV screen. "If they made textbooks more like video games or comic books, I'd do a lot better in school."

"You know what? I'll write an email to the Dean for you. That should change things," James sarcastically responds.

Ignoring James, Daquan puts the game on pause and asks Taylor, "You wanna take on the reining champ?"

"Nah, I'm good. All my boys back home loved those games, but they just don't do it for me."

"What?" Daquan asks dumbfounded. "What'd you do in high school?"

"Played ball, mostly. And watched a lot of TV, when I wasn't reading or hooping."

"Read? As in books?" Daquan asks, his eyes growing wide at the thought.

"Yeah," Taylor answers with a shrug of his shoulders.

"Told you, James, our Jersey boy here is wack. Reading outside of school is forbidden where I come from. In West Baltimore, you get attacked for even looking like you can read. Crabs in a bucket, yo."

"Crabs in a bucket?" James asks. "What are you talking about?"

"Yeah, what are you talking about?" Taylor asks.

"You telling me you boys from the 'burbs have never heard of the crabs?" Daquan responds.

"No," James and Taylor both answer at the same time.

"All righty, let me pontificate then. Yeah, don't be shocked, that word's from a book. I study when I need to," Daquan replies and then shoots both of them a look of "don't mess with me." "If you put a bunch of crabs in a bucket, all they want to do is climb out to a better place. They don't know where they're going, but they know they want out of *that* bucket. They'll walk, fight and claw each other to death if they have to. Anything to get out of that bucket faster. And the lower in the bucket they start, the harder they'll fight to get out. See, the projects is the bucket and me and my peoples are the crabs."

"Got it, man," James responds with a laugh. "That's really enlightening."

"You think I'm kidding?" Daquan asks. "I didn't make that up. That's common knowledge where I come from."

"Good to know," Taylor sarcastically answers.

"Forget you suburban jokers," Daquan responds with a wave of his hand and then turns back to the TV and his video game. "And just in case you uneducated fools were wondering," he shouts over his shoulder. "I'm up twenty on the computer right now."

"We weren't wondering," Taylor answers.

"Couldn't agree more," James replies. "Hey, Socrates. What'd you say we get out of here?"

"And one! Count the basket! Wait, what'd you call me?" Daquan asks, looking over at James with alarm.

"Relax, D'," James responds with a smile. "Socrates was an ancient Roman philosopher. It's all good."

"He was actually a Greek philosopher," Taylor corrects James.

"Right, like I said, he was a Greek philosopher. You sure?" James asks Taylor.

"Yeah, I'm sure."

"I think you're right D', our Jersey boy here is wack," James tells Daquan and then turns and lightly punches Taylor in the shoulder. "Hey, Socrates. C'mon, man. Turn that game off so we can get outta here."

"Fine by me," Daquan answers. "The computer's no match for me anyways. No one can take down the king!"

"I like that. The King of Greek Philosophy," James bursts out laughing. "I think that's what we'll call you from now on."

As James keeps laughing, Taylor and Daquan have no choice but to join him as the players' silliness overtakes the room.

CHAPTER 51

As the three players walk casually from Essex Hall to Fraternity Row, the quiet campus surrounding them provides the perfect backdrop to talk more seriously than before. Brought together by age, basketball and talent, they've slowly grown over these last few months to become the most important thing they can be to each other—friends.

"Yo, where's your boy Irish tonight?" James picks up lull in the conversation.

"I thought we agreed we're gonna call him Emmet The Sturdy," Daquan asks.

"He took off to visit Emily," Taylor answers, pretending not to hear Daquan.

"Does that mean you got your place all to yourself?" Daquan asks.

"Yeah, it's just me and the four walls."

"I wish I could say the same thing," James replies with a laugh.

"Whatever, yo," Daquan responds, then playfully pushes James with his forearm. "Double-A, maybe you'll meet a fine young thing tonight and use that empty room to your advantage," he cocks an eyebrow at Taylor as he says this.

"Whatever. We'll see," Taylor responds with a shrug his shoulders.

"Why doesn't Emmet just transfer to Emily's school?" James asks. "That way instead of drooling over a life size poster of his girl, he can do it in person anytime he wants."

"Not sure," Taylor answers with a chuckle. "But I don't think he was recruited there. I guess their coach doesn't appreciate the European game the way the *Mac Man* does."

"For real, that boy is crazy weak!" Daquan shouts, flexing his arms as he says this. "If he left here, I know I wouldn't miss his eighth grade girl's body."

As Taylor and James laugh at Daquan's joke, Daquan keeps talking, "What was it like growing up in New Jersey, man?"

"What do you mean?" Taylor asks.

"Is it true mobsters are hanging out all over the place?"

"What are you talking about?" Taylor replies, looking over at Daquan perplexed.

"Every mob guy on TV or in the movies is from New Jersey. At least, that's how I see it," Daquan tells him.

"Yeah, it's just like that D'," Taylor responds with laugh. "Every kid in my high school had an Italian last name. I'm the only one who didn't."

"Really?"

"No, man! I'm kidding! I come from a hard-working middle-class town. There's no organized crime in Longwood Hills. Unless you count the old people who sit down during the freshmen basketball game and don't get up until after the varsity game is over."

"That's weak," Daquan replies with a shake of his head. "It'd be a lot cooler if there were mobsters everywhere."

"How'd you get to this school, man?" Taylor asks Daquan.

"Coach Banks. He and my high school coach are boys from summer ball."

"It all goes back to Coach Banks," James jumps back in.

"What do you mean?" Taylor asks.

"Coach Banks' fingerprints are all over all three of our recruitments. He's also practically Andray's dad."

"What are you talking about?" Taylor asks.

"You don't know?" James replies.

"Nah," Taylor answers with a shrug.

"Coach Banks is Andray's legal guardian."

"What? C'mon, man. For real?"

"Yeah, for real. Andray lived with Coach Banks his last three years of high school. And when Andray blew up his senior year, Coach Banks used their relationship to jump to a job here."

"Coach Banks is a climber," Daquan backs up James.

"But my man can recruit. So the *Mac Man* gives him whatever he wants. But still, I betcha Coach Banks is outta here the minute he can ride Andray's coattails to a new job as a head coach at some other big name school or an assistant's job on a pro bench somewhere. As soon as he can, Coach Banks is a goner."

"For real, it's all just a big game to the coaches," Daquan backs up James again. "They don't care about us. All they care about is their jobs and their paychecks. We're just the mules to bring it to them."

"You think that's always true?" Taylor asks. "I can see what you're saying about Coach Banks. But what about Coach McCallom? He's been here forever. I don't think he's going anywhere."

"Would you leave this place if you were him?" James asks Taylor. "He's God in these parts. And if he keeps getting players like us to commit to this school, they're going to have to bury him in that arena."

"Good," Taylor answers. "Part of the reason I came here was so I can play for the same coach each year."

"All we're saying, Double-A, is this ain't high school anymore," Daquan steps back in. "You've got to look out for

326 / Adam Poe

number one. I know we're all friends right now, but if they wanted to, the coaches could make us hate on each other in a second. All they've got to do is tell us only one freshman is going to play from now on. And damn, they still might do that just for fun."

"Hopefully, they won't," Taylor responds and then changes his tone when he realizes he doesn't want to think about such a thing…"See James, I told you your roommate's not dumb," Taylor forces a sideways smile. "Just like the crabs, he knows the truth when he sees it."

"Whatever, man," Daquan answers and then goes to playfully push Taylor in the chest for retribution; Taylor jumps out of the way, crouching down low into an exaggerated fighting stance.

"See James, I told you Double-A is not a depressed loner," Daquan responds with a smile and a laugh.

"We all have our things," James tells Daquan. "And my thing right now is to smack you upside the head," James reaches out and slaps Daquan in the back of the neck, then jumps next to Taylor, crouching down low into the same fighting stance.

"Man, you two are lucky I like you both. 'Cause this definitely ain't a fair fight," Daquan warns and then takes off running after them in a comical gait.

When the three players finally reach the fraternity house, they are confronted by a long line of partiers that starts at the front door of the red brick mansion and wraps around the side of the building. After taking one look at the long line, the players ignore it and walk right up to the front, where James yells over to the house brother who's working the door, "What's up with this line, man?"

Since the three players are at least a half-of-a-foot taller than everyone else in the line, the house brother smiles like a kid in a candy store when he sees the players. At the front of the line, waiting patiently to get into the party are two overweight girls wearing skinny jeans that are *way* too small for their large bodies and matching black sweaters their friends told them look slimming, but aren't fooling anyone. When the two girls see the house brother invite the players into the party without waiting, they shoot him a look of disgust. Seeing the girls' expression, the house brother tells them, "They're on the basketball team," as if that explains everything—*but it does.* Basketball players are social capital on the Maryland State University campus. The players know it and the fraternity houses know it, with each using the other to get what they want. In this case, the players get a hassle-free night of partying, while the fraternity house gets bragging rights for the week for convincing the players to show up.

When James, Daquan and Taylor walk into the fraternity house packed with wall-to-wall bodies, they're enthusiastically greeted by the rest of the house brothers and their pledges, all of whom are wearing island-themed clothes for tonight's "Beach Bash" party. With a foot of sand spread across the dance floor, green plastic blow-up palm trees, large hollowed-out bamboo sticks and colorful beach balls decorating the rest of the fraternity house, the players feel like they've let campus and entered a different world entirely. It's a much needed break for all of them.

Within minutes of walking into the party, Daquan takes off to find a bathroom and James leaves Taylor to chase after a girl he's been eyeing up from his English class. Suddenly alone and feeling vulnerable, Taylor walks over to one of the large plastic bins filled with ice cold cans of beer and takes one with him to the nearest wall. Standing with his back up against the wall, he watches the party happen in front of him, once again feeling separate from everything around him.

As far as Taylor can tell, everyone at the party is having a great time; which makes his mind race with its usual string of unanswerable questions, *"Is something wrong with me? Am I the only one who doesn't like college?*

Maybe I am a depressed loner?" No sooner do these questions grab hold of him, does he get overwhelmed by feelings of being homesick again. Homesick for the life he left behind in Longwood Hills and the person he was there.

Closing his eyes, he leans back against the wall and wonders how long he has to stay at the party before he can leave. With the music rattling the wall, sending deep earth-moving beats of bass reverberating through his bones, a painful pit of discomfort takes root in his stomach, making him feel even more sad and alone than he was only minutes ago. So engrossed in what's going on inside his own head, he doesn't even notice at first the cute girl standing next to him with eyes that shout, *"Talk to me!"*

Not sure what to do, he does nothing but sip his drink as the music keeps blasting at an ear-splitting level. Finally gathering the courage, he turns and looks down into her pretty face, "Place is crowded, right?"

"What?" she shouts back.

"I said, the place is crowded, right?"

"Yeah, I know...Are you okay?" she leans in close as she asks this question.

"Why? Does it look like something's wrong?"

"You look lonely, that's all," she answers, her eyes dancing and sparkling inside her head as she stares at him.

"Is it that obvious?"

"Yes," she giggles. "Aren't you that basketball player? The one everyone is always talking about."

He wants to scream back at her, *"I used to be that basketball player! Now I just sit on the bench and watch! If I could tell you all the things I was told to convince me to come here to "play" basketball, you'd laugh! Now all the coaches do is yell at me and tell me how wrong I'm doing things! I don't even know which way is up anymore! And that's just the coaches! The players all seem to hate me, except for the two guys I came here with and my roommate, who's a total clown! Do you mean that basketball player?"*

"I saw your picture in the school newspaper," she tells him. "At least, I think that was you?"

"Yeah, that was me," he responds.

"That's sooooo amazing, getting your picture in the paper like that," she scrunches her nose as she says this.

He's immediately struck by the fact that if she thinks having your picture in the school newspaper and being on the basketball team is exciting and not lonely and isolating, maybe just being a normal freshman is a whole lot worse.

"Thanks," he responds as a renewed sense of confidence begins to take hold. "Being in the media can be cool sometimes."

"I thought you were cute when I saw your picture in the paper," she tells him with a mischievous smile. "Then, when I saw you standing over here by yourself, without a girl next to you, I thought I'd see if I could talk to you. I'm Lauren, by the way," she extends her soft small hand in his direction.

"I'm Taylor," he answers, taking her hand.

"Yeah, I know that already," she giggles. "Remember, I recognized you? You must be really good to be on the basketball team?"

"I'm not bad, I guess," he answers, feeling better by the second.

He suddenly wants to tell her everything, all about his fears, anxieties, loneliness and anger. That he's better than the nine minutes and 3.2 points per game he's averaging. How he's thinking of transferring to Central New York University, a place that he knows will appreciate him. He desperately wants her to make all his problems go away.

"That's really impressive," she answers. "I could never be on a college sports team. I'm not that disciplined. Do you know one of the reasons I came to this school is because it has good football and basketball teams?"

"No," he answers with a shake of his head.

"That, and the partying...I mean, education," she giggles at her slip-up.

"Where are you from?" he asks.

"Columbia, Maryland."

"Where's that?"

"It's outside of Baltimore. You should really get to know Maryland if you're going to go to school here," she tells him.

"Good point. I'll work on that," he answers with a smile.

"You're from New Jersey, right?"

"Yeah, how do you...The article, I forgot."

"Did you come to the party alone?" she asks.

"No, I came with two other players from the team. But I haven't seen them in a while," he answers with a shrug. "You, uhm, want to get a drink or something?"

"Sure," she answers with a big smile, not sure what else she had to do to get him to ask this question.

As they head over to the makeshift bar in the corner, Lauren reaches out and takes Taylor by the hand, interlocking her soft small fingers into his. With her free hand, she slyly waves to a group of girls standing on the other side of the room; some of them smile back at her, but most of them just shoot her looks of jealousy and contempt.

A few hours later, after dancing, drinking and shouting back and forth over the noise, Taylor and Lauren leave the party together drenched in their own sweat and fatigued from too many bodies packed into too small of a space. As soon as they step outside the front door of the fraternity house, the cool night air washes over them like a comforting blanket, providing them instant relief, but most importantly, breaking the intensity of the buzzing going on inside their heads.

"It's getting late," she tells him as they stand on the sidewalk, still hand-in-hand. "Is there anything else you might want to do tonight?"

"Uhm, I'm not sure," he responds, hesitating to ask the question that's been on his mind for hours. "I was thinking, uhm, if you were into it, we could, you know, head back to my dorm room."

"That sounds like fun," she answers, tightening her fingers around his to let him know how excited this thought makes her.

After taking the long walk back to Kent Hall, Taylor gives a casual wave to the guard on duty and leads Lauren by the hand into the first empty elevator he sees. As soon as the elevator doors close, they dive into each other's arms like two long lost souls, their tongues dancing and wrapping around each other in a heated embrace. Neither one of them comes up for air until Taylor realizes the elevator has already stopped on his floor and the doors are about to close. Acting quickly, he jumps into the doorway and invites Lauren to walk off first—a chivalrous move— which also lets him admire the view as she walks away.

Once Lauren is completely off the elevator, Taylor turns and looks into the video camera secured to the top corner and gives it a big thumb's up. While he has no idea where this video feed goes, maybe, just for tonight, he can at least be a star there.

With his long right arm draped over Lauren's feminine and undefined shoulder, the two lonely freshmen walk together down the hall in silence to room 408, neither of them wanting to say anything that might ruin the moment. When they step into Taylor's dorm room, instead of turning on all the lights, he turns on the lights for only one half of the room. Unfortunately, he chooses Emmet's half.

"Wait! What is that?" Lauren shouts at the sight of the poster of Emily. "Is that thing for real? Who is that girl? Is she your girlfriend?"

"What? Huh? I don't have a girlfriend," he answers in surprise, forgetting for a second the poster of Emily is even there. "And, if I had a girlfriend, do you think I would get something like that made of her?"

"I don't know," she shouts again in alarm. "We just met, remember? I don't know what you're capable of."

"She's *not* my girlfriend," he tells her. "I promise."

"Then who is she?"

"She's my roommate's girlfriend."

"You have a roommate?"

As Lauren looks around the semi-dark room for the first time, she sees there are two beds in the room and not one. For some reason, she just assumed every basketball player would have his own room, "Oh...Sorry...I don't want to cheat with anyone's boyfriend. Especially with someone who has a poster of his girlfriend in his room. That thing is completely embarrassing."

"Tell me about it. I wish I could throw it out, believe me. The day I moved in, I thought it was a joke. No one has a poster of their girlfriend like that. A couple of small pictures, maybe. But a poster?"

As the two of them break out into uncontrollable laughter, Taylor walks over to Emmet's side of the room and flips over the poster of Emily, so her face is now staring at the blank wall. This way, Emily can't watch what is about to happen between the two live people in the room.

CHAPTER 52

With only Thanksgiving and the day after Thanksgiving off for practice, Coach McCallom invites all the players over to his house for a traditional Thanksgiving Day turkey dinner. Even though he lives less than a mile from the "Arch on Arm," and many of the players live too far away from campus to make it home for the holiday, only one or two take him up on his offer. The rest, including Taylor, make alternate plans.

After saving up enough money over the last few months for gas, food and a nice hotel room, Deborah drives down to Washington Springs to have Thanksgiving dinner alone with her son at a restaurant along Armstrong Avenue. Over dinner—and with her guilt still eating away at her—Deborah once again pushes Taylor to make amends with his father, repeatedly suggesting Taylor call Bill to wish him a Happy Thanksgiving. Even though Taylor doesn't have any interest in doing so, he does as his mom asks. In what can only be described as a Thanksgiving Day miracle, when Taylor calls his dad's cell phone, it goes straight to voicemail.

Deborah's short two-day stay in Washington Springs moves way too quickly in her opinion and while she gets the sense her son is adjusting nicely to his new life and surroundings—perhaps even better than she first thought—something about him feels different. But after three months away from home, it could be as simple as he looks more like a man now than she can ever remember him being.

During this visit, Deborah lets Taylor know she'll be coming to see him play in person for the first time in early January when the Revolutionaries visit Newark, New Jersey, to square-off in a nationally televised out-of-conference game on a neutral court; and she'll also be coming back down to Washington Springs at the end of January for a long weekend to watch him play at home in the Liberty Arena.

While Bill has yet to also see Taylor play a college game in person, he keeps calling Deborah to make sure she lets Taylor know he'll be coming to a game real soon and Taylor should keep an eye out for him.

As far as Thanksgivings go, it's a fulfilling one for Deborah and Taylor. It's been a long time since they spent so much mother-son quality time together; not to mention, it's extremely comforting for them to find out extended separations, both now and in the future, won't have any effect on their relationship.

When Taylor closes the door to his mom's car and watches her drive off at the end of her short stay, there is a familiar smile on his face, a reminder, if only briefly, of how things used to be.

CHAPTER 53

Time is ticking. When the second week of December rolls around, Taylor learns through the grapevine the Revolutionaries are heavily recruiting a nationally known high school senior who also plays multiple positions on the court, plus at least one other small forward, along with a few guards. While he heard all of these same rumors during the early signing period for high school seniors in November, that time period came and went without anyone signing on the dotted line to come to Maryland State University. But now, with the late signing period just over four months away in mid-April, he can hear the footsteps of his future competition coming his way and it's getting louder by the day.

To make things worse, on the Wednesday of that same week, four days before The State War, the annual basketball game between the Maryland State University Revolutionaries and the Maryland Tech University Sturgeons, a negative article appears in the state's largest newspaper and on its website, calling out Taylor and the rest of his recruiting class. While the architect of this article doesn't outright call Taylor a "bust," he does save his harshest criticism for the freshman from New Jersey, calling him…*"A major disappointment for not coming close *to living up to expectations."* This same sportswriter goes on to state very clearly that he doesn't believe the Revolutionaries can make a serious run at a conference title or a post-season college basketball tournament bid if Taylor and the team's other two promising freshmen, James Knight and Daquan Mayes...*"Don't get real good, real fast."* The article doesn't mention Emmet at all.

Once this article goes live, it instantly becomes a hotly debated topic on sports talk radio and online in cyberspace. To help his freshmen players deal with what he refers to as "white noise," Coach McCallom calls a meeting in his office for the Friday of that same week to instruct his young players on how to handle a situation like this. Supported by the assistant coaches, Coach McCallom turns this meeting into a "teaching moment," telling the players, "You need to figure out a way to ignore what the media has to say, whether it's good or bad. The only opinions that count are the people in this office right now and the rest of the players in the locker room. While easier said than done, each one of you needs to find a way to concentrate on playing basketball only and helping the team win."

After the players leave this meeting, the coaches stay back to talk amongst themselves about the direction of the team. While the Revolutionaries are off to a nice 7-2 start, they've looked a lot worse at times than this winning record suggests; which is why the coaches can understand the media coming down so hard on the team at this juncture in the season. They also know from experience that if they can't right the ship soon, it's only a matter of time until this white noise gets louder and louder, until all they're doing is managing this noise and not coaching the team. And if that happens, there's a good chance the season could be lost for good.

During this informal strategy session, the coaches decide now is the time to give Damon more quality game minutes, which means moving Andray to the two guard position when they're both on the floor together. This decision leaves Coach Banks to convince Andray to see this change as a positive move that will help the team find its footing, while also freeing him up to score more. The coaches also talk briefly about how they can close the divide in the locker room between the upperclassmen and the freshmen, but even they know this is a hard hill to climb, since the only currency that matters on a college basketball team is playing time and right now the upperclassmen are doing most of it.

The next day, the second Saturday of December, the entire Maryland State University men's basketball team, the coaches and a small army of support personnel board a private luxury bus to make the hour and a half drive to play Maryland Tech University in its home arena. This much-anticipated annual game between the state's two largest public universities has dominated the sports pages, talk radio stations, online blogs and student conversations on both campuses since the Monday after Thanksgiving—bringing out the best and worst in everyone.

As Taylor sits in a row by himself at the front of the bus, he puts on his headphones to start mentally preparing for another humiliating day of watching basketball from the bench—in front of thousands of people—instead of playing it. With tonight's game also being broadcast live on national TV, not only will the sold-out crowd in the arena watch The Great Scott sit on the bench in his warm-ups, a national TV audience at home will do the same, including most of Longwood Hills.

With the bus rolling along toward Maryland Tech University, Taylor stares at the houses and trees rushing past his window, feeling lower than ever. He reasons that out there beyond his window, life is being lived by real people in the real world and not on this bus by him—some stupid college kid who's supposed to be able to put an orange ball through an orange rim better than almost everyone else in the country, but now can't seem to be able to even do that. *It feels as if the world is growing exponentially larger and he's only getting smaller.*

Like most college basketball players, the game itself is Taylor's identity. Without it, he doesn't know who he is and has no real way of communicating with the world. So each game he doesn't play more than a few minutes, it feels as if the air he breathes is slowly being taken away from him, while his soul is being crushed by the weight of not knowing when, if ever, the situation will change.

"What are you listening to?" Coach Banks turns around from the row in front of Taylor with a friendly smile.

"Huh?" Taylor answers as he pulls off his headphones.

Laughing a little, Coach Banks repeats himself, "I said, what are you listening to?"

"Just my usual pre-game mix. A little rap. A little hip-hop. A little top forty. Why?"

"Nothing important, I'm just curious what a player like Taylor Scott listens to in order to get prepared for a big game. You ready for tonight?"

"Yeah, I guess," Taylor answers with a shrug of his shoulders.

"You guess?" Coach Banks responds, the friendly tone in his voice suddenly gone. "The whole state's going to be watching! Make sure you're ready to go when Coach McCallom calls your name. This could be your time to shine. You hear me?"

"Is he toying with me?" Taylor thinks silently to himself as he replies in a flat voice, "Sure, Coach. I'll be ready. Don't worry about me."

"Good," Coach Banks answers with a stern look on his face. "And keep your head in the game, no matter what."

"Sure, Coach," Taylor responds, before watching Coach Banks turn back to the front of the bus, leaving him as confused as ever by his coaching methods.

After placing his headphones back over his ears, Taylor turns the volume of his music up to full blast, while pushing his forehead against the window so he can once again watch the world fly by at sixty miles per hour. With months of frustration slowly rising to a raw irritating burn, he wants to grab Coach Banks by the collar and scream at him, *"Why did you just tell me to be ready for tonight's game if you didn't mean it? And why does being a part of this team mean I have to take so much heat from the coaches? Why can't I be a great basketball player and just be myself?"*

As Taylor violently bites his bottom lip, he presses his forehead even harder against the window to try and keep his emotions in check—*but it's no use.* From somewhere deep within his aching heart, in a place he thought he'd locked away forever, his emotions move swiftly from his heart to his throat and then to his nose, making his eyes fill with wet tears. Not wanting anyone to see, especially Coach Banks, he tries to hide what is happening by tapping his forehead against the window in rhythm to the song blasting from his headphones, *"Please make all of this go away!"* he cries out in silence. *"I need to feel whole again! Someone please help me!"*

Within seconds, his feelings change from helplessness to confusion and then to a million more mixed-up emotions about the direction his life has taken. Feeling overwhelmed, overmatched and mentally broken, the intensity of the moment rages on as he continues to tap his forehead against the window in rhythm to the song. At the same time, thoughts of his dad unexpectedly pop into his head. While he's always kept his dad at a distance—even after his mom asked that he forgive him and let him back into his life—he mostly ignored her. *But things are different now.* He wants to tell his dad how much he loves him and how he wishes they could have a real father-son relationship. That he desperately needs his dad to be proud of him, as he's the only dad he'll ever have. *But thinking about his dad only makes him angrier!*

Clenching his fists, he puts his hands under his legs to stop himself from doing anything stupid. But he wants nothing more than to get up and tell the bus driver to pull over to the side of the road so he can call his dad and yell at him. To tell him how much he hates him for everything he did to their family, for everything he did to him. That he despises feeling second rate and being the constant reminder of a failed marriage. *That his dad is an unethical rotten human being that doesn't deserve to live, let alone receive his love!*

With his angry emotions blazing with fury, Taylor thinks about how his dad's new family got all his love, support and money, while he and his mom struggled each day to make a life for themselves. How every dollar spent in his house was discussed and analyzed, with no mistakes allowed or the financial consequences would be severe. How he went that first time to the new house his dad bought for Cindy and their kids, wanting nothing more than to punch those kids in the face for being spoiled and taking away all the things he was supposed to have—that his life should've been easier. But most importantly, he wants his dad to know he's *not* a throwaway child. He's so much more than that. He's a good kid on his way to becoming a great man. Even if all these ruthless bastards who call themselves his teammates don't think he's worth a grain of salt right now. *Someday soon, he's going to show them too!*

As the bus continues to roll toward Maryland Tech University, no one even notices Taylor's outburst. Not even Coach Banks, who's sitting less than four feet away.

Later that night, in front of a sold-out crowd of 16,390 screaming fans, Taylor plays eight minutes, scoring 4 points and grabbing two rebounds to help the Maryland State University Revolutionaries beat the Maryland Tech

University Sturgeons by a score of 74-68. A victory that makes Coach McCallom smile in a way Taylor hasn't seen in a long time.

CHAPTER 54

Taylor's dream is as vivid as anything that he's ever experienced awake...

...Using his forearm, he shields his eyes from the sun so he can focus on his surroundings. While nothing looks familiar, something about where he is feels almost perfect. But where is he? And why is he here?

As he looks off into the distance, he now sees her. It's as if she appeared out of nowhere. She's dressed exactly the same as the day they met—a tight yellow V-neck T-shirt hugging her body, white jeans accentuating her curves, silver open toe sandals highlighting her red painted nails, her wavy blond hair pulled back into a pony tail and no makeup, just her natural beauty radiating a warm glow. Kelly is even prettier in his dream than he remembers her to be in real life.

Feeling a tap on his shoulder, he looks down to see Jimmy smiling, telling him to go over and say hi; and not to worry, it's a safe move. She's been asking around about him.

Without waiting for his response, Jimmy starts walking in Kelly's direction alone, begging him to come along. Finally unable to control his desires, he yells at Jimmy to stop!

As he starts walking toward Kelly, his arms instinctively reach out to embrace her...

...The neighbor's door across the hall slams shut and jolts Taylor from his deep sleep. Jumping up into a sitting position, he turns wide-eyed toward the small window near his bed and pulls the blankets up to his shoulders. It's still pitch dark outside.

Suddenly aware of what it's like to be marginalized and pushed aside so other people can shine, the more he thinks about Kelly, the more he's overcome by feelings of shame and disgust for what he did to her. And while he has no idea if she's forgiven him—or even thinks of him at all—he knows he has to get in touch with her.

When the library doors open at 7:30 a.m., he practically runs up to the third floor to find an open computer so he can start typing his long overdue apology. Uncertain if she still uses the same email address, this doesn't stop him. He writes and rewrites his heart-felt apology, over and over again, until he can't figure out what it is he's even trying to say anymore. Finally erasing everything he's written, he decides to type the only words he thinks she might want to hear.

To: <Kelly Raymond>
From: <Taylor Scott>
Subject: Too Little, Too Late

Kelly:

I'm sorry for what happened.
I hope one day you can forgive me.

- Taylor

Later that day, alone in her dorm room, Kelly stares at her computer screen, mesmerized by the unopened email in her inbox. With her heart in her stomach, she thinks about what she should do—open it or delete it? She's spent the last eleven months getting over what happened that night at Susan Jamison's party and while she knows Taylor is struggling right now—*who from town doesn't?*—should that even matter?

Eventually giving in to her curiosity, she opens the email, reading it silently to herself.

CHAPTER 55

The rain pounds hard against the windows high above the Rosenberg Center practice courts as the once lush and brightly colored giant oak trees planted just outside the Rosenberg Center's walls now scrape their bare and empty winter branches angrily against these same windows each time the wind howls across campus—creating an eerie and dream-like atmosphere inside the gym. With the women's team using the Liberty Arena for their game, Taylor and the rest of his teammates line up along the baseline and wait for Coach McCallom's direction.

Standing in the center of the hot and stuffy gym, with his normal angry scowl cemented on his face, Coach McCallom warns the players in a gravelly voice to make sure they run at a pace he deems worthy, before blowing his whistle, signaling for them to start running suicide sprints—white team first, blue team second. As he blows his whistle time and time again, he watches closely for any sign of quit in his players, a mental weakness he refuses to tolerate. With each step becoming more difficult and labored than the one before, sharp pain shoots through every bone in Taylor's body, while he can't seem to get enough air into his burning lungs fast enough to ease the unnatural sensation of pushing his body beyond its physical limits.

As the pace of each suicide sprint continues at a breakneck speed, the players focus their attention on trying to get through this abysmal moment in time— completely unaware of the poetic struggle of the oak trees taking place against the backdrop of the afternoon's grey menacing sky just outside the Rosenberg Center's walls. That is, everyone except Taylor, who in between running his guts out and trying to manage his difficult breathing, stares in awe and wonder at the scene unfolding high above the practice courts. A reminder he's not alone in his epic battle to survive.

With the wrath of the King unchecked and out on full display, the Maryland State University men's basketball players are once again being reminded the Revolutionaries are not a democracy; it's Coach McCallom's kingdom and they're only visiting. When the anger of the King finally dies down, the players take the court again, separating into their usual teams, white team starters versus blue team reserves. With the Revolutionaries barely winning their road game the night before against a conference bottom-feeder, the players hardly had enough time to fly home and get some sleep before finding themselves back on the court today.

From his customary spot a few feet above the three-point line, Coach McCallom directs the players to run through the offensive and defensive sets he was unhappy with from last night's game, telling the players with his usual borderline rage, "You're going to get it right this time! No matter how long it takes!"

With his body still numb from the suicide sprints, Taylor is assigned to cover Maurice Barnes, a defensive assignment, which in all likelihood should keep him more than focused—but when the drill starts droning on and on, he can't help but let his mind once again drift to the thought of what it would be like to transfer to Central New York University. While he now sees how difficult it is to succeed on the big-time college level, he believes, without actually knowing why, that Coach Horner's practices have to be a lot easier than Coach McCallom's and he can't possibly yell as much as the *Mac Man*.

A few minutes later, and with his mind still wandering, Taylor misses his defensive rotation, letting Corey Lawrence get behind him near the basket. Since there's no way he can listen to another angry barrage from Coach McCallom, Taylor tries to make up for his mental error by blocking Corey's dunk as hard as he can. Instead of succeeding, his overly physical play sends Corey crashing awkwardly to the floor, where he lands with a loud thud. The sound of Corey's body crashing into the hardwood catches the trainers' attention and sends them sprinting onto the court.

Before the trainers can even reach Corey, he jumps to his feet and glares with fury at Taylor; while Taylor simply shrugs his shoulders and moves back to his defensive position on Maurice Barnes. Rather than let his anger get the best of him, Corey lets Coach McCallom take care of things for him, "Goddamn it, Taylor! What are you doing?"

"Just playing hard, Coach," Taylor answers, keeping his eyes fixated on Maurice as he responds.

"When are you going to learn? Everything matters! Don't do in practice what you wouldn't do in a game!"

"Screw you, Coach! Leave me alone!" Taylor shouts inside his head as he keeps his eyes fixated on Maurice's back. *"You hardly played me last night! Why do you even care?"*

"Look at me, Taylor!" Coach McCallom yells. "This is my job. I'm not a teacher. I'm not an accountant. I'm a basketball coach. And I only coach players who want to be here. I demand your attention and your discipline. Not just today, but always. Got it?"

"Yes, Coach," Taylor answers flatly.

"Do you?" the vein in Coach McCallom's forehead bulges as he asks this question. "Because the sooner you understand what I'm saying right now, the sooner we'll get along better."

"Yes, Coach," Taylor answers flatly again.

Shaking his head in disgust, Coach McCallom finally turns toward Corey to make sure he's okay. Corey nods back he's fine.

"Let's go!" Coach McCallom yells as he claps his hands. "No more stupid fouls! Enough of this goddamn lazy basketball! Do you hear me? Enough!"

After retaking his position above the three-point line, Coach McCallom looks closely at Taylor. What he sees is the same scared and pained look he's seen a thousand times before from his young players. It's a look that tells him he might be losing his prized freshman to the "process." Every freshman has to be broken down and taught to play the game the right way—*the Maryland State University way*—before they can be put back together again; even the high school All-Americans.

When the team's five-on-five drill starts back up, Andray passes the ball to the wing and sprints down the center of the lane to set a screen on Taylor, his eyes fixated on him the entire time. When Andray reaches Taylor, instead of standing still on his screen, he leans in and throws both elbows into Taylor's ribs as retaliation for fouling Corey so hard. Gasping for air, Taylor tries to move around Andray's screen, but he's too late. Maurice flies right by him and easily lays the ball into the basket.

As soon as the ball falls through the net, Coach McCallom ignores the look he just saw on Taylor's face and starts yelling at him for not playing hard enough on defense. The louder Coach McCallom yells, the louder the chorus inside Taylor's head gets, the hotter Taylor's now simmering temper boils.

Having seen enough, Coach McCallom loudly blows his whistle and tells the white team and blue team to switch offense-defense. It's time for the white team to show the blue team how defense should be played.

On the blue team's first offensive possession, Taylor catches the ball a step above the elbow and squares up to the basket. Rather than pass the ball to the wing and screen away like the play calls for, *he's already decided it's time to shut everyone up for good.* Pump-faking Maurice off his feet, he takes one hard dribble down the lane and readies himself to explode toward the rim. Right before he can do this, Andray slides in front of him and violently slaps at the ball. With his wrists burning in pain, and the ball lying softly on the court, Taylor looks over at Coach McCallom for a whistle—but all he gets in return is a stare that says, *"Don't complain! Keep playing!"*

Angrier than ever, Taylor retakes his position on offense, determined to make everyone notice him—*no matter what.* Watching the next play develop, he sees James set a high ball screen on Andray, which frees Damon up to drive to the basket. As soon as Damon jumps off the floor to attack the basket—which is the exact same moment Andray leaves his feet to try and block Damon's shot—Taylor arrives to the play, shoving his forearm hard into Andray's chest. The blow sends Andray flying sideways through the air, where he lands on the court with a loud bang. *Unfortunately for Taylor, Andray doesn't stay down too long.*

Bouncing right back onto his feet, Andray goes straight after Taylor like a dog attacking an intruder. With electrifying speed, he clean lifts Taylor high into the air and power drives him into the hardwood. Using his oversized forearm, Andray grinds Taylor's face and nose, making it feel as if Taylor's face is being attacked by an army of flesh-eating ants. Summoning all his strength, Taylor tries to get Andray to stop attacking him, *but he can't.*

With blood spilling from Taylor's nose and whistles blowing from all directions, Tim and Daquan are the first ones to arrive to this one-sided fight. As the two players pull Andray off Taylor, Andray begins screaming loud enough for the whole world to hear, "What'd ya have to say now? Huh, freshman? You're a loser, man! You think you're better than the rest of us? Well, you ain't! Take your ass back to New Jersey! You're nothing! You hear me? Nothing!"

"That's enough!" Coach McCallom shouts as he takes a step toward Andray. "I'll handle it from here. Tim, take Andray down to the other end of the floor and help him calm down."

"What?" Andray asks wide-eyed.

"I said, get yourself down to the other end of the floor and calm down," Coach McCallom repeats with force.

"I got it, Coach," Tim jumps in and throws his arm over Andray's shoulder, leading him away from the altercation.

Spinning on his heels, Coach McCallom now turns his powerful gaze on Taylor, "What the hell is wrong with you?" he dresses Taylor down in front of the rest of the team. "You know what? Don't answer that. Just take yourself out of my gym. You're done for the day. You hear me? *Done!* We might battle each other in practice, but we don't ever, I repeat *ever*, attack one of our own! You crossed a line today, son! Now get the hell out of my gym!"

"Yes, Coach," Taylor answers in a barely audible voice.

"Wait!" Coach McCallom shouts, pointing his commanding index finger at Taylor. "I know I just dismissed you, but you're not done for the day. When practice is over, I want you to come back here to finish your *Bag Crew* duties and when you're done with your own responsibilities, I want you to take care of everyone else's too. If you want to stand separate from this team, well...you just got your wish. You're also not practicing with the team tomorrow. The next time I want to see you is in my office at eight o'clock tomorrow night. Got it? Now take yourself out of my sight!"

A few minutes later, Coach McCallom sends Coach Foote to the locker room to check on Taylor. When Coach Foote opens the locker room door, he finds Frank already with his arm draped across Taylor's shoulder, consoling his young friend. Taking a seat next to Frank, Coach Foote tells Taylor he definitely needs to spend some time thinking about what he did today, so he can learn and grow from his mistake, but he can't let what happened today define him. The last thing Coach Foote tells Taylor, before leaving him alone in the locker room to his thoughts, is that he should think long and hard about the answers he's going to give to Coach McCallom's questions tomorrow night, because his future with the Revolutionaries might very well depend on how that conversation goes.

CHAPTER 56

The next night, at exactly 7:58 p.m., Taylor steps off the elevator leading to the office of the Maryland State University men's basketball team, the same way he did just eight months earlier. With his heart pounding rapidly in his chest, he walks slowly across the office's unmistakable sea of blue carpet—that not too long ago symbolized only glory and success—and now symbolizes something else entirely. As he heads in the direction of Coach McCallom's private office in the back, *all he can think about is how much he hates this blue carpet right now.*

Since it's almost eight o'clock at night, the men's basketball team office is completely empty, except for Coach McCallom, who's sitting alone behind his desk looking out into the empty Liberty Arena with a glass of whiskey in his hand. As Coach McCallom stares out into the vast darkness below him, his mind churns away with what he should do with Taylor. He spent so much time and energy recruiting Taylor to the school, but he can't let that cloud his judgment right now—and while there's still no doubt about Taylor's limitless talent, even he has to admit, he underestimated how fragile Taylor's psyche is.

In Coach McCallom's personal experience, kids raised by a single parent often arrive at his doorstep a lot more fragile than kids raised in a two-parent household and Taylor has done nothing to refute this. He also knows it takes a while for players to warm up to his strong and abrasive personality, but for over twenty-five years, his "tough love" approach has proven to be nothing but successful, which only reinforces his belief he shouldn't have to change his ways for any one player, no matter how badly he needs this player to win.

As Coach McCallom unconsciously jiggles the ice cubes in his glass, he finally makes the decision to do what he's always done—*trust his instincts.* While many things have changed since he first started coaching college basketball all those years ago, he still believes deep in his heart that kids are kids. Each generation likes to think they're different from the one before it, but as far as he can tell, an eighteen-year-old kid is an eighteen-year-old kid, no matter when they were born. They all crave the same thing, a strong and consistent male role model in their life to deliver a delicate balance of discipline and approval.

When Taylor reaches Coach McCallom's office door, he takes a deep breath and knocks lightly on the outside for permission to enter. Hesitating ever so slightly when he hears Coach McCallom invite him inside, Taylor walks deliberately through the door, while wondering for the thousandth time since yesterday what his punishment is going to be for what he did to Andray.

"Over here!" Coach McCallom waves Taylor over to the same leather arm chair he sat in during his recruiting visit and waits for him sit down. "As you know, I called you here tonight so we could talk privately about what happened yesterday. But before we do that, I think we should talk about a few things that have been happening with the team lately."

"Okay," Taylor quizzically answers.

"Let me start out by letting you know I realize there's some internal tension on our team and while you might think this has gone unnoticed, I want to assure you, it hasn't. To be honest, it's not hard to imagine why some players on this team believe they're being treated differently than others. This has been my mistake and I take full responsibility for not dealing with it sooner."

Taylor quietly breathes a sigh of relief when he hears this.

"I also want to let you know this hasn't been my only meeting on this subject. I've been getting ready to execute a plan to alleviate some of this tension, but unfortunately, you took this issue to a whole different level yesterday."

"I...I'm sorry, Coach," Taylor replies, his head falling forward in regret.

"Truthfully, there are many reasons why I need to fix this problem," Coach McCallom keeps talking, ignoring Taylor's apology. "But the most important is I believe this tension is holding our team back from reaching its full potential. If it doesn't get fixed, we won't achieve our goals for the season, not to mention what our fans and alumni expect from us."

"I understand, Coach. It's just..."

"Before we talk more about you," Coach McCallom ignores Taylor again. "I need to share some sad news about your roommate."

"Sad news?" Taylor asks.

"Yes, we got Emmet's mid-term grades back earlier this week and it doesn't look very good for him. It appears Emmet isn't cut out to be a student-athlete here at Maryland State University. Actually, I'm not sure Emmet is cut out to be a student-athlete anywhere."

"How bad is it?" Taylor asks, his brow furrowed.

"I don't normally share a player's grade point average with anyone that's not a coach, but I'm sure you'd find this information out one way or the other, so I might as well be the one to tell you. Emmet's mid-term grade point average was zero point eight. He's failing every subject except math. If he stayed, the best he could hope for is academic probation."

"If he stayed?"

"Yes, if he stayed. Even with my influence, I'm not sure I could keep Emmet from being kicked out of here. I met with him earlier today and told him I thought it was best if he found another place to enroll. I recommended a community college instead of another four-year university right away. It's not a matter of intelligence with Emmet. It's a matter of him not being ready to handle the responsibilities of going to a university like this."

"When is he leaving?"

"I gave him the option of finishing out the semester, but he chose to leave campus immediately. He's back in your dorm room right now packing up."

Blindsided by this news, Taylor's mouth falls wide open.

"I asked Emmet not to leave campus until the two of you could say your goodbyes, but he was so upset, I'm not sure he's going to listen."

"That's really sad," Taylor answers, almost to himself. It's all he can think to say. He's been so worried all semester about his own problems, he never even noticed how much trouble Emmet was having finding his way.

"I don't like to admit my failures, especially to the media," Coach McCallom states in a serious tone. "But I was the one who recruited Emmet, just like I was the one who recruited you. So Emmet's failure is all on me. Even though I'm still not sure how I got it so wrong. I spoke to Emmet's high school coach in Tennessee and all his coaches back in Ireland many times and none of them ever said anything about how lazy he is in the classroom, or how much he likes to drink. It's really a shame, because I still believe one day he's going to blossom into a very serious player. It always takes big men a lot longer to develop and when they do, it usually happens over a period of months, not years. Our sports information department is going to send out a press release later today to let the media know Emmet has decided to leave the team right now to get treatment for an undisclosed injury and then we'll follow that up with another press release over winter break stating Emmet has decided to transfer to another school. Since I never played Emmet very much, I'm hoping this story will go away quietly on its own. And if it doesn't, well...I'll do what I always do. I'll take care of it. My job here is never done."

"Thanks for letting me know, Coach. I had no idea. Emmet and I were on such different schedules, I only saw him at practice, or at night sleeping in his bed. I guess, now that I know, I could've been a better roommate, or friend, or done something to help him out."

"Don't lose any sleep over it," Coach McCallom responds with a dismissive wave of his hand. "I don't think there's anything you or anyone else could have done to stop what happened. I talked to Emmet several times in private before this, warning him that if he didn't get his act together, bad things were going to be heading his way. I also had Coach Foote and Coach Dougard do the same, yet Emmet never changed his behavior. I honestly believe he just didn't want to be here."

"Okay...I guess," Taylor replies, although deep down he knows he should've done something to help Emmet.

"Now that we're done discussing your old roommate, I think it's time we turned the conversation back to you. After all, that's why we're here. You're a smart kid, Taylor, so I don't have to tell you what you did yesterday was *way* over the line. One of my goals is to always create as competitive an environment as I can in practice. But as I said yesterday, I don't under *any* circumstances allow players to attack each other. Ever."

"I know, Coach. I'm sorry. It won't..."

"Stop right there!" Coach McCallom loudly responds, putting his hand halfway across the desk to cut Taylor off. "I know you're sorry. I could see it in your body language when you walked into this office. It's also written all over your face. I know you probably think you're a difficult person to read, but truthfully, you're not."

"I don't know what to say, Coach. Except, I promise it won't happen again."

"Taylor, stop! *Please.* I'm sure I could sit here all night and listen to you apologize for what happened yesterday. But I'm not going to. What happened, happened. It's over. We need to move on. I'm also going to work under the assumption that from this day forward you won't ever do something like that again."

"Never, Coach. I promise," Taylor answers, hoping against hope that might be the end of it. He couldn't be more wrong.

"First things first," Coach McCallom forcefully tells Taylor. "You're suspended one game, effective immediately. You're not going to suit up this weekend when we play West Virginia A&M University down at their place. You'll travel with the team, completing all of your *Bag Crew* duties along the way, but you'll watch the game from the end of the bench in your street clothes, right next to the trainers. I'm also going to hold you out of practice until after the weekend. That means I don't want to see you back in my gym until Monday afternoon. But let me be clear, I'm not giving you a vacation. I want you in the weight room and I also want you to find some time to shoot a basketball. As a matter of fact, I'm going to ask Coach Foote to work with you one-on-one over the next few days during your suspension. It will be good for the two of you to spend some quality time together."

"I understand, Coach," Taylor softly answers, as if he had a choice.

Staring deep into Taylor's eyes, Coach McCallom's voice now gets even more focused, "Taylor, please listen carefully to what I'm about to say next. You have to stop asking yourself, *why me?* You have to stop feeling sorry for yourself. I feel like you do this a lot more than you lead on. This campus is one step away from the real world out there," Coach McCallom points outside his office door. "And out there, they don't care if you feel sorry for yourself, or what you think you had to overcome to get where you are. Outside of your family, your friends and someday, your wife, *no one else cares.* You might as well get all this through your head right now and start working on changing the narrative. Do you understand me?"

"Uh, huh," Taylor grunts back. It's as if Coach McCallom can read his mind, which makes him believe maybe he's not that hard to understand after all.

"Taylor, I now need to ask you an extremely important question. And I need you to answer it honestly."

"Okay."

"I need to know if you're still committed to what we're trying to accomplish here?"

"What do you mean?"

"Are you still one hundred percent committed to this university, or have we already lost you to another school? Because if the answer is we've already lost you, then we should have that conversation out right here and now. There's no need to wait."

Caught off guard, Taylor's mind spins as he readies to give perhaps the most important answer of his college career. *It's time to pick a side of the fence and stay there.*

"I'm committed, Coach...I want to be here."

"Good," Coach McCallom responds, while quietly breathing a sigh of relief. With Emmet leaving, he can't lose both recruits he personally delivered to campus at the same time. Not to mention one half of a recruiting class he was so excited about before the season started.

"The reason I asked you this question is I know Central New York University came in a close second this past spring when you were deciding where to play. So I just wanted to make sure you weren't thinking things would be any easier up there. You have to understand, the grass isn't always greener on the other side. Most of the time, it's usually the same color. And while I personally don't know Coach Horner, I can guarantee you, just like me, he doesn't hand out playing time on potential alone. You have to earn it."

"I understand, Coach...I..."

"Let me finish, Taylor. Even the best college basketball players only have four years of eligibility to show the world what they can do. *That's it.* Those four years amount to one hundred twenty to one hundred forty-five total games, depending on how good your teams are. Except for the lucky few who go on to play professionally, all college basketball players' careers come to an abrupt end after four years. The games suddenly stop. There's no more cheering, bright lights, headlines and definitely no more girls telling you how great you are. It's only once your eligibility is up do you find out what kind of player you really were. Because when that time comes, for better or worse, all you're left with are your memories. I know you think right now cheering crowds are deafening, but wait until no one cares anymore about how many points you score, rebounds you pull down or assists you hand out. I can tell you from experience that silence is what's deafening. For all of us in life, time is always ticking. It moves quickly and opportunities are limited. But for college basketball players, the stark reality is time is ticking to a precise end point from the moment they step foot on campus..."

A half-hour later, Taylor leaves Coach McCallom's office feeling more connected to his coach than ever before, while also relieved at his relatively short punishment for attacking Andray. Determined, now more than ever, to prove to Coach McCallom he's not only mentally and physically strong enough to survive on this level—*but thrive*—he makes a promise to himself to take advantage of every opportunity he's given from this point forward, no matter how big or small.

Once again, he's so focused on himself, he almost forgot about Emmet. When he finally reaches his dorm room, he opens up the door to find Emmet's half of the room is already empty. There's not even a note. It's like Emmet had never even been there.

CHAPTER 57

The day Taylor returns to practice, Coach McCallom is once again in a foul mood. With the Revolutionaries losing over the weekend on the road by a score of 65-61, their overall record now stands at 9-3. At the same time, the loss exposed many of the Revolutionaries' weaknesses—the same weaknesses that have been worrying the coaches since the season started—which prompted yet another conversation on the plane ride home about needing to keep tweaking the team's rotation in order to get things just right.

In addition to their normal responsibilities, each assistant coach has been assigned to keep a close eye on Taylor during today's practice. While all the reports from Coach Foote during Taylor's suspension were positive, Coach McCallom wants to make sure Taylor's head is completely screwed on straight now that he's back.

Less than ten minutes after Coach McCallom blows his whistle to start practice, Taylor gives Coach McCallom the answer he's looking for, and then some. It's as if an entirely new Taylor has come in and replaced the old one. With a raw hunger usually displayed only by the upperclassmen, Taylor jumps, dives, rebounds and hustles as if his life depends on it.

During the team's white team starters versus blue team reserves five-on-five half court drill, Taylor shines and even dominates for long stretches of time. His energy and enthusiasm is not lost on his teammates, all of whom stare in confused wonder at what seems to be a brand new player wearing Taylor's practice uniform.

Later, during this same practice, Coach McCallom watches over a big man drill run by Coach Davis, where Taylor is matched up against Corey Lawrence. Each time Corey catches the ball on offense, Taylor plays extremely tight defense, making it difficult for Corey to shoot, let alone score. When Coach Davis blows his whistle for the two players to switch positions, Corey starts out by slamming his forearm hard into Taylor's lower back, a reminder he hasn't forgotten about what happened between the two of them. This well-directed blow knocks the wind straight out of Taylor, but instead of looking to Coach Davis for a foul call, or retaliating in some stupid way, he stands his ground and calls for the ball exactly as he was taught.

Taking the pass from Coach Davis, Taylor fakes going to the middle, before spinning to the baseline. This quick move makes Corey fall slightly off-balance. Using one strong power dribble, Taylor grabs the ball with both hands and explodes off the floor. In one electrifying motion, he cups the ball behind his head and slams it through the rim with resounding force. The rim snaps thunderously back into place as Taylor lands triumphantly back on the floor—he immediately looks to Coach McCallom for approval.

Seeing Taylor's stare from across the court, Coach McCallom simply shrugs his shoulders and loudly tells him, "Good job! Now let me see you do it again! But only harder!"

As Taylor readies himself again on offense, steadfast in showing how easily he can repeat this move, Coach

McCallom turns his back on the drill and starts walking away, a grin of absolute pleasure spread across his face.

At the end of practice, Taylor fulfills his *Bag Crew* duties, but now there's a lot less tension in his body. After picking up the water buckets he's assigned to, he puts both buckets onto the dolly, takes the elevator one floor down, wheels the dolly into the equipment room, dumps out the remaining water and ice, showers, puts his street clothes back on and heads over to Heritage Hall to eat dinner with the rest of the team. The entire time he does this, he doesn't talk to any of the players, except James and Daquan, something he knows he needs to change real soon if he truly wants to make Maryland State University his home.

In his first game back from suspension, Taylor plays ten minutes and scores 2 points in a win inside the Liberty Arena and in his second game back, he plays twelve minutes and scores 5 points in a loss on the road. While these results look almost identical to the outside world as the rest of the games he's already played in, things couldn't be more different. With his sour and emotionless demeanor replaced by what can only be described as a passionate determination, his metamorphosis appears to be well on its way.

The biggest highlight, however, isn't how everyone's opinion of him is improving each day, or how well he's been playing in practice—it's the speed of the game—it's finally slowed down to a pace that reminds him of high school. For the first time since October, he's seeing the team's offensive and defensive plays develop in real time and not *after* they've already happened. It's as if his eyes and brain have caught up to his body.

By the end of the third week of December, Taylor can hardly wait for the team's Saturday night conference home game against the defending post-season college basketball champions and highly-ranked Monument University Red

Demons. Every team and every coach loves beating Monument University, not to mention every student. There's just something about taking down the mightier than thou Red Demons that can't easily be put into words. The anticipation for this game has gripped the Maryland State University campus and become so extreme, students have been sleeping in tents in front of the Liberty Arena for over a week just for the chance to see this game in person.

On Saturday night, before the game even tips off at 8:00 p.m., the sold-out crowd of 15,000 cheers non-stop from warm-ups through player introductions, creating an adrenaline-charged party atmosphere inside the Liberty Arena of no equal in any college basketball arena.

Unfortunately for Taylor, when the referee throws the ball into the air to start the game, he once again finds himself sitting on the bench watching the action, the same way a national TV audience is doing at home. While he'll never get used to the idea of watching a basketball game he believes he should be playing in, over these last few weeks he's quietly embraced the embarrassment that comes from not playing as much as he wants at this point in his career, no matter how badly it hurts.

With the game unfolding on the court at breakneck speed, Taylor can't help but let his mind once again retreat into itself. In the middle of the bedlam and noise consuming the arena, his eyes drift into the stands, where they come to rest on a food vendor. Focusing on this food vendor, he immediately starts speculating about his life, *"Who are his friends? What does he do for fun? What kind of car does he drive?"* No sooner does this last question pop into his head, does he see a large shadow appear in his line of vision. Looking up with surprise, he sees Coach McCallom staring back with concern.

Shaking his head, Coach McCallom almost walks away, but then decides to stick to his gut again—sending Taylor into the game to replace Corey, who's been struggling since tip-off.

The arena is still a madhouse of noise when Taylor pulls off his warm-ups and checks into the game with eight and a half minutes left to go in the first half. It's so loud, Corey doesn't even hear Taylor tell him he's being replaced, even though Taylor is standing less than three feet away when he does.

Taking his position on defense, Taylor shakes his arms and legs to try and get loose, while breathing in deeply to calm his rapidly pounding heart. The excitement of the moment feels like it might completely consume him, but instead of succumbing to it, at the sound of the referee's whistle, he immediately starts playing like he has been in practice—and how everyone has always expected him to play—relaxed and under control on offense and a menace on defense. The entire time he's on the floor, the coaches shout non-stop instructions—but instead of confusing his once cluttered mind, he absorbs and executes everything they tell him as if it's second nature. Having more fun on a basketball court than he can remember, he plays the last eight and a half minutes of the first half, never returning to the bench. It's the longest stretch of continuous playing time he's received since arriving at Maryland State University.

Even though the Revolutionaries head into halftime down by a score of 38-34, Taylor doesn't disappoint himself or Coach McCallom, finishing the first half with 5 points, three rebounds and two steals, including a three pointer, his first in four games.

After spending most of the halftime break sprawled out in exhaustion on the chair in front of his locker—wishing for nothing more than to hear his name called out to start the second half, so he can continue living out his dream—when the second half starts, he once again finds himself back on the bench watching the action.

The good news is he doesn't have to wait too long for his real life fantasy to return.

With a little over thirteen minutes to go in the game and the Revolutionaries down 52-46, Corey misses two straight shots from close range and then picks up his third foul out of frustration. Disgusted by Corey's play again, Coach McCallom skips over his usual rotation and inserts Taylor back into the game. Well rested and feeling as alive as ever, Taylor steps back onto the court, *ready to go*.

Over the next five minutes, Taylor plays like he knows he's the best player in the game—seemingly fueling the Revolutionaries' comeback all by himself—scoring 7 points and grabbing four rebounds to cut the Red Demons' lead down to a single point.

With the home crowd continuing to cheer at an ear-splitting level, the Red Demons are granted a momentary reprieve when the referees are forced to call a TV timeout at the eight minute mark. A stoppage in play like this can sometimes slow a team down, *but not tonight*. The Revolutionaries come out of this TV timeout the same way they went into it—*on a tear*—and over the next minute and a half, they establish what looks to be an insurmountable 71-64 lead.

Sensing his team is running out of time, the Red Demons head coach is forced to burn one of his timeouts to try and stop the bleeding. Away from the prying eyes of the TV cameras, he challenges his players to not let this key conference road game slip away and to do it *as soon as they step back onto the court*. Filled with an indescribable sense of urgency, the Red Demons retake the floor and immediately hit a three pointer from the right side, followed by a steal and uncontested dunk to cut the Revolutionaries' lead back down to two points in what feels like the blink of an eye.

With a look of unstoppable determination, Andray takes the inbounds pass from Maurice Barnes and calls out play #1 as soon as he steps over half court. Running the play exactly as Coach McCallom drew it up, Andray passes the ball to his left and cuts down the center of the lane, before popping out to the wing to receive a return pass, a step above the three-point line. Faking high, then low, he dumps the ball into the post to Tim Daulton—who's immediately double-teamed. Pivoting in the lane, Tim turns his shoulders and throws a cross-court diagonal pass to Taylor, standing wide open behind the three-point line. Stepping comfortably into his shot, Taylor rises high off the floor and watches as his wrist snaps down in picture perfect form and his three pointer hits nothing but net.

With the Revolutionaries lead back up to five points and the crowd standing on its feet, cheering with everything it has, Taylor comes across the lane on defense and helps turn an easy shot by Monument University's center into a difficult one. This missed shot is aggressively rebounded by Tim, who spins away from the basket and safely outlets the ball to Andray's waiting hands.

A few steps over half court, Andray once again dribbles the ball with focused intensity as he calls out a high screen and roll with Maurice. Dribbling hard to his left, Andray takes Maurice's screen and turns the corner, forcing his defender to come over the top. Instead of using this small opening to go all the way to the basket, Andray stops his dribble and pulls up for a bank shot from ten feet away. The ball spins perfectly off his fingertips as it finds the glass and calmly falls through the net—sending the crowd into an even *louder* frenzy.

As Taylor runs back on defense, he can hardly hear himself think. The Liberty Arena is once again proving itself to be an impossible place for opposing teams to play. Positioned a step above the three-point line, Taylor watches the next play unfold as if it's happening in slow-motion. With Andray hounding Monument University's point guard and the crowd continuing to make it impossible for the Red Demons to communicate with each other, Andray forces the point guard to turn his back.

Reacting instead of thinking, Taylor leaves his man and runs up from behind the play to steal the ball. All alone now on the other side of half court, he races toward the basket as if he's gliding on air. When his feet hit the lane, he rises into the sky with his right arm stretched out to the heavens and his right hand cupping the ball. At the height of his jump, he swings his arm down through the rim, sending the ball scorching through the net and shaking the basket down to its foundation.

When he finally lands back down on earth, his momentum carries him into the first row of fans, where he's grabbed, embraced and patted on the back by what feels like a million sets of hands, all at the same time. As the entire arena erupts into a celebration of white noise, a noise so loud it makes his eardrums shake and the hair on the back of his neck stand on end, he looks up into the stands and sees all 15,000 Revolutionaries fans, standing on their feet, yelling and screaming in excitement—*yelling and screaming for him!*

Freeing himself from the fans' grasp, he starts running back on defense, but not before he slows down his pace so he can return the crowd's love. With his body tingling from head to toe, he starts screaming at the top of his lungs in euphoria, "YEAH! YEAH! YEAH!" Clenching his fists, his joy explodes out of every pore, "YEAH! YEAH! YEAH!" This feeling is worth more than all the money in the world, "YEAH! YEAH! YEAH!" He couldn't describe it to anyone if he tried, "YEAH! YEAH! YEAH!" With every ounce of pain and frustration from the last four months unleashing itself in a river of emotion, he continues to scream as loudly as his body will let him, "YEAH! YEAH! YEAH!" But no one can hear him, "YEAH! YEAH! YEAH!" The mayhem of noise inside the arena is just too loud, "YEAH! YEAH! YEAH!"